FALLEN ELITES

FALLEN ELITES

THE MILITARY OTHER
IN POST-UNIFICATION GERMANY

Andrew Bickford

Stanford University Press
Stanford, California

Stanford University Press
Stanford, California

Printed in the United States of America on acid-free, archival-quality paper

Library of Congress Cataloging-in-Publication Data

Bickford, Andrew, 1966- author.
Fallen elites : the military other in post-unification Germany / Andrew Bickford.
pages cm
Includes bibliographical references and index.
ISBN 978-0-8047-7395-9 (cloth : alk. paper)--ISBN 978-0-8047-7396-6 (pbk. : alk. paper)
1. Germany (East). Nationale Volksarmee--Officers--Attitudes.
2. Germany (East). Nationale Volksarmee--Officers--Social conditions.
3. Retired military personnel--Germany--Attitudes. 4. Retired military personnel--Germany--Social conditions. 5. Germany--History--Unification, 1990. I. Title.
UB415.G3B53 2011
355.10943'109049--dc22   2010043611

Typeset by Bruce Lundquist in 10/15 Sabon

For
Gabrielle Fisher

Everyone imposes his own social system as far as his army can reach.

JOSEPH STALIN

Having once attributed a real existence to an idea, the mind wants
to see it alive and can effect this only by personalizing it.

JOHAN HUIZINGA,
The Waning of the Middle Ages

Men possess thoughts, but symbols possess men.

MAX LERNER

Contents

Acknowledgments

FIRST AND FOREMOST, I would like to thank the officers and their families—from both the East and the West—who opened up their homes and lives to me, and who shared their experiences of the Cold War and German unification. I am deeply grateful for their help and support.

A number of friends and colleagues have helped with this project over the years. I'd like to thank Uli Linke, Roger Lancaster, Dorothy Hodgson, Louisa Schein, Omer Bartov, Paige West, J. C. Salyer, Charles Smith, G. S. Quid, Robert Marlin, Stephanie Marlin-Curiel, Catherine Lutz, Ken Mayer, Jerry Mayer, Janine Wedel, Lesley Gill, Art Walters, Linda Green, Susan Terrio, David Vine, Melissa Fisher, Katherine McCaffrey, Angelique Haugerud, Hope Harrison, Erik Jensen, Elena Mancini, Sabine Kriebel, and Jiro Tanaka for their thoughtful suggestions and criticisms over the years. At George Mason, my friends, colleagues and students have been very helpful and supportive: thanks to Jeff Mantz, Bhavani Arabandi, Susan Trencher, Linda Seligmann, Hugh Gusterson, Ann Palkovich, Tom Williams, and James Snead. And a special thanks to my students Kristin English and Nate Crow for their help with the final versions of the manuscript. I would also like to thank the two anonymous reviewers at Stanford University Press for their extremely helpful comments and criticisms during the review process.

In Germany, a number of people provided invaluable support, help, and friendship, and enriched my research and fieldwork: Herbert Becker of the Deutscher Bundeswehrverband, Professor Dr. Egbert Fischer, Dr. K. P. Hartmann, and the members of the Arbeitsgruppe Geschichte der NVA, Dr. Rüdiger Wenzke at the Military History Research Center in Potsdam, Karin Goihl at the SSRC Berlin Program, Ute Guenther, Ina Dietszsch, Helga and Ulli Ortmann, Marja Dempski, and Felix Seyfarth.

My research was made possible by generous grants from the Wenner-Gren Foundation, the Social Science Research Council Berlin Program for

Advanced German and European Studies, Fulbright II, and a Woodrow Wilson Center Archival Research Grant. Early drafts and ideas were worked through at the Social Science Research Council Berlin Program for German and European Studies seminar, the Rutgers Center for Historical Analysis, the German Historical Institute's Young Scholar's Seminar, the Havighurst Center for Russian and Post-Soviet Studies at Miami University, and the Culture, Power, Boundaries Seminar at Columbia University. I would also like to thank George Mason University for a semester writing sabbatical. All translations from the German are my own, as are any mistakes and/or omissions.

I'd like to extend a special thanks to my editor at Stanford University Press, Joa Suorez, for guiding me through the submission and review process, and for her great feedback and comments on my manuscript. I would also like to thank Mariana Raykov, my production editor at Stanford University Press, and Andrew Frisardi, my copy editor, for their help in making this a much stronger book.

Most of all, I want to thank Gabrielle Fisher for her love, support, encouragement, coffee, and patience.

Prologue

IT TOOK ME OVER A YEAR to finally sit down with Klaus-Dieter Baumgarten, the general in charge of the Grenztruppen der DDR—the East German Border Guards. I had slowly worked my way up the "chain of command" that still regulated much of my work, including whom I could talk to and whom I could meet. While it was generally not a problem meeting with lower-ranking officers and their families, gaining access to high-ranking former officers was a tricky process of vetting, knowing who to talk to, observing military courtesies and customs, of using the right words and phrases at the right time.

I often had the feeling that among a certain group of former NVA officers, a "shadow government-in-waiting" existed, a group of men who had held power, and who—however tenuously—clinged to a hope that they would one day have power again. They were a group of men who had had power, lost it, were still dazed by the loss, and had not quite recognized that power had slipped away from them forever. These men still used their ranks, observed the hierarchy of the NVA, and demanded a strict observance of the hierarchy. Working one's way up the chain meant observing the hierarchy, of paying deference at each stage of the ladder.

One afternoon, I received a call from Baumgarten's "adjutant," a former NVA *Volksmarine*—"People's Navy"—captain. My request for a meeting with General Klaus-Dieter Baumgarten had reached him, and he had decided, based on discussions with other officers who had met with me and who I had interviewed, that he would present my request to the general. If successful, I would receive a call from the general himself in the next few weeks.

A few weeks did indeed pass. As I was getting ready to go to the archive one morning, the phone rang. A slightly gravelly voice began, "Are you Herr Bickford, the American student interested in the National People's Army of the German Democratic Republic?" I was somewhat taken aback by the abrupt question, but realized quickly that the person on the other end of the line was Baumgarten. "Yes, I'm Herr Bickford," I answered, and waited for him to continue. "Good," he said. "This is General Baumgarten. I have received your request to meet with me and discuss the experiences of the officers of the National People's Army and Border Guards of the German Democratic Republic. I will meet with you tomorrow. You will do the following: Take the S-3 train to the Erkner station, arriving at eleven A.M. You will have a copy of tomorrow's edition of *Neues Deutschland* with you. Proceed down the steps from the station, and stand under the third light post on your right. You will see a Trabant appear. I will flash the lights at you twice, whereupon you will transfer your copy of *Neues Deutschland* from your right arm to your left. I will flash the lights twice again. I will know it is you and pick you up. Click."

With that, our conversation was over, and our meeting had been arranged. I felt like Richard Burton in *The Spy Who Came In from the Cold*, although, unfortunately, I didn't own a trenchcoat.

I arrived at Erkner shortly before eleven. It was—perhaps wonderfully—a typical winter day in Berlin: cold, gray, dreary, and wet. What better way, I thought, to meet the former head of the Border Guards, the man who had issued the shoot-to-kill orders for the Berlin Wall, and who was now serving time for murder for issuing those orders. The weather only enhanced my feeling that I was taking part in a Cold War thriller, heading out to some secret meeting from which I might never return. I didn't really think I would never return, but it definitely added to the fantasy-performance of Cold War intrigue. Of course, ten or twenty years earlier, a call such as that from Baumgarten indeed would have carried the threat and menace of the possibility of not returning.

It was raining steadily when I found the third lightpost on the right. There were a few people around, but otherwise, it was a very quiet and subdued morning. I stood by the light post, but I really wasn't sure how to stand. I put my copy of *Neues Deutschland* under my arm and leaned against the light post. But was that the right way to stand? I wanted to look nonchalant, but not disinterested. I didn't want to stand completely upright, either, looking as if I were standing at attention for the general. These things meant a lot, I had learned; body posture among former officers could communicate indifference or disrespect, deference, and sincerity, and set the tone of the interview. I finally figured out a compromise: I would stand up straight and lean against the light post. I felt like a slanted matchstick.

I have no idea if Baumgarten saw me trying to figure out how to stand, or if he did, if he knew what I was doing. Shortly—mercifully—after figuring out my posture, an old Trabant approached me slowly. As it came closer, I squinted to see the driver, but because of the rain and mist, I couldn't really see into the car. The car stopped. Twice, the lights flashed. I slowly shifted my copy of *Neues Deutschland* from my right arm to my left. The lights flashed again, this time a bit more quickly. The Trabant's engined roared, as Baumgarten pulled up in front of me. "Get in!" he growled. I got in. I had entered a time machine.

Abbreviations and Terms

AR   *Armee Rundschau* (Army Panorama; East German military magazine published between 1956 and 1990)

BA-MA   Bundesarchiv-Militärarchiv, Freiburg (German military archive in Freiburg)

Die Bundeswehr   Cold War West Germany military, and the name of the post-unification German military

DDR   Deutsche Demokratische Republic (German Democratic Republic)

Deutscher Bundeswehrverband   German Army Association

FDJ   Freie Deutsche Jugend (Free German Youth; East German youth organization)

FRG   Federal Republic of Germany (Cold War West Germany, also post-unification Germany)

GDR   German Democratic Republic (East Germany)

GST   Gesellschaft für Sport und Technik (Society for Sports and Technology; East German youth group)

GT   Grenztruppen der DDR (Border Guards of the German Democratic Republic; East German Border Guards)

ISOR   Initiativgemeinschaft zum Schutz der sozialen Rechte ehemaliger Angehöriger bewaffneter Organe und der Zöllverwaltung der DDR (Association for the Protection of the Social Rights of Former Members of the Armed Forces and Customs Agency of the German Democratic Republic)

JP   Junge Pioniere (Young Pioneers; East German youth group)

KPD   Kommunistische Partei Deutschlands (pre–World War II German Communist Party)

KVP   Kasenierte Volkspolizei (Garrisoned People's Police)

Landesverband Ost   Eastern State Association of the German Army
Association

NVA   Nationale Volksarmee (National People's Army of the German
Democratic Republic)

SAPMO   Stiftung Archiv der Parteien und Massenorganisationen der
DDR im Bundesarchiv (Foundation Archives of the Parties and
Mass Organizations of the GDR in the Federal Archives, Berlin)

SED   Sozialistische Einheitspartei Deutschlands (Socialist Unity Party
of Germany; East German Communist Party)

SS   Waffen SS (Armed military wing of the German Nazi party)

VP   Volkspolizei (East German People's Police)

Die Wehrmacht   World War II German military

FALLEN ELITES

PART ONE

Becoming Militarized

MY BROTHER, MY ENEMY

The man over there with a gun
could be my brother
but what is a brother?
Cain killed Abel
fairy tales tell of brothers who are enemies
but that doesn't prove anything
The man over there who could be my brother
may be gentle and peaceful
but he has a gun
and obeys his superiors
who are my enemies
The man over there standing with a gun
could be my brother
but he believes in "Home into the Reich"
and is a cheap tool of conquerers
a heartless weapon of murders
human, perhaps my brother
but nonetheless useful for murder
and therefore my enemy![1]

CHAPTER 1

The Military Imaginary

SOLDIERS, MYTHS, AND STATES

I WANT TO OPEN THIS BOOK with a bold proposition: the soldier is the state. The soldier is the personification, the sign, the representation of the state; its arm, its agent of violence, the tip of the spear, the means by which the state comes into being, is maintained, and continues to be. Soldiers represent the imagined community of the state in living, active form; they are homogenized into a single identity of the state, and represent this imagined ideal of homogenization. States write the mythology of soldiers, turning soldiers into mythic creatures. This kind of myth-work elevates soldiers above "mere" civilians, removing them from the quotidian and placing them into the unquestionable. According to the state, the soldier is the ideal citizen, the best kind of person the state can produce. Soldiers in uniform are living memorials to the state and its history, walking monuments to memory—they just are not made of stone, like other war memorials, though they may appear as cold, hard, lifeless, and unfeeling. Soldiers are monuments to previous wars and the preformed memories of as-yet unfought wars to come. The soldier represents the congealed historical memory of the violence of the state, and is the state in its most concrete, literal, purest human form. This image is, of course, drilled into the soldier.

And into civilians.

. . .

At least, this is how states would like soldiers to be and be perceived. Because they would like this, states go to great lengths to insure that soldiers—and representations and imaginings of them—approach these ideals. States can be seen as vast experiments in social construction, and militarization plays a key role in this; states make soldiers both to "be" the state and to defend the state. But how are soldiers "made" into this ideal, and how are they "unmade" when the desired image changes? What happens when men, made into the soldierly ideal of one state, find themselves absorbed into another state, a state with a very different idea of what it means to be a soldier? What does it mean to live as a sign of the state, and what happens when meanings and signification shift? What are the material ramifications of shifts in the symbolics of militarized identities? These were the sorts of issues involved in the experiences of former East German army officers in the context of German unification in 1990; the sorts of problems and processes they faced resulted from these issues.

In *Fallen Elites*, I examine the cultural politics of what it means to be a soldier in Germany by focusing on the lives of a group of East German Army and Border Guard officers, both before and after unification, and on the ways in which memories and representations of the World War II German military and soldiers—the Wehrmacht and SS—continue to shape ideas of what it means to be a good and proper soldier and man in postunification Germany. By focusing on East German army officers who had power and then lost it, this book studies up, and then down again, providing an ethnographic perspective on elites and power in the modern state. I examine the idea of "soldiers" in political life, the construction of citizenship and national identity, and the legitimation of the state and military. I look at how states use soldiers—who counts, how, why, and when—in the political life of the state, and how the deployment of ideas about soldiers affects the symbolic and material lives of men identified—positively and negatively—as soldiers. This is an examination of German unification as seen through what I call the "military imaginary" of the state: the ways in which the necessity, implementation, and desired outcomes of (compulsory) military service and training are imagined and envisioned by the state, and the ways in which these tropes are linked to normative ideas of the "proper" soldier and man, legitimate violence, morality, and military tradition.

There are multiple military imaginaries in a state: those of the state, of the military, of soldiers themselves, and of civilians. The military imaginary of a state is linked to the past, to memories and representations of soldiers and their actions, their heroism, deeds, and defense of the state. In a sense, these imaginings of the proper soldier function along the lines of myth, achieving a mythic status, and occurring in a mythologized time.

They are also linked to the economic system of the state: soldiers are expected to fight and die for the state's political and economic viability.

Fallen Elites is about the Cold War contest between the capitalist West and the communist East, and the lingering effects of competing military and economic blocks. As Germany works through complications brought about by unification, ideas, prejudices, and mindsets formed and lived during the Cold War continue to effect it. Lingering on in corners of the state are contentious notions of what it means to be a good and proper "German soldier"; these competing ideas of what it means to be a soldier act as a metadebate about the past forty years and the history and memory of German soldiers in World War II. East German officers (and their families) are products of their time and context, products—and producers—of a vast exercise in militarization, extensions of a history that shaped and continues to shape their lives and worlds. War and economics, history and memory coalesce in these men's lives and experiences, making them the living exemplars of militarization policies. Within the shaping of national histories, personal histories and narratives of militarization take shape. I trace the life histories of men who became elites in the German Democratic Republic (GDR) in a context of military-political power, specifically, the Cold War context of the post–World War II rivalry between the United States and the Soviet Union. These men lost their status and power when the Cold War ended. Officers of the East German Nationale Volksarmee (National People's Army; NVA) held and wielded power, and symbolized and represented power and the state. After unification, they lost their power and status but continued to symbolize and represent militarism, oppression, and totalitarianism within a context in which they no longer are seen to fit and in which they no longer have power.

Examining German unification through the lives of NVA officers reveals the contentious and unfinished nature of unification, the cumbersome and contradictory attempts by the German government and military to come to terms with the military of a dictatorship, and the problematic and often disturbing use of Germany's military past in state discourse and narratives. This book explores what happens to fallen elites—in this case, military officers—when they lose both the state they were sworn to defend and the status that goes with this duty and "privilege." I follow the lives of men who held power and lost it overnight, who went from being official heroes to being official villains. I also examine the practices and actions of West German elites as they consolidated their power over both the military itself and representations of the German military and soldiers. Through the use of Cold War tropes of "proper" militarized masculinity, as well as the deployment of specific memories of World War II, West German elites have created an internal "other" and rehabilitated certain forms of German military history, tradition, and identity as a means of shoring up legitimacy for the newly unified state and appeasing the German military. Conversely, some NVA and Border Guard officers have used West German military policies of exclusion as a way of "explaining away" human rights abuses and military authoritarianism in the GDR, making themselves, in their own eyes, the "victims" of unification. As such, I examine the rational world of elite victims: the ways in which they see and process their experiences in light of the contexts from which they came and in which they find themselves. From the outside, what they say and do might seem irrational and offensive; for officers, their responses and understanding of their situation make perfect sense to them, and are ways to make sense of their lives after unification. Only by trying to understand their "rationality"—even if we find their comments and remarks offensive and off the mark—can we come close to understanding how former elites construct themselves as victims, see themselves as victims, and create victimhood narratives as a way to make sense of their fall.

States rarely leave militarization policies or the creation of "soldiers" to chance. Drawing from the German experience, I theorize the ways in which states use the military as a means of creating "ideal" men—and ideal citizens—through the inculcation of military values, worldviews, and "hegemonic" masculinity. In *Fallen Elites*, I ask two main questions: Do the political uses and representations of militarized masculinity change when states or governments change? In what ways does military identity intersect with political economy, memory, political processes, gender, semiotics, and citizenship? Through a consideration of the lives and experiences of East German NVA and Border Guards officers, I examine the fact that men must be made into soldiers by the state. Soldiers do not come "ready-made"; if they did, states would not need to expend effort, resources, or expense to make men into soldiers. Rather than relying on sociobiological or psychological models to explain why men become soldiers, we need to examine the role of states, governments, political economy, education policies, history, and the creation of gender roles as the formative factors in creating militarized masculinity and soldiers.

A VERY COLD FUSION

Despite official narratives of a relatively smooth transition, of the merging of "those things which belong together," German unification and the formation of a new German state have been an uneven project filled with friction and animosity. While the West German government celebrated the "victory" of unification, and stated that all East Germans wanted unification, one group of East Germans did not look forward to the dissolution of the GDR and their absorption into the West German state: members of the East German military, the NVA. Disbanded immediately upon unification on October 3, 1990, the overwhelming majority of NVA officers were immediately unemployed, stripped of their status as officers and "defenders" of the state, portrayed by the West Germans as the perpetrators and "losers" of the Cold War. This was a group of people who, contrary to most East Germans, I would not characterize as happy about the demise of socialism. For these men, unification was not a joyous, desired event; rather, unification represented the "end" of their careers, security, status, identity, and the state they had pledged their lives to serve. The "fall" into democracy for these men was from the start fraught with uncertainty, disappointment, anomie, and a profound sense of loss. Unification in 1990 signaled a radical transformation in the political, economic, and symbolic lives of East Germans, despite the promises by the Kohl administration of a "blooming landscape" of economic prosperity. The collapse of the GDR and the merger of the two states meant instability, lost jobs, lost homes, and lost income for many East Germans, as well as the stress of adapting to capitalism and learning how to consume. With unification came widespread unemployment and disruptions in daily life and life courses; by 1991, out of a population of roughly 16 million, 4 million East Germans were out of work.[1] The experiences of NVA officers after unification are characteristic of East German experience in general, but they differ in a number of important ways. These differences illustrate the role and use of the military in the state; how state elites operate and perceive the state, the military, and violence; and how the "banal practices" of state elites impact the lived experience of the state.

On October 3, 1990, all NVA soldiers and officers over the age of fifty-five were immediately released from the military, and all officers above the rank of lieutenant-colonel (*Oberstleutnant*) were relieved of duty.[2] The Einigungsvertrag—the treaty unifying East and West Germany—stipulated that the Bundeswehr (the Cold War West Germany military, and the name of the post-unification German military) was to be reduced to 370,000 soldiers by 1994; 25 percent of the Bundeswehr was to be filled by former NVA soldiers and officers. The Bundeswehr initially accepted twenty thousand NVA soldiers and officers into its ranks; these were primarily specialists to train Bundeswehr personnel in the use of Soviet weapons and weapons systems taken into the Bundeswehr. The overwhelming majority of these soldiers and officers were released from the Bundeswehr within two years. By 2002, only 5 percent of the Bundeswehr was made up of former NVA soldiers and officers;[3] as of 2006, there were approximately eight hundred former NVA officers left on active duty in the Bundeswehr.[4]

German unification was not simply the joining of two halves of a long-separated whole; it was about fusing together two diametrically opposed systems, two distinctly different ways of seeing the world, the state, economics, fairness, human beings, the military, and conflict. In this context, memories of World War II and the actions of German soldiers loomed large, playing a key role in the shaping of the new German state. Perhaps most important, unification was the fusing of two radically different ways of imagining "Germany," what it should be and represent. It included the supposed merger of two different systems of defense and what it meant to be a "defender" and soldier of the state. It was the unequal merger of two militaries sworn to defend diametrically opposed political-economic systems, and soldiers trained and indoctrinated to believe each was the one true system. The GDR was ultimately a militarized dictatorship (though the debate is open as to what degree), and the NVA and Border Guards were integral parts of the system: they helped develop and maintain it, protect, and preserve it. In one of the great ironies of history, however, when it came time to actively save the GDR, the NVA and Border Guards decided that it was not worth saving in the state it was in, and did not fire a shot or intervene to keep it from collapsing. These are the soldiers who many see as the men who let socialism slip away. It is due to their actions (or inaction) that German unification was allowed to proceed peacefully—without a shot fired to stop it.

For Germans on both sides of the political divide, the Cold War was experienced as a cultural division, a splitting of the "family" of Germans that included an intense rivalry over legitimacy.[5] Indeed, much of the political battle between the two Germanys revolved around representations of their respective armies, their actions, and their relation to the past. Just as the two Germanys constituted a "mirror" for the other, so too did the two German Cold War militaries.[6]

As Frykman and Lofgren have noted, identity formation often takes the form of a negative example; that is, by stating that another group acts in a certain manner, or has certain characteristics, the identity of one's own group is defined in contrast, by what it is not.[7] In regard to the former GDR and the NVA, I argue that such a process is occurring in the representation of former East German soldiers by West German state actors and by the new, formerly West German Bundeswehr. A former NVA general summed up the attitudes of many former NVA soldiers about portrayals of the NVA as an aggressive military, and the trials of former Border Guards and GDR government officials when he stated: "Hey Germany, look here: we've found someone who is guilty. Now we can be satisfied."[8] This feeling of being the victims of "victor's justice" runs deep with former NVA officers, and frames the ways in which they view the post-unification German state and their experiences in the new state.

Representations of the officers and soldiers of the NVA as highly aggressive and concerned solely with preparations for the invasion of Western Europe or the suppression of internal dissent within the GDR elide the extremely complicated political, social, and economic dynamics within the NVA, and the role of the military in East German society. As Lesley Gill, Cynthia Enloe, and Ruth Seifert have noted, militaries serve to create hierarchies among men.[9] I argue that a similar process is at work in post-unification Germany: the former NVA and its officers are coded as the "bad" Germans who served an "illegal" regime and lost the Cold War, while the West German army and its officers are the "good" Germans who served the "legitimate" Germany and won the Cold War. This is not to excuse the human rights abuses of the Border Guards, the *Kadavergehörsamkeit* ("corpse-like obedience") of the NVA, or the brutality of overarching compulsory military service. Rather, it is to point out the inconsistencies, inequalities, and unevenness of the unification process and the ways in which history, memory, and gender came together in the German military after unification.

States emerging from periods of dictatorship must often come to terms with officials and soldiers who have committed war crimes or human rights abuses; Chile, Argentina, and post–World War II Germany come to mind.[10] The German case is unusual, as the East German military never fought in a war, did not resist its own demise, and willingly participated in the dissolution of the state it was sworn to defend. Germany was also forced to come to terms with a dictatorship for the second time in the twentieth century, and confront the actions of soldiers in the service of an unjust regime. While Border Guard officers and soldiers could be brought to trial for easily identified human rights abuses committed on the Berlin Wall and intra-German border, NVA officers could not necessarily be held accountable for their actions during the existence of the GDR. Despite the harsh discipline and bellicose rhetoric of the NVA, it never actually did much that would have involved its officers in war crimes trials or other sorts of trials for crimes against humanity. Although the overwhelming majority of NVA officers could not be tried in court for clear-cut crimes or abuses, they could still be "punished" through extrajudicial means, such as cuts in pensions, symbolic marginalization, and their removal from the cult of German military honor. Given the Cold War rivalry between the Bundeswehr and the NVA, and the fact that no former GDR or NVA officials or officers were in power and in a position to contest such actions,[11] West German elites felt that they could do as they pleased with NVA officers. This followed a general trend in the early years of unification, when large numbers of GDR officials, bureaucrats, teachers, professors, and anyone whose loyalty to the new German state was seen as questionable, lost their jobs, posts, and positions, and were replaced with West Germans, or East Germans who were considered politically reliable.

As McAdams writes, one of the forms of justice used by West German elites to punish East German elites was "disqualifying" justice; that is, even if they could not be held directly responsible for abuses or illegal actions in the GDR, they could still be disqualified from full rights and participation in the new state, based on their past affiliation(s) in the GDR.[12] They were punished not necessarily for what they did, but for who they were in the past, regardless of wrongdoing, and because they "should have known better" than to have served in what to West Germans was the "illegal" military of a "state without the rule of law" (*Unrechtsstaat*). In some instances, this may be true, but as a blanket condemnation of all NVA officers (and by extension, their families), it creates problems for the unification process. In the Bundeswehr, this was expressed more as retribution, and not justice, vis-à-vis the NVA. Bundeswehr officers saw NVA officers as both expendable (in terms of the reductions stipulated by the Unification treaty), and as threats to their careers.[13] The NVA was seen as traitorous to the "German nation," as a military that upheld the GDR state, and helped perpetuate the Cold War. Perhaps most important, the NVA was allied with the Soviet Union and the Red Army, Germany's primary enemy in World War II. Given the carryover of fascist and anticommunist sentiment in the West German military from World War II (the Bundeswehr was founded and heavily influenced by former World War II Wehrmacht officers, who—unofficially—carried over the traditions and worldview of the World War II German military), this was seen as the most grievous sin of NVA officers.

By looking at the politics and practices of military representation and the seemingly banal questions of military honor, we can see how the state uses soldiers to link itself to an idealized version of the past that upholds legitimacy in the present. I examine who controls representations of Germany's military past and its soldiers, who gains and who loses, who is valorized and who is marginalized by these representations and the subsequent material and symbolic ramifications they engender. As an examination of power relationships centered on the military, policy, and representation, I focus on ideas about "proper" soldiers and the "proper" relationship between the military, men, and citizenship, and how these ideas shape, as Eric Wolf writes, who can "direct and initiate action to others" and how these "others who [have] to respond" do in fact respond.[14]

My primary field site was Berlin. Berlin was in many ways the quintessential Cold War setting: heavily militarized, the trip-wire city of the folly of war and the possibility of suicidal war to come. Divided by the Wall, the site of countless intrigues, personal dramas, political dilemmas, and death, Berlin symbolized the division of Germany in concrete form. The Berlin Wall came to symbolize the Cold War and the division of Germany like no other structure, and the men who maintained the Wall and protected the GDR were seen in the West as servants of an unjust and inhumane regime—soldiers harkening back to the recent history of a criminal military. They were, in many ways, the personification of Cold War injustice. Snaking its way through the center of Berlin, and encircling West Berlin, the Wall was—and still is—*the* signifier of repression and militarization in post-1945 Germany.

Berlin was the logical site to study the cultural politics and memories of soldiering in post-unification Germany. Most importantly, a large number of former NVA and Border Guard officers still live in Berlin; the political contexts may have changed, but they and their families have remained. The headquarters of the German Army Veterans Association (Deutscher Bundeswehrverband), which handles the veterans groups of former NVA officers, is located in Berlin. I also know Berlin well, having lived there for a number of years; it was the site of my military experience and my initial experiences with the NVA, the Border Guards, and the Wall. For the most part, the Wall is gone, though sections have been preserved as a memorial to those killed, wounded, and imprisoned for attempting to cross into the West, and to serve as a reminder of the brutal nature of the East German regime (a reminder that is deeply offensive and misguided to many former NVA and Border Guard officers). While remnants remain, the Wall as an active military barrier, a barrier that gave structure to their lives, is gone. Literally and figuratively for them, only remnants remain, remnants of a former life of power, status, and stability.

Here, the Cold War was the surface level of a series of complex layers of memory: decisions made in Berlin shaped the course of history, both personal and public, leading to the deaths and distress of countless millions. Berlin has a long history of militarization, as a site both of military expansion and of military death and destruction. From the capital of the German Reich, to the Third Reich, to the partitioned camps of East and West Berlin, Berlin has been associated with war, militarism, and militarization for most of its recent history. Even after the fall of the Berlin Wall and the return to normalcy, the remnants of militarization—both physical and mental—haunt the landscape and the memories of its inhabitants, and shape the experiences of its visitors.[15] Remains of the Wall continue to attract visitors, and work a strange and eerie legerdemain on both landscape and emotion. The hulking remains of World War II anti-aircraft towers—too large and strong to be demolished—form cumbersome squares of painful memories in fashionable districts. The Cold War presence of the Allied militaries—U.S., Soviet, British, and French—form a network of landmarks, tourist sites, and spaces converted to civilian use. And sprinkled throughout the city, like the horrid memories of a childhood pox, lay the various memorials to the victims of what was perhaps the most militarized state and system in history. These are the material remains of militarization, the concrete reminders of the (pre)dominance of the military and militarization in German social, cultural, and historical life. Somehow forgotten in the midst of these concrete realizations of militarism are the experiences of the men who created, maintained, and defended the GDR and the Wall—those who made militarization real.

In many ways, I consider this to be a "siteless" ethnography. *Fallen Elites* is an ethnography of the soldiers of a no longer existing army of a no longer existing state who find themselves in a new state that will not necessarily let them forget who they were in their former state. I was not able to conduct research on an NVA base, for example, nor to see the NVA and its officers "in action." Nor could I talk to Border Guards as they manned the Wall, or even observe the Wall as it divided the city and people. But this did not mean that I could not conduct fieldwork on the NVA or Border Guards. It meant that my fieldwork in many ways focused on their sense of loss: The loss not only of their careers but of their state, the physical trappings of their professions, and the meanings they gave to the physical structures and markers that helped create their identities as soldiers and officers, structures that helped make them who they are.

But of course, this is not a siteless ethnography. I examine the "echo" of East German militarization in the new German state, and the ways that militarization in the GDR continues to impact those who went through it, embraced it, and promoted it. A certain version of Berlin may no longer exist, a certain militarized understanding and reception of Berlin may be gone, but Berlin is still there, and the people who served the East German state and made it work are still there. For them, Berlin is a ghost town: a shadow of its former GDR past, the spectral past of their lives and careers, an urban environment of militarized history, changed contexts, changed signs, and charged meanings.

FIELDWORK AND INTERVIEWS: PREPARING FOR WAR IN FOUR TIMES AND PLACES

Like most ethnographies, this one has the ubiquitous "entry to the field site" story, though mine is fairly different. My work with the NVA began years before I even imagined becoming an anthropologist. I enlisted in the U.S. Army in 1984, when I was seventeen-years-old, as a way to go to college, and arrived in West Berlin in 1986 as a twenty-year-old army linguist. I spent the next three years in West Berlin, leaving the army shortly before the fall of the Wall, having experienced the Cold War division of Berlin and Germany firsthand.

As part of the U.S. "army of occupation" in Berlin, we were referred to by the military as "proud defenders of freedom stationed on an island of democracy, 120 miles within a sea of tyranny." Fundamentally, however, we were on our own, cut off 120 miles behind "enemy" lines, with little to no hope of rescue or relief if actual combat had occurred. We knew that the NVA and the Soviet Army were to attack and capture West Berlin if war started, though few of us really thought a war would ever start (or if it did, that we would actually survive). As I was to later learn during my fieldwork, my experiences in the army would prove invaluable as a way of establishing rapport with NVA officers. My time in the military helped me understand their experiences of military service and militarization on a different, visceral level, making me something of a "native" ethnographer of the military.

This is a story of militarization in four times and contexts: the Cold War rivalry of East and West Germany, post-unification Germany, and the United States. Woven throughout are my experiences of the military, of East and West Germany, the Cold War, and unification. While this book is, of course, not about me, I found that I could not entirely distance or remove my experiences from my fieldwork or the writing of the book. My experiences of militarization and military service played a key role in my ability to conduct fieldwork with NVA officers, and opened up productive areas of discussion and inquiry. In the majority of cases, the fact that I had military experience had a positive effect on my relationships with former officers. As many officers told me, it proved to them that I was "serious" about my subject, and that I was "honorable," even though I had been on the other side.

A decade and a different world later, having decided that I was interested in studying militarization, I returned to Berlin in 1997 to conduct exploratory fieldwork. I knew that many former NVA and Border Guard officers still lived in Berlin and the surrounding towns and cities, but I had no idea how to contact them.

Even though I thought it might be a long shot, the day after arriving in Berlin, I looked up the number of the Bundeswehr press office in Berlin, which I thought might have some useful information. After explaining that I was an anthropologist interested in the NVA, the press officer told me to come by, and that he would see what he could do for me. The following day, after showing up at the press office, the press officer told me to go to the Berlin headquarters of the Deutscher Bundeswehrverband. He explained that a large number of former NVA officers were now members of the association, so someone there might be able to help me.

I took the S-Bahn train toward Nikolaussee, a posh and upscale neighborhood in the southwest of Berlin, and found the headquarters. It was located in an old villa, complete with turreted rooms and gothic towers, with a large German flag and Bundeswehr pennant flying from the flagpole in the courtyard. I was politely—though somewhat coldly—received by a former NVA noncommissioned officer who worked for the Bundeswehr-

verband. As I described my interest in the NVA, he simply sat there, gaz-
ing at me with a look that expressed bewilderment, amusement, and a
hint of annoyance, all of which combined seemed to reveal his thought of
"why me?" He heard me out, uttered a low, drawn out, "hmmm," and
then picked up the phone to make a call. Clearly hoping to be rid of me, he
rapidly dialed the phone. "Egbert, I've got an *Ami* (German slang for an
American) here who is interested in the NVA—do you have time for him?"
Placing his hand on the receiver, he asked "Do you want to go over to his
house?" I nodded and said yes, so he told Egbert that I'd be right over, a
slight smile of relief emerging from behind the receiver.

"Egbert" turned out to be Professor Doktor *Oberst* (Colonel) Egbert
Fischer, a former NVA colonel and historian, who lead the "Arbeitsgruppe
Geschichte der NVA und Integration ehemaliger NVA Angehörigen in
Bundeswehr und Gesellschaft"—the "Working Group on the History
of the National People's Army and Integration of former NVA members
in the Bundeswehr and Society." The Arbeitsgruppe—comprised of former NVA historians, sociologists, and political-economists who held important teaching and research positions at NVA military academies and
research institutes—writes counterhistories to what they see as views and
analyses of the GDR and NVA written from a West German bias.[16] Prof.
Fischer offered me the chance to take part in the monthly meetings of the
Arbeitsgruppe, and his support greatly eased and facilitated my entry in
the NVA community. He also introduced me to Oberstleutnant Rainer
Wulf, an influential member of the NVA veterans groups association, who
opened up the NVA veterans network for me, introduced me to countless
officers, and took me along to veterans groups meetings in Berlin and
elsewhere in eastern Germany. Rainer Wulf was my "key informant,"
an invaluable resource, and a wonderful interlocutor. My meeting with
Prof. Fischer was fortuitous—it came about by my looking in the phone
book—and would make fieldwork both possible and successful.

TALKING TO "THE CLASS ENEMY"

My primary method of fieldwork consisted of semiformal and informal
interviews and conversations with officers, either at their homes or at bars;
monthly meetings and special events with the Arbeitsgruppe Geschichte

der NVA; and participant-observation at NVA veterans groups. Over the course of my primary fieldwork (1998–2000), I attended veterans groups meetings and spoke with officers in Berlin, Oranienburg, Gera, Rostock, and Bad Saarow. Meetings with officers were generally one on one, though I often met groups of officers at bars, and discussions at veterans groups were usually with a number of officers.

I was initially concerned that it would be difficult to find former officers willing to take part in my project. I was not sure if former soldiers would willingly and openly speak of their experiences with me. I was concerned that "Cold War" assumptions about me would get in the way: a former U.S. soldier asking questions about militarization, life in the NVA, and so on. Fortunately, I was wrong. After assuaging their initial suspicions, former officers were more than willing to speak to me, and said that it was because I was American and a "scientist," and could therefore be "objective" (as I was repeatedly told). Had I been West German, they would never have agreed to speak with me. West Germans, they said, were simply out to demonize them and hold them responsible for the Cold War. And because I was a former soldier, they said they felt I could better understand them: their experiences, reasons for joining, concerns, actions, and motivations. Of course, as I will discuss in later chapters, many officers had very specific reasons and goals in mind when they spoke to me. My concerns about Cold War rivalry did play a role, but in a humorous way: I was often referred to by the East German term for NATO, Imperialists, and Americans: *der Klassenfeind*—the class enemy. This was used as a term of acceptance and inclusion, as an ironic mark that I had finally been accepted and trusted. I was often greeted with a slap on the back, a handshake, and "Na, Klassenfeind, wie geht's Dir?"—Well, Class Enemy, how are you doing?

Between 1997 and 2000, I conducted interviews with sixty-seven former NVA officers and eighteen Bundeswehr officers, as well as seventeen NVA conscripts and one conscientious objector. I was able to interview the last minister of defense of the GDR, Admiral Theodor Hoffmann, the head of the NVA military intelligence service, General Alfred Krause, and the head of the Border Guards, General Klaus-Dieter Baumgarten. I conducted interviews with the wives of eight NVA officers whom I had previously interviewed, and I spoke with both East and West German civilians concerning their experiences and opinions of both German militaries, and unification in general. In 2003 and 2006, I returned to Berlin to carry out follow-up interviews with NVA officers and their families, and I attended meetings of the Arbeitsgruppe Geschichte der NVA to follow their work and research. Interviews focused on questions about informants' lives in the GDR and the NVA, their experiences as soldiers, their family histories, their interactions with men, women, and children, as well as soldiers and officers in the NVA, their views on warfare, violence, and killing, their experiences after unification, and employment and economic situations.

When not speaking with officers, I conducted archival research focused on GDR militarization policies, military and paramilitary training, military education policies in schools, and reports concerning the need to militarize families and familial relationships. This included research on the Ministry of Defense, the State Security Council, and the Ministry of Education. Archival research in Berlin was conducted at the SAPMO (Foundation Archives of the Parties and Mass Organizations of the GDR in the Federal Archives) and the Staatsbibliothek zu Berlin; in Potsdam at the Militärgeschichtliches Forschungsamt (Military History Research Center); and at the Militärarchiv Freiburg. I had access to formerly classified documents from the NVA concerning the goals, methods, and evaluations of militarization programs, paramilitary training, military discipline, and reports on the methods necessary for the creation of the "socialist military personality," all of which helped detail the structures and policies of militarization in the GDR.

FIELDWORK AND THE KAMERADSCHAFTEN

A good part of my fieldwork was centered on the lives, actions, and experiences of former NVA officers in the Kameradschaften, the NVA veterans groups. I usually attended Kameradschaft meetings with Rainer Wulf. He made sure to tell me when we first met that he had not been a member of the STASI, as he had been *vergauckt*, that is, cleared by the Gauck-Behörde, the group charged with investigating the STASI, and initially led by the former pastor Joachim Gauck (hence the wordplay of *vergauckt*, meaning cleared and given a clean bill of "moral" health by the Gauck group). Herr Wulf always made sure to introduce me at the meetings by saying something along the lines of, "Tonight, we have a special guest, an American ethnologist and former U.S. Army sergeant who is conducting research on our situation since unification." At this point, everyone in the room would turn and stare at me (if they had not already done so), and I would stand and give a short nod by way of introduction.

My trips to these meetings brought back memories of my time in West Berlin in the mid- to late 1980s. These were the men that I had expected to fight if a war started, and now I was meeting with them. It was a curious feeling, a mix of intense interest and curiosity, fascination, and apprehension: what if something had happened? What would I have done, or what would they have done? In later conversations, when this topic came up, many told me that they had had the same feeling. It struck me that therein lay the power of military thinking: eight years after unification and the end of the NVA, both they and I still had lingering feelings of uncertainty and curiosity, tinged with a slight feeling of possible danger. My relationship with these men was summed up by a comment that Franz, a former political officer, made to me late one night in a bar: "You know, I would have killed you during the Cold War, no problem. But that's over, so now we can be friends."

While never hostile, my reception at a new Kameradschaft was never terribly warm, either, and seemed to generate a combination of curiosity, suspicion, and caution. Initially, I found meetings at the Kameradschaften somewhat bewildering. I was very much the outsider: I was much younger than everyone else there, and I was never quite sure what members made of me. Meetings were usually very formal, with a rigid and well-defined set of points of order and procedures (at the end of the meeting, people would relax, and officers would mingle and chat). It generally took a while for people to become comfortable with my presence; I was later told that many thought I was from the CIA or the military, that I had come to investigate them and their activities after unification. Surely, I was told, the U.S. military was still interested in them, as the NVA had played a major role during the Cold War, considered second only to the Soviet military in combat capabilities and strength. As my fieldwork progressed, I suspected—and was told—that many former officers actually hoped that I was from the CIA or the military, as this would have been an indication that they were still in fact seen as important, key players in global military-political affairs. In an ironic twist to the usual fieldwork experience, I always felt that I was letting them down in some way when I told them that, no, really, I was not a CIA or military spy. For many of these men, to be spied on was a high compliment. To be spied on was to be important in the eyes of the state, to represent something that required attention, respect, and a certain amount of fear. To be spied upon meant that you were dangerous, and many of these men, I was to learn, desperately wanted to still be seen as dangerous.

ANTHROPOLOGY, MILITARIZATION, AND THE STATE

Anthropology is concerned with deciphering cultural logics, analyzing normative ways of being, and considering how people speak and act in context. An anthropological perspective focuses on the insider's point of view, or rather, "their" world from their point of view, and is concerned, as Michael Herzfeld states, with understanding "commonsense" notions of the world.[17] Ethnographic analysis provides a microlevel analysis of everyday life and experience, and views society and culture as systems; as such, anthropology seeks to link microlevel analysis to these larger social systems and structures in order to investigate the relationship between behavior, practice, and culture. To become and be a soldier is to take on a political-economic identity situated in time and space, specific to a given cultural context and historical epoch.

In *Fallen Elites*, I see militarization as "the contradictory and tense social process in which civil society organizes itself for the production of (military) violence" (my addition of "military" to the original quote).[18] Lutz's definition of militarization as "the shaping of national histories in ways that glorify and legitimate military action" is also particularly useful in thinking through militarization programs in the GDR, the effects of these programs after unification, and the ways in which the new German state creates a new military identity and ethos.[19]

As Sharma and Gupta write, an anthropological perspective on the state allows us "to pay careful attention to the cultural construction of the state—that is, how people perceive the state, how their understandings are shaped by their particular locations and intimate encounters with state processes and officials, and how the state manifests itself in their lives."[20] Soldiers are never simply "soldiers," "warriors," or the mere instruments of violence: soldiers are the congealed ideal of propriety and violence, of how the state sees itself—and wants to be seen—as strong and legitimate. Soldiers lend the state a certain "international" image or face. It is of great importance to the state that soldiers accurately reflect how the state wants to be perceived.

An anthropological approach to the military and soldiering allows for an examination of the ways in which states and military service influence and shape the identities, worldviews, and life courses of individuals, including how they cope with life in the civilian world after military service. It is also a window into the ways in which state bureaucracies work, both in tandem and in conflict, to create the political structure of the "State," and to examine the practices and techniques of power that state agents utilize in the consolidation of power and legitimacy. In the case of German unification, we see the bureaucratic methods and strategies of identity valorization and marginalization, the ways in which historical memory is mobilized to uphold political and military policy, and how the state codifies, imagines, and deals with soldiers who no longer fit within the state's military imaginary or political structure.

States, according to Weber, claim to have a monopoly on legitimate violence. And as Tilly writes, war makes states.[21] Of even more significance here is that while war makes states, states make soldiers to make war; through this cycle, war shapes and forms a key part of the political structure and identity of the state. States not only claim the monopoly on legitimate violence, but also have a keen interest in maintaining the monopoly on the representations and images of the men (and increasingly, women) who are to commit violence; that is, they claim a monopoly on militarized gender identities, on who is considered a legitimate, proper man or soldier. This monopoly on militarized identities includes not only the present, but also the past, for it is more often from the past that role models and traditions are sought. Soldiers of the past combine emotion, kinship, and memory: they are one's father, grandfather, brother, or uncle, a close relative who fought and possibly gave his all for the state, the fatherland, and the nation (and increasingly, as noted, they are also mothers, sisters, wives, daughters, aunts, and girlfriends who give their lives). States play this emotional trump card to create and maintain legitimacy and support for the military.

The "state" is understood here as "a set of organizations invested with the authority to make binding decisions for people and organizations juridically located in a particular territory and to implement these decisions using, if necessary, force."[22] This process often entails the state "simultaneously expressing several contradictory tendencies,"[23] and an anthropological examination of the state can examine how these "contradictory tendencies" can be expressed in people's lives through the "banal practices of the state" and the "cultural struggles [that] determine what a state means to its people, and how it is instantiated in their daily lives, and where its boundaries are drawn."[24] In addition to banal practices, Corrigan and Sayer note that one of the main things states do is *state*, that is, make statements, about inclusion and exclusion, about who is part of the state and who is not, and about how history and memory coalesce with the political life of the state: "States, if the pun be forgiven, *state*; the arcane rituals of a court of law, the formulae of royal assent to an Act of Parliament, visits of school inspectors, are all statements. They define, in great detail, acceptable forms and images of social activity and individual and collective identity; they regulate, in empirically specifiable ways, much—very much, by the twentieth century—of social life. Indeed, in this sense, 'the State' never stops talking."[25]

While states make statements concerning history, memory, gender, and propriety, the various administrative units (and administrators) of the state are often at odds with one another with regard to just what form these statements or pronouncements should take, and how to transform them into policy and practice. States are not to be considered "homogenous" units; to do so would be to reify the state and fail to examine the often contradictory actions of the various organs of the state.[26] Indeed, as Herzfeld writes, research on the state should focus on "what bearers of power actually do—

how they direct institutional controls and classifications to the pursuit of particular ends."[27] This has particular resonance here, as questions of classification and naming—and the power to classify and name—are one of the contested fields of power between the two former Cold War enemies. Rather than simply examining discrete elements, we need to attend to the process and flow of state formation and militarization, as a process of unequal power relations and political opportunity.[28] This is evident in post-unification Germany, where the official goal, as articulated by the German state, is the complete and equal unification of East and West; yet, in terms of the German military, this is seemingly not the aim. As Bald has written, the doctrine of the Cold War—of being threatened by the East—has had a delayed effect; the previously "external enemy" (the GDR and the NVA) is now instrumentalized internally, allowing the NVA to remain a "threat" to the post-unification German military.[29] The post-unification Ministry of Defense and Bundeswehr have instituted policies to prevent the full integration of former East German officers into the military, national identity, and "positive" historical narratives, thus shoring up the claims of West German elites that they are the "legitimate" German military and inheritors of the "proper" German military tradition, a tradition which draws both officially and unofficially on the Nazi-era Wehrmacht and Waffen SS. This draws on both institutional tradition and the perceptions of the "honor" and military acumen of World War II German soldiers.

IMAGINING SOLDIERS AND MAKING THE STATE

In many ways, soldiers are imaginary beings, mythic creatures dreamed up in the minds of politicians and generals; myth and folklore provide models for this process, the imagining of the warrior-hero who saves and protects the group, one who is seemingly invincible and almost always noble. Soldiers also occupy the imaginations of civilians, who see them as heroes and protectors, cowards and criminals. And soldiers, too, imagine themselves in various ways: as the heroes and protectors of the state; strong, virtuous men; agents of destruction and death; conquerors; those who merely carry out the armed policies of the state; and those who simply have a "job" to do. Image is everything to a military and state, and soldiers are expected to uphold this image, acting and performing as imagined.

Of course, soldiers are real: they are real people who can commit real acts of violence against real people and implement policies of domination, terror, and control. They often uphold and support repressive state policies and do the violence work of the state. To think otherwise is to enter a realm of pure fantasy, a realm in which extreme constructivism and relativism holds sway, where victims are made to disappear and violence is just another discourse. The point I wish to make here is that ideas, imaginations, fantasies, and conceptions of soldiers do have very real material effects. Ideas—and the power to make ideas a reality—bring soldiers into being. If we go from the fact that states make soldiers, we have to attend to the process of making, the "hard poetics" of soldiering,[30] the aestheticized production of a militarized political identity that must be made both materially and symbolically palatable, desirable, and useful to those who are to become these imagined soldiers and those who will support these soldiers.

I see militarization programs—particularly with regard to the two Cold War Germanys—as competing forms and visions of the state and the moral universe of the state,[31] and I examine how these competing visions produced different types of soldiers and citizens. Capitalism and communism—and their respective military blocs—created different rationales for different types of militaries, soldiers, and citizens. These competing visions contained different moral economies that shaped ideas about soldiering, killing, allegiance, human rights, conceptions of justice and law, and conceptions of political economy. These visions also created moral economies of worry. Militarization is much like Benjamin's "state of emergency": it only works if a state of emergency—a perpetual state of fear, threat, and preparedness, and a manufactured feeling of the need to be prepared—exists. As the slogan for the East German youth group, the Young Pioneers went, "Young Pioneers: Be Prepared!" And the refrain: "Always Prepared"—the cultivation of a perpetual state of preparedness, a perpetual state of worry and emergency, contingency and concern.

Militarization is an intentional process, something a state must set out to accomplish. No one is born a soldier, although this kind of sociobiological rhetoric of "man the warrior" plays well in certain discourses of the state. States must develop ways in which to make men—and women—into soldiers, and to convince citizens that it is a natural progression, part of the natural life-course of a person to become a soldier, to have an innate and "uncoerced" willingness to fight and die for their country, homeland, fatherland-motherland, or people. While biological notions of "man the warrior" are politically convenient, and seem to explain away all sorts of theoretical and moral dilemmas,[32] these arguments elide questions of power and process in the state, and in fact can be used to naturalize politics and violence employed by the state.

Militarization is dependent on the establishment of deep networks within the state, and on the deployment of discourses about courage, strength, honor, masculinity, femininity, credentials, health, marriage, violence, and identity. Broadly speaking, militarization is about the transformation of civilians into soldiers,[33] about the creation of certain types of men and citizens through the creation of certain types of soldiers.[34] It is a process of social, political, and military reproduction, the reproduction of the state through military values and identities, the naturalization of the creative and (re)productive violence of the state in and through the very bodies of its citizens. In terms of citizenship, I follow Gill, in her discussion of the relationship between military service and the creation of proper citizens and men, and Biess, in his discussion of World War II German prisoners of war and their experiences in the development of the two postwar German states.[35] Biess examines military service and citizenship, and sees citizenship as a "concept of belonging and a marker of subjectivity that is located at the intersection between state and society."[36]

SOLDIERS IN THE STATE

Soldiers occupy a special niche in the state—they are either heroes or villains, saviors or murderers, good men or bad, the best of the best or chattel, detritus, or cannon fodder. They are rarely, if ever, viewed neutrally. Regardless, soldiers do the dirty work of the state, and the state needs to maintain the illusion that soldiers are valued members of society, even though they are the ones to be sent to fight and die, kill and maim, and live to think about it for the rest of their lives. And, of course, the killing soldiers do must be justified by the state, made to seem necessary, and above all, legal. One state's murder is another's martial prowess; one state's murderer is another state's hero. The ways in which this killing is codified and legalized, and the ways in which soldiers are valorized or demonized for carrying out the dirty work of the state are the focus here: Who counts as a proper and legal soldier, and why, and how, and when? What does it mean to be a legal soldier versus an illegal soldier, war criminal, or murderer? Who decides who counts as a "real" soldier, and how is that decision made definitive? For example, it is illegal to state that a member of the Bundeswehr is a murderer, though it is permissible to make such a statement about a former NVA officer or Border Guard officer (which, in terms of the Border Guards, may be true; I will expand on this point later).[37] The point here is: how does the state decide when a soldier—as a member of an entire army—is either a murderer or defender, even though soldiers are tasked with killing the "enemy," which itself is differentially defined in time and space by the state? How does the state convince its citizens that its soldiers are good, proper soldiers and men, while those of other states or groups are not? The lifespan of the two Cold War Germanys was short; during this short life, West Germany was seen by the West as the "good Germany" and East Germany was seen as the "bad Germany," even though both states were heirs and results of the Third Reich. Just as labeling an entire group of soldiers "heroes"—as in the United States— elides the complicated reasons and pressures for joining the military in the first place, so too does labeling an entire military of a subsumed state— that of the GDR—as murderers, criminals, or "illegal" soldiers, elide the complicated role of the soldier in the GDR, the reasons for joining, and the experience of being a soldier and carrying out orders in the GDR. It also dodges and deflects questions of legitimacy with regard to the Bundeswehr.

THE MILITARY IMAGINARY:
SIGNS, SOLDIERS, AND THE STATE

The "military imaginary" of the modern state includes the ways in which the necessity, implementation, and desired outcomes of military service and training—whether compulsory or voluntary—and the ways in which these tropes are linked to normative ideas of citizenship and gender identity, are imagined and envisioned by the state.[38] This is based on Kerzer's analysis of the symbolic dimensions of power and politics, Taylor's discussion of the social imaginary, and Anderson's notion of "imagined communities" of citizens connected through various discourses,[39] discourses and ideas that become so real for those involved that they are willing to fight and die for them.[40] Taylor sees the "social imaginary" as "the ways people imagine their social existence, how they fit together with others, how things go on between them and their fellows, the expectations that are normally met, and the deeper normative notions and images that underlie these expectations."[41]

Soldiers are very much a part of the military imaginary of a state; as Walzer describes the process, "the state is invisible; it must be personified before it can be seen, symbolized before it can be loved, imagined before it can be conceived."[42] Soldiers make the state visible through their personification of the state and identification with the "positive" virtues of the state. Much of what it means to be a soldier, to become a soldier, and to make a soldier revolves around symbolism, representation, ritual, and the imagination. In many ways, the power of the state revolves around the ability to use and manipulate symbols and images, to manipulate perceptions along unequal lines of power and access, to make the relationship between the imagined and the real, the name and the thing appear natural and normal. As Kerzer writes, people gain their basic political ideas through the society in which they live, ideas determined largely by those who exercise power and control over society.[43]

The work of Voloshinov is important in this regard.[44] Voloshinov shows that signs are saturated with political meaning, even if they are as opaque as the social relations in which they are produced. Voloshinov points out that signs are the true center of class—and political—struggle.[45] For Voloshinov, the sign is the site where the dominant class(es) attempt to stabilize and fix the meanings of signs according to their own interests and agendas.[46] Ideology and hegemony become a struggle over who controls the "legitimate" meaning of signs; dominant ideology attempts to enforce its conception of meaning upon those below, who constantly receive and rework some signs but not always all of them. As the site where the "historically contingent configuration of social relationships" is contested,[47] dominant groups attempt to fix the meaning of signs; an appreciation of how signs are created allows us to see ideology and hegemony in action.

The central task of hegemony is to limit the ways in which signs can be interpreted and understood. In the case of the Bundeswehr and the NVA, it comes down to an unequal political struggle centered around meanings and representations of "Germans," "soldiers," and "German soldiers," as well as representations of German history and military history. As West German elites attempt to delimit understandings and perceptions of the GDR and the NVA, former NVA soldiers resist these attempts to fix political signs and meanings centered on them. It is one thing to think about signs as things; it is another thing entirely to live as a sign, to be made to signify in an unequal system of signification.

To speak of the "NVA" or the "Bundeswehr" is to speak and imagine a name and a political entity; these "names" or entities are in fact networks of cultural and political practices, networks which, while on one level imagined into being, entail the real activities and lives of people engendering real inequalities of power.[48] To imagine the "NVA" or the "Bundeswehr" is to also invoke an imagination of space and place, as each was a military dedicated to defending—and through defense, making—a certain bounded geographical entity.[49]

In *Mythologies*, Roland Barthes uses an apposite example to illustrate one of the key points of his theory of signification and myth: the image of a Franco-African soldier on the cover of a glossy French magazine.[50] Barthes explicates the various meanings, submeanings, connotations, inferences, and metaphors attached to this image, the ways in which the soldier signifies for the state. But Barthes leaves out one key point (though obviously not a point he was interested in for his argument): What did it mean to *be* that soldier, the soldier who signifies, who connotes, denotes, infers, and spins out metaphors and meanings in the public and private spheres, who literally represents France, and who, through his actions, in many ways makes France? Who was this soldier, and how did he feel about living as a sign of French imperial power and ambition, as the signifier of past, present, and future French martial glory and prowess? Soldiers are metasigns of the state, and represent the mythology of the state. But what does it mean to live as a sign of the state? As a sign of protection and defense? As a sign of violence, killing, and death, whether condoned or decried? And what does it mean to live as a sign of a state that no longer exists, when the signification system has changed, when your sign no longer has power?

As semiotic systems of the state, soldiers are perhaps *the* political sign. This semiotic valuation plays a large role in the life of the soldier and the ways in which the soldier is understood, interacted with, and treated. Soldiers live at the nexus of multiple meanings and readings, of varying registers of signification, differentially valued, received, and imagined. These imaginings and readings have concrete, material effects: they drive policies, influence employment possibilities, determine procurement budgets and weapon systems design, and shape who is considered a part of the nation-state. To attempt to understand German unification and the role of the military is to trace out the swirling relationships between images, ideas, and memories of World War II German soldiers, West German Bundeswehr soldiers, East German NVA soldiers, and the soldiers of the post-unification German military.

As the focal point of power projection, soldiers are metaphors of the state. This is not to say that soldiers are merely signs or floating signifiers out in the ether. Of course, soldiers are flesh-and-blood human beings in place and time, who cause and suffer real pain and violence. As soldiers, not only do they prosecute war for the state, they represent the state, and as such, they represent, signify, stand in for the state and an idea, the ethos or ideology or worldview of the state or system to which they are sworn and must serve. And as soldiers, they must oppose, fight, contest, wound, incapacitate, or kill other human beings, not simply because they are human beings, but because of what they represent and stand for: one god over the other, good versus bad, up versus down, how profit is created and shared (or not)—what they stand for over and above their humanity. This is why we use terms like *enemy, threat, combatant, soldier, commie, class enemy, collateral damage,* and the rest. Militaries have to turn other human beings into a representation in order to get its state-represented-human-soldiers to kill other human beings, not because they are human beings, but because they are signifiers of something other than themselves.

Politics is primarily an act of symbolism, the deployment and use of symbols to shape reality, actions, and material processes. As Kertzer argues, little that is political involves the use of direct force; material resources—

crucial to the political process—are largely used and distributed through symbolic means.[51] This does not mean that politics is purely imaginary or made up; rather, ideas and symbols drive actions and practice, policies and inequalities, marginalization and massacres. Conceptions of war, peace, the military, and soldiers all involve a great deal of work on the level of imagination, work that draws on the past. Wars of the future, writes Sam Keen, are first imagined and fought in the minds of men.[52] The ability to create and shape these images, and to convince the majority of people that these representations are in fact the only representations and conceptions possible, is very much the work of politics and hegemony, the coalescence of symbolism and political power in everyday life.

Memories and the imagination come together in the social construction of soldiers and the military. The representational dimension of soldiers is a manifestation of the amount of time and money states invest in creating and crafting the image of the soldier and ensuring that there is only one possible "reading" of its soldiers. This image work goes a long way in securing the position of the soldier in civil society, promoting a positive view of the military and soldiers, and perhaps most importantly, insuring that young men will want to join the military. Of course, this positive image creation requires a negative image: the creation of the image of the enemy, of improper soldiers, of those who fall outside the imagination and the morality of the state. This image work depends on the memory of soldiers and war, on remembrances of heroism and war crimes, the deeds and actions of "good" soldiers and "good" men, or those of cowards and criminals. To cathect soldiers to the state, the French Marshal Lyautey acknowledged, they had to be treated not as brutes, but as Frenchman.[53] But what about former soldiers of an "enemy" state who find themselves incorporated in a new state? After unification, would former NVA officers have to be treated as Germans, or as brutes?

WRITING MILITARIZATION, NAVIGATING MEMORY AND POWER

To write about militarization is to navigate between contested fields of power, to enter into the debate on the representations of the GDR after unification. On the one hand, the GDR was a militarized state, heavily dependent on the saturation of civil society with military structures and values as a way to insure and maintain political control and claim legitimacy. On the other hand, to write about the GDR as a militarized state is potentially to replicate West German and Western discourses of the GDR as a continuation of Prussian militarism and the fanaticism of the Third Reich, to paint a picture of a highly ordered, "jackbooted," totalitarian state. This is precisely where ethnography and anthropology come into play: we can examine militarization as a process and system, as a form of structural violence, but that only gives us one part of the picture. Anthropology allows us to examine the lived experience of militarization and soldiering, to examine how people enacted military policies, how they complied, how they resisted, and how militarization continues to shape and impact lives and worldviews. If anthropology "explores how different cultural constructions of reality affect social action,"[54] then the point is to see how cultural constructions of reality based on military values affected the social action of NVA officers both before and after unification.

Examining the militarization of the GDR ethnographically reveals a different picture of life in a militarized society, uncovers the nuances and tensions of everyday life, and complicates our understandings of the GDR as a militarized state. We can see the ways in which East German citizens dealt with the incursion of the military and military values into their lives, how they accommodated the state and militarization programs, and how they resisted. To see the GDR simply as a militarized state without resistance, without the weapons of resistance employed by the (politically) weak and dominated,[55] is to paint a picture that is not only distorted and inaccurate but also reinforces Western political rhetoric from the Cold War and right after unification. Conversely, we cannot ignore the overarching attempts by the East German state to militarize its citizens, and the programs designed to create a socialism intimately tied to military service, values, and honor, including the lingering effects of military socialization, effects connected to both Prussian and Nazi-fascist militarization. The GDR was a militarized state, and to argue otherwise, or to "underwrite" militarization in the GDR would be to do an injustice to those who were forced to undergo military socialization, conscription, and the everyday violence of military service.

To speak with former officers, NVA conscripts, and GDR citizens, and to study NVA and SED documents on militarization policies, is to hear and read a chronicle of never-met goals and expectations, of the frustration of officials as they comment on the "insufficient" fear and appreciation of the threat by NATO, West Germany, and the United States, and hear the resistance strategies of everyday civilians trying to make do. While the GDR was a militarized state, militarization was never a completely successful state project. It was an uneven and contested process, a process of partial compliance, accommodation, and resistance, of differing intensity at different times. The majority of East Germans were suspicious and distrustful of the military, even if they did willingly complete their compulsory military service, take part in party organizations, and seemingly go along with the party. In the end, however, all of the military preparation and linkages between the military, the party, and citizenship could not save the GDR from implosion and dissolution.

FALLEN ELITES: STUDYING UP AND STUDYING DOWN

The study of elites—even discredited or fallen elites—is instructive, though fraught with potential pitfalls and moral quandaries.[56] NVA officers in East Germany were elites, occupying positions of power and influence. These were men who enjoyed the benefits of militarization, and carried out militarization programs and policies. While the military was never loved in the GDR, it did command a grudging respect, given the prominence of the military in everyday life and in the government power structure. With unification, officers lost their status overnight: when not simply forgotten, they were considered pariahs, hard-line communists, or simply anachronisms, relicts of a gray, stern past. My focus is on the unequal experience of German unification and the role of military identity, masculinity, and historical memory in the process of state formation and citizenship; in no way do I seek to legitimate or relativize human rights violations committed by former NVA officers or East German Border Guards. I take seriously Robben's caution that when "studying up" with military officers, one must be on guard for the "charming officer."[57] From early on in my fieldwork, it was clear to me that the NVA officers with whom I worked had an agenda they wished me to publicize: namely, that they were not "bad" men or "war criminals." I was well aware of their agenda, and that they were not talking to me simply because they wanted to help an anthropologist write a book about them. Many of the officers were crafty political operators, having honed their skills in the Byzantine political structures of the NVA and the East German Communist Party. I realized that they saw my research as a way of "rehabilitating" their reputations, identities, and honor, and of getting their side of the story into the public sphere.

Nonetheless, one of the problems associated with working with fallen elites, or in some cases, people who have committed human rights abuses, is that on a personal level, you might actually like them, find them charming. And in many instances, they are charming and friendly, offer fascinating insights, tell compelling stories, and use their charisma to great effect. I did strike up a friendship with a few of the officers, and had friendly interactions with the majority, though I felt that I had to maintain a certain distance in order to remain as objective as possible. This is not to say that I distrusted everything I was told by my informants. I also felt the need to carefully consider statements and comments from West German officers, who, with few exceptions, took a very hard line against former NVA officers, and who also saw me as a way to "prove" their point that NVA officers are simply carryovers of the Wehrmacht and SS. By studying up and down, I put myself squarely in the middle of competing agendas and competing versions of German military history, memory, and politics. Willi, a gregarious and strong-willed former NVA political officer, told me—and other officers, whenever we were together—"this young man has no idea what kind of political firestorm he's getting in the middle of."

Working with "power"—with those who had it, wielded it, used it, and lost it—can be difficult. Not simply because of what they did (or might have done), but because they often seemed normal and ordinary, and generally likable (at least initially), which sometimes makes it difficult to imagine the things they had done or ordered or found acceptable. I often felt that I was hanging out with my grandfather, hearing stories and talking about a past I was interested in, a past I partially knew and had experienced from the other side. But interviews often devolved into a sort of "trial by dialogue": as my interviewees' anger and bitterness built, as they slipped into a sort of "time warp" of shifting guilt and justification, I would feel myself slipping into a different time, a time when armed borders, shoot-to-kill orders, and the prerogatives of the Cold War were still alive. They knew that I was interested in their situations and histories, and I knew that no one had taken an interest in them or listened to their stories. Six- to eight-hour discussions were not uncommon, and occasionally, I would sit for ten to twelve hours listening, asking questions, taking notes, and recording. At the end of an interview—and after numerous cigarettes and cups of coffee—I would make my way slowly to the U-Bahn or S-Bahn train station, where I would invariably stop at an Imbiss for another coffee, more cigarettes, and a *döner kebap*. In the end, it was worth it to see the bitter face of power lost and known to be irrecoverable.

BECOMING MILITARIZED, BEING MILITARIZED

The role of the soldier in German society has a long and complicated history, replete with questions of class, masculinity, hierarchy, domination, aesthetics, and of course, violence. Beginning with the Prussian state, and the valorization of the military, of military values and virtues, the idea of the soldier in German culture and society found firm footing. The idea of the strong, brave, loyal, and obedient soldier became the ideal of male identity, the sine qua non of masculinity, status, and legitimacy. The soldier was to represent all that was good about Germany, and the good and supremacy of Germany was to be represented by the soldier.[58] After World War II, however, soldiers were blamed for the destruction of Germany, and there was a dramatic drop in the appeal of being a soldier and the social standing of soldiers in general, in both East and West.

The history of the two German Cold War militaries offers an unparalleled view of the relationship between militarization and society, and of the processes by which states turn men into soldiers. The mirroring of German Cold War military masculinity offers a comparative approach to the process, showing just how the state goes about valorizing and marginalizing soldiers. Chapter 2, "Emotions, Generations, and Death Cults: Militarization and the Creation of Socialist Military Personalities," draws on archival and ethnographic data to examine the relationship between gender and militarization in East German society. The chapter highlights the most important features, events, dates, and trends in the militarization of the GDR, examining the various organs of the East German state charged with the creation of the "new socialist man," such as the Young Pioneers, the Free German Youth, the Society for Sports and Technology, and the NVA.

In Chapter 3, "Coming of Age in the NVA: The Master Narratives of Militarization," I focus on the lived experiences of militarization through an ethnographic analysis of the lives and life histories of NVA officers and conscripts, and the role of state propaganda and pressure in making men into soldiers and citizens.

As a way to set up the experiences of NVA officers during the chaotic months prior to unification, and to highlight the growing sense of unease and the awareness of what was to come for them after unification, Chapter 4, "The Writing on the Wall: The NVA Surrenders," follows the attempt of one officer to navigate and outwit the political process that would lead to his dismissal from the military, and the end of his career.

Shifting my analysis to post-unification Germany, Chapter 5, "A War of Signs, Images, and Memories: German Militaries in the Cold War and Unification," explores the "unmaking" of the new socialist man after unification, and the ways in which this "unmaking" are used to consolidate (West) German claims to governmental legitimacy, facilitate post-unification German state formation, create a new military identity through a material and symbolic denunciation and "victory" over the GDR (and those considered close to the East German state), and recuperate and reclaim portions of German military history.

Chapter 6, "'Unification Has Ruined My Life': The Political Economy of the Military Other," places the experiences of NVA officers and their families in Berlin during and after unification within the overall context of the East German experience of unification.

In Chapter 7, "As Germans Among Germans: Life in the *Kameradschaft*," I examine the lives of former NVA soldiers in East German army veterans groups—the *Kameradschaften*—and what these groups provide former officers and their families. Veterans groups give former East

German army officers an official, military forum from which to tell their side of unification and German history. They are also "training grounds" in which to explore the transition from state socialism to market capitalism, come to terms with unification, and learn how to become citizens in a completely different state and social system.

In Chapter 8, "'We're the Jews of the New Germany': Heroic Victimhood, Fallen Elites, and the Slipperiness of History and Memory," I examine the links NVA officers make between the Third Reich, the Holocaust, and the victims of Nazism as a way of making sense of their own situations and treatment by the Bundeswehr and the German government after unification. The combination of symbolic othering and economic distress has led many NVA officers to conceptualize their experiences, and the types of policies employed by the Bundeswehr, as akin to the exclusionary and genocidal policies of the Third Reich.

Drawing from the German experience of the Cold War, and the experiences of NVA officers after unification, in the concluding chapter, Chapter 9, "Death and Allegiance: Toward an Anthropology of Soldiering," I theorize the ways in which states use the military as a means of creating "ideal" citizens, and in so doing, legitimate the use of violence.

CHAPTER 2

Emotions, Generations, and Death Cults

MILITARIZATION AND THE CREATION OF
SOCIALIST MILITARY PERSONALITIES

It has been proven again: the more and the better we are able to use
commanders, staff officers, political (officers), party functionaries, and all
communists in ideological training, the greater success we can achieve in the
consciousness education of all army members and Border Guard soldiers.
To always make ideological work the point of all party organizations in
order to make all soldiers into communists, that's what it's about.

GENERAL HEINZ KESSLER,

Minister of Defense of the German Democratic Republic,

in a top secret report to the National Defense Council in 1985.[1]

The Fatherland may demand every sacrifice

Nothing is too valuable for the Fatherland

Vom Sinn des Soldatenseins,

a handbook distributed to all NVA soldiers and officers

Militarization in the GDR wasn't preparation for

war. It was preparation for peace.

KARL,

former NVA Agit-Prop officer

AT THE END OF WORLD WAR II, the idea of a new German army, or
two new German armies for that matter, seemed an impossibility, a gro-
tesque idea. Within ten years, however, two new and diametrically opposed
German armies would emerge, key players in their respective military
blocks and in the internal politics of each state, and important international symbols of the political and economic ideologies they represented.

Both the United States and the Soviet Union saw their respective spheres of influence in Germany as a way to contest the other, to fight a battle of social, cultural, and economic prestige, and insure security and peace in Europe through the status quo of the Cold War. The Soviet Union saw East Germany as a potential "showcase of socialism," and as a potential "chit" to be played in the increasingly tense relations with China.[2] The United States saw West Germany as a bulwark against Soviet expansion and influence in the West, and as a base from which to shape and influence Western European economies and governments through the Marshall Plan and "Americanization." The formation of both armies was under the control of the two superpowers—the United States and the Soviet Union—and was seen as a way to further control Germany. Additionally, by linking the two states to international security blocks, the control of Germany was internationalized.[3] Each army reflected the internal political system of its state: socialism and democracy in the workers' and peasants' state of the East, and a capitalistic market economy and parliamentary democracy in the West.[4]

In this chapter, I examine the international and national political, cultural, and military contexts in which former NVA officers were raised and lived, contexts which they also helped to create, shape, and maintain: NVA officers are products of the Cold War contest between the East and the West. I examine the structures, mechanisms, and goals used and desired by the SED and the NVA to create compliant citizens, shape political and gender identities, and create a system that upheld the values and ideals of the state and party—a system in which certain men would embody the state. It is a "history" of militarization through an analysis of the structures and contexts of power that shape and form people's lives, worldviews, fields of actions, and possibilities in the sense of history that Eric Wolf describes: not simply "one damn thing after the other," but "one that is concerned not so much with the flow of events as with the history of societal arrangements and transformations."[5]

To use Eugen Weber's felicitous phrase, militarization is about turning "peasants into Frenchmen."[6] Military service promotes the idea of a unified national identity, turning regional identities into a national identity and an imagined community.[7] The history of the state in Europe is arguably a history of militarization policies, a drive to create a bond between citizens and the state through military service.[8] As Braudy argues, it is the integration of the army and the political state.[9]

Of course, this integration is stronger or weaker in certain states at certain times, but it is nonetheless a process of attempted integration, of the saturation of everyday life with military values and concerns. The structure of the modern state as we know it is based on the use of the military to create not only a national identity, but the feeling of a nation-state that needs defending. State formation entails the development and construction of a citizenry that identifies with the state and sees the success and defense of the state as part of their own success and well-being.

National armies demand a loyalty to the nation-state and a willingness to subordinate oneself and accept the goals and organization of the state one has pledged (or been conscripted) to serve. Through seclusion, segregation, and a commonality of experience, men from diverse and differing backgrounds are to come to see themselves as soldier-citizens of the state. Bartov, Grossman, and Nolan contend that national armies (such as the Bundeswehr and NVA) tend to represent nations (in Europe) better than most other state institutions, since soldiers are recruited by universal (male) conscription and thus drawn from all walks of life and age cohorts.[10] Of course, in the case of the two Germanys, it was (and is) about turning Germans into "West" Germans or "East" Germans or "unified" Germans. Soldiers must be convinced of the naturalness of the state they are sworn to defend, of the impossibility or desirability of a different type of economic or political organization; the two must blend together seamlessly and effortlessly.

MILITARIZATION, MASCULINITY, AND THE STATE

After World War II, both Germanys experienced a "remasculinization," as both states sought to find new models of "proper" masculinity, particularly in relation to the military.[11] Rearmament and (re)militarization—as well as remasculinization in East and West Germany—followed different paths, but both paths were linked in, and in many ways directed by, the respective political-military blocks that controlled them, and by the recent past of Nazi militarism and atrocities. The establishment of both militaries was also part of a project to come to terms with, and refute, the Nazi past, and to come up with viable foundation myths for both states.[12]

Rather than simply taking militarized masculinity as a biological given or constant, we need to ask: how are "proper" soldiers created? How are history, memory, violence, and political economy used to create ideal soldiers in space, place, and time? What does it mean for people to become soldiers, and be identified as soldiers? A more productive way to understand soldiering is to examine it as a political process and goal of the state, to see the militarization of identity as a constructed state identity "offered" by the state to prospective recruits, or simply forced upon the majority through conscription, to examine soldiering as "intertwined ideas about war and masculinity."[13] The work of Arkin and Dobrofsky, Enloe, Frühstuck, Gill, Gusterson, Higate et al., Janowitz, Kanaaneh, Lutz, Moon, and Seifert, for example, focuses attention on the importance of theorizing the militarization of men and society as an intentional process, as the creation of political identities based on military service.[14] Mosse, writing from a cultural history standpoint, examines the process whereby nations actively induced men into militaristic identities and linked these identities to ideas of propriety and "normality."[15] Ideal forms of male identity—"hegemonic masculinity"—are often predicated on military prowess and virtue, portrayed by the state as the pinnacle of male identity.[16] This is of particular salience in the military, as the state must legitimate the link between masculinity, military service, violence, and the morality, ethics, and legality of killing for the state. It is not that states simply want soldiers who will commit violence; rather, states want—indeed demand—soldiers who will commit the right kind of violence at the right time and in the right manner, at a time determined by the state, and in ways that benefit the state. The linking of the ideal man to the fiat to kill for the state is perhaps the most visible expression of the power of the state to shape the perceptions and actions of its citizens. The state may claim a monopoly on violence, but it is the expression, timing, and type of violence that defines the soldier, which in turn defines the state, and in so doing, is to lend legitimacy to the state's claim to the monopoly on violence. Fundamentally, in order to claim and maintain a monopoly on violence, a state has to have people and/or citizens willing to carry out this violence. This kind of unreflected emotional willingness on the part of its citizens to fight and die for the state and party is precisely what East German politicians and officers attempted to create through the idealized, hegemonic masculine ideal of "socialist warriors." And it is this image of militarized masculinity that continues to shape the lives of former NVA officers, making them politically "radioactive."

Militarization policies were directed at creating a form of hegemonic masculinity that was to become the "base line" by which all other ways of being a man were measured. Officers of the National People's Army were to embody this ideal of hegemonic masculinity and be the ideal men of the GDR. In the later years of the GDR, this version of masculinity and identity lost purchase. As Cornwall and Lindisfarne describe it, hegemonic masculinity defines successful ways of being a "man," and in so doing, defines other sorts of masculine behavior as inadequate or inferior.[17] Hegemonic masculinity provides an extremely useful vantage point from which to investigate masculinity, for it supersedes notions of masculinity that focus on men's dominance of women and allows for an understanding of the ways in which some men dominate other men.[18] Militarization policies are very much a process of men dominating other men (and women and children). Carrigan and colleagues state that "hegemonic masculinity . . . is, rather, a question of how particular groups of men inhabit positions of power and wealth and how they legitimate and reproduce the social relationships that generate dominance. An immediate consequence of this is that the culturally exalted form of masculinity, the hegemonic model, so to speak, may only correspond to the actual characters of a small number of men. Yet very large numbers of men are complicit in sustaining the hegemonic model."[19]

As Cornwall and Lindisfarne point out, masculinity and male identity can mean many things at once, in the same places and in different places.[20] Following Hodgson, I approach the study of masculinity and gender with the belief that "masculinities (like femininities), are multiple, historical, relational, and contradictory."[21] Rather than considering masculinity as some sort of universal concept, Cornwall and Lindisfarne argue, it should be viewed as location- and context-dependent: what might be considered hypermasculine behavior in one locale may be considered as effeminate or deviant in another.[22]

One of the most useful and productive approaches to thinking about military masculinity and identity is offered by Collier and Yanagisako,[23] who state that masculinity is fluid and ambiguous within spatial and historical contexts, thus demonstrating that no sort of universal "man's point of view" exists.[24] Militaries are concerned with the creation of ideal forms of male identity within certain historical and political contexts; however, there is no one type of militarized male identity within a military, or indeed between militaries. There may be similarities, but by parsing out the subtle differences between ability, tactics, strength, courage, weakness, cowardice, and so on, the political contestation between militaries is played out. This is particularly true of the Cold War and post-unification struggles in Germany for definitions and truth claims concerning "proper" soldiers, militaries, and violence.

THE NVA AND THE BUNDESWEHR

German rearmament was a contentious issue on both sides of the Cold War divide, given the nearness of the war, the destruction caused by German militarism and expansionism, and the unease and trepidation of Germany's neighbors to a reconstituted German military.[25] Despite internal and external unease and distrust of a rearmed Germany—or two rearmed Germanys—both the Allies and the Soviet Union felt increasingly compelled to establish military forces in their respective zones of influence.

In 1952, in an attempt to drive a political wedge between the Allies, Stalin pushed for a united, but neutral, Germany. The "Stalin Notes," as they came to be called, were not taken seriously by the Allies, nor, as it came to pass, by the Soviets themselves. Stalin never seriously believed that the Allies would withdraw their troops from Germany, and in fact saw the presence of American, British, and French soldiers on German soil as a guarantee against the resurgence of German fascism.[26] The American position was fairly similar to the Soviet's. The United States publicly declared support for a united Germany, provided Germans on both sides were given the chance to choose freely for themselves. With regard to the division of Germany, U.S. Secretary of State John Foster

Dulles told Eisenhower in 1959 that "there was a great deal to be said for the status quo, but this wasn't a position we could take publicly."[27] Even though the overall command of each military would rest with the commanding generals of NATO and the Warsaw Pact, German politicians in both zones agitated for new military structures and forces, as each Germany increasingly saw the other as a threat to its own survival and security. Both West German chancellor Konrad Adenauer and SED party chief Walter Ulbricht in East Germany saw the formation of a national military as a way of gaining a measure of sovereignty and political leverage that would secure their own positions.[28] Adenauer and Ulbricht were both able to manipulate the political situation to their benefit, carrying out policies that often not only aggravated their allies but that frequently ran counter to U.S. and Soviet strategic goals.[29]

The West German Bundeswehr was founded first, on November 12, 1955; after long and contentious debate, West Germany decided on a conscript army of five hundred thousand men.[30] This was seen as a means of consolidating the new West German state, placating the political desires and goals of West German politicians, appeasing the large number of former Wehrmacht soldiers and officers in West Germany who were increasingly political and vocal, and helping counter fears of a Soviet expansion into Western Europe. The establishment of the Bundeswehr in 1955 and the acceptance of the Bundeswehr into the NATO defense structure represented a failure of Soviet attempts to prevent a West German alliance with the West.[31] As a result, the Warsaw Pact was formed and the Soviets increased their support for the GDR.[32] The NVA was founded on January 18, 1956, when General Heinz Hoffmann issued Order 1/1956, establishing the NVA with a strength of 120,000 soldiers.[33] Unlike West Germany, denazification and the antifascist program of the SED prevented the political participation of former Wehrmacht officers in East German politics, although a small number were involved in the early days of the NVA. Rather, militarization and rearmament, as internal political projects, were more concerned with shoring up the legitimacy of the SED, insuring that East German citizens would be socialized according to the will and goals of the party, and that internal dissent and dissatisfaction with SED social, political, and economic policies (which reached a critical mass in the 1953 uprising) could be curtailed, contained, and controlled.[34] For East German politicians, the militarization of the GDR and the founding of the NVA were to show the Soviets that the GDR was a staunch and reliable ally—a move designed to prevent the USSR from backing away from the GDR and allowing it to dissolve.[35] In turn, from a purely military-political standpoint, the GDR—and the East German military—were envisioned by the Soviets as key buffers to any attack from the West; as such, the Soviet Union took great pains to strengthen the GDR and NVA to insure the safety and security of the new state.[36] Over time, the GDR became the Soviet's most dependable and steadfast ally, and the NVA the most powerful Warsaw Pact military, after the Red Army.

FROM PEOPLE'S POLICE TO NATIONAL PEOPLE'S ARMY

The creation of the new East German army was a delicate political operation, given the open wounds of the recent world war and the widespread antiwar sentiment among East Germans. Initially, the NVA was conceptualized as a volunteer army, hoping to draw on the enthusiasm and commitment of the *Aufbau* (reconstruction) generation—the postwar generation of men and women committed to the construction of a new, socialist, progressive, antifascist German state.[37] The NVA drew its initial members from the Kasiernierte Volkspolizei (Garrisoned People's Police; KVP), and mandated a two-year period of service for its soldiers. In order to shore up support for the newly created NVA, and to play up its "national" character, a character that was to lend the NVA legitimacy as a "German" rather than East German army, a uniform very similar to the former World War II Wehrmacht uniform was introduced.[38] This was an attempt to show that while the NVA was a "new" type of German military, a military based on Marxist-Leninist principles, it was still a "German" army, linked to German military traditions and prowess. The NVA also used a helmet design based on the iconic World War II *Stahlhelm* ("steel helmet"), and retained the Prussian and World War II "goose step" of the Wehrmacht.[39] Ironically, NVA soldiers looked very similar to World War II German soldiers—the very soldiers and military from whom they wished to distance themselves. This proved controversial, as the uniforms and helmets historically and aesthetically linked the new NVA to the World War II Wehrmacht in a way unintended by the SED and the NVA, allowing the West—and East German citizens as well—to emphasize the totalitarian nature of the new East German army by linking it to the fascist German military.

The impetus for the founding of the NVA came from the Soviet Union and Stalin, who told leading East German politicians, "Create a people's army, but quietly [Volksarmee schaffen-ohne Geschrei]."[40] Concomitant with the creation of a new army was the militarization of East German society as a means of establishing political and social control, to speed along the establishment of a socialist society and "new socialist men and women" who would embrace the party-state. As Mary Fulbrook describes it, militarization was a "battle for the souls" of postwar East Germans.[41] Fulbrook's choice of the word *battle* to describe military socialization is apt, as it was a struggle to socialize people not only to prepare for battle but also to forego the memories and remnants of Nazi and fascist socialization, to effect their rapid transformation from former citizens of the Third Reich into new socialist citizens. Militarization was one method the East German state could employ to control East Germans, bringing them under direct governmental control through employment in the various military, paramilitary, and defense organizations. Eventually, over 10 percent of the entire East German workforce was connected to the various defense organizations, and over 3 million men passed through the NVA.[42]

The advent of militarization policies in the GDR came as a result of pressure from Stalin in 1952, as well to begin the formation of a "youth service–premilitary training [Jugenddienst–vormilitärische Erziehung]," in which youths were to learn to shoot and to complete paramilitary training.[43] The Gesellschaft für Sport und Technik (Society for Sports and Technology; GST) was founded in 1952 as a result. Originally called Schutz der Heimat (Homeland Defense), the name was changed to give it a more politically palatable, "civilian," and less military feel.[44] The Freie Deutsche Jugend (Free German Youth; FDJ) was to be the primary ideological and paramilitary group in the GDR, and the GST was to further the paramilitary training of East German youths, and co-opt them in terms of "useful" and "productive" time, by keeping them busy with party and military education and activities at the expense of other types of activities.

It was only after the construction of the Berlin Wall that conscription was introduced.[45] On September 20, 1961 (a little more than a month after the Berlin Wall was built), the People's Parliament (Volkskammer) issued a new *Verteidigungsgesetz* (defense law), making service in the NVA legally required of all men between the ages of eighteen and fifty.[46] The minimum enlistment time for a career officer (*Berufsoffizier*) was set at twenty-five years, which effectively precluded any other employment opportunities or training, and which ensured that these men were completely brought into the fold of the party, with almost every aspect of their professional and personal lives controlled by the military and military priorities. Active military service in the NVA consisted of eighteen months of conscripted service; there was also a thirty-six-month enlistment as a noncommissioned officer (*Unteroffizier auf Zeit*), a ten- or twenty-five-year enlistment as a career noncommissioned officer (*Berufsunteroffizier*), and a fifteen-year enlistment as a warrant officer (*Fähnrich*).[47]

One advantage of a conscript army over a volunteer army is that it makes military service a concern for all families, not just those of volunteers.[48] In this way, the entire GDR was brought into the militarization process and national defense programs. Conscription is the nationalization of risk and commitment through military service. Rejection or acceptance of the government's military policies no longer had a detrimental impact on manpower quotas; one either reported for military service or faced the consequences. Additionally, pacifists could be made useful through service in the *Bausoldaten*, units of soldiers who did not carry weapons and who were used for road repair and construction projects. *Bausoldaten* were seen as politically suspect, and subject to harsh conditions and harsh treatment for their refusal to carry a weapon. Rather than relying on already "motivated" citizens to fill the ranks of the army, conscription was a way to turn soldiers into motivated citizens who would internalize the goals and logic of party policies.

While the SED and the NVA were attempting to draw even more of the population into the "defense" of the GDR, and were engaged in a militarization program on an immense scale, they rejected the idea that what they were doing was in fact militarizing the East German state.

Rather, they denounced labels such as "militarization" as attempts by the West to defame and slander the GDR and its "peace Program"; Politburo member Egon Krenz, then head of the Free German Youth, told GDR head of state Erich Honecker: "In the political-ideological work, we have to be aware that the enemy, in his 'crusade strategy' is also attacking the civil defense preparedness of the GDR and its role in the national defense system, slandering and defaming this system as a 'total militarization of society.'"[49]

Corey Ross notes that throughout the history of the GDR, the SED devoted a considerable portion of its propaganda efforts to denouncing militarism. According to Marxist-Leninist doctrine, militarism and war are integral elements of capitalism, where the logic of ruthless competition, ever-expanding markets, and the constant striving for ever-greater profits inevitably leads to imperialist expansion and, ultimately, military conflict.[50] Because the GDR was a socialist, and not a capitalist, state, there could be no militarism in the GDR, a claim the SED maintained throughout its existence.

The majority of officers I interviewed were adamant that they never served in an army of conquest; rather, they had served in an army that defended socialism against aggression and conquest, and therefore had helped maintain peace in Europe. Kurt, an NVA tank officer, claimed that while in hindsight one could consider the GDR to have been a militarized state, there was no "war enthusiasm" (*Kriegsbegeisterung*); rather, militarization was the creation of "peace enthusiasm" (*Friedensbegeisterung*). This type of doublespeak was fairly common among former officers; militarization was peaceful, in much the same way that Carol Cohn discusses the doublespeak of U.S. nuclear weapons scientists, who use nonthreatening terms to speak about—and come to terms with—the deadly power of nuclear weapons.[51] In the view of NVA officers, and in the official view of the SED and NVA, "militarization" was a characteristic of the West and NATO, and in particular, the West Germans. West Germans—and the Federal Republic—were merely a continuation of Nazi and fascist traditions, and as such, were the "true" militarists bent on aggression, a desire for war, and the destruction of the GDR. It was they who forced the GDR to take measures to defend itself.

THE STRUCTURES OF MILITARIZATION

Militarization in the GDR was a curious mix of Soviet and Nazi practices and structures; the SED (under pressure from the Soviet Union) developed organizations similar to those in the Soviet Union, but also drew upon the recent experiences and structures of the Nazi era. Military socialization in the GDR was accomplished through a merger of schools and educational facilities, and through the creation of mass organizations such as the Ernst Thälmann Junge Pioniere (Ernst Thälmann Young Pioneers), the GST, the FDJ, and the NVA.[52] Beginning with the Young Pioneers and continuing through middle age, this process was designed to constantly reinforce and promote support of the SED and its policies, as well as inculcate support and "love" of the Soviet Union and the other "brother states" of the Warsaw Pact. Military education and training were envisioned as one of the primary paths to the socialization of the East Germans into the tenets and goals of socialism. Mass organizations were to function as the "transmission belts between the party and the masses."[53]

After the Young Pioneers, children and youths were expected to join the FDJ and the GST. The FDJ was responsible for the ideological training and indoctrination of youths, whereas the GST was the primary paramilitary organization in the GDR. The GST was mandated with the development of *Verteidigungsbereitschaft*—defense preparedness—in students and the preparation of all youths in various military and military-technical skills that would allow them to move quickly into the NVA; as such, the GST was known as the *Schule des Soldaten von Morgen*—the "school of the soldier of tomorrow."[54]

The GST was to provide a constant reserve force in the event of war. The GST, however, did not function completely as desired or designed; interviews with people who took part in GST activities show that while they enjoyed the opportunities to scuba dive, parachute, or learn how to use radios, many people took part in the GST primarily to obtain their driver permits, which they could do for free and more quickly than through other venues. The FDJ was designed to provide for the ideological training of youths and serve as the primary pressure group to entice young men to join the military for longer periods or to make it a career. The ultimate goal of the FDJ was "to turn all Free German Youth members and young army members into class-conscious and 'steeled soldier-personalities [gestählten Soldatenpersönlichkeiten].'"[55]

Through *Wehrerziehung* (military education), East Germans were to be convinced of the necessity and ultimate victory of socialism, and to promote the expansion and protection of socialism in the GDR and abroad.[56] Socialist military education was based on a statement by Lenin, who stressed the need and desirability of creating a strong "disposition to defend the state," which required the implementation of paramilitary training for the entire populace.[57] The need to militarize socialism, Lenin wrote, meant that the "masses" must be given a basic knowledge of military matters, and learn to fight for the defense of socialism under the leadership of the party.[58]

The necessity of training and socializing young men into military and socialist values was of the utmost importance to the SED and the NVA. There was always a sense of urgency to this perceived need; even in the 1980s, a document detailing the military socialization programs in the Weissenfels district stated:

We have no illusions that in regard to military education, particularly in regard to young men, we have to assume that in the case of imperialist aggression, we will have to enter armed combat with the level of consciousness (in young men) that we have achieved by that date. For this reason, the commission on socialist military education sees its general mission to form unshakable foundational beliefs (in young men) which will be tested, in unimaginable ways, by the political-moral, psychic, and physical demands of armed warfare.[59]

This comes from a report concerning premilitary education for high school students; the teenagers impacted by these programs had not yet entered the military. The commission recognized the "need" to establish "unshakable" qualities in young men prior to military service to prepare them for combat, and to insure that they, as potential combatants, would be ready and willing to fight and die. The report later states that the "military preparation of our entire *Volk* is an important, peace-securing factor, which the imperialist warmongers will have to take into account."[60]

NATURALIZING WAR, DENATURALIZING PEACE:
CREATING SOCIALIST MILITARY PERSONALITIES

As the militarization of the GDR intensified, the concept of the "socialist personality" was subsumed under the rubric "socialist military personality."[61] The personification of this ideal would be the development of soldiers and citizens who demonstrated "loyalty to socialist ideals, proletarian internationalism, socialist patriotism, solidarity, resilience in the face of adversity, courage, discipline, knowledge of how to achieve victory, loyalty to the party of the working class, willingness to sacrifice one's self, and hatred of the class enemy."[62] An additional goal of the early inculcation of these attributes was to offset and counter any form of pacifism or unease about military service, to naturalize and depoliticize war, and "denaturalize" peace by politicizing it.

Mandated by law, compulsory military training was designed to inculcate differing identity attributes according to gender. In 1969, a secret agreement between the Ministry of Education, the mass youth organizations, and the East German Red Cross, under the aegis of the SED, provided for the "unconditional preparation of all male students for military service"; the aim was to provide for "the unity of the political-moral, military- and military-technical, physical, and psychological abilities of students in preparation for military service."[63] Despite rudimentary training in marksmanship and atomic-biological-chemical (ABC) protection, girls and young women were only expected to complete courses in first aid and civil defense, and to attain qualifications in the German Red Cross.[64] While both male and female students received military education, and to some degree participated in the same sorts of training, military education and training were always focused on males; eventual military service was to be seen, by both men and women, as a "natural" part of a man's life, and the fulfillment of a man's *Ehrendienst*, his "duty of honor." To refuse military service was to be a "dishonorable" man, a failed socialist, and to fall outside of civil society. While women were allowed to join the military in certain fields, a military career for a woman was viewed as something of an aberration, and this was only looked upon as a positive development in the late GDR. As Gerd and Paul, two former artillery officers, made explicit during a discussion about women in the military, "We didn't want our women to have the burden of military service—that was our burden. We thought you Americans were barbarians for having women in your army."[65]

Furthering this process, the Military Service Law of 1982, the final and most all-encompassing law with regard to the increased militarization of East German society, stated explicitly: "State organizations, as well as factories, leading industrial groups, concerns, installations, associations, societal organizations and groups are mandated with the preparation of all citizens for military service. . . . Preparation for military service is the main focus of education and pedagogy at comprehensive schools, installations for career training, trade schools, high schools, and universities."[66]

The desired efficacy of this law, and the intense pressure that was to be applied to young men in high school to join the military for longer periods of time, are demonstrated by the fact that at the end of 1982, the number of young men leaving high school who were to choose to become career officers in the NVA was to increase from the yearly average of 520 to 3,730.[67] While this could be understood in purely military terms, it is also an indication of the desire of the SED to increase the number of "loyal" party members in leadership positions in the military to insure the proper ideological training and level of obedience in the military, as well as the number of men directly linked to the state via the military and the party.

ARMEE RUNDSCHAU: DREAMING OF SOLDIERS AND WIVES

The SED considered the control and use of the media as one of the most important aspects of social and political control, and the coupling of the media and the military was a prevalent feature of GDR propaganda efforts.[68] The media and aesthetic agitation were used to support and reinforce images of strong socialist-warriors defending the state, the family, women, and children. These images were used to promote strong families as the "anchor" of defense, and to promote traditional gender identities and dynamics considered important for the support of the GDR.

Armee Rundschau (Army Panorama) was one of the most widely circulated and read magazines in the GDR, with an average monthly readership of 1.5 million.[69] Founded in 1956, *Armee Rundschau* was designed to be a "popular" magazine devoted to the newly formed NVA and military subjects. From the outset, *Armee Rundschau* was meant to be a readily available and entertaining platform from which to extol the virtues and glory of the NVA, SED, and GDR, and to create interest in military subjects. More importantly, *Armee Rundschau* promoted an idealized view of socialist military families and relationships focused on both the defense of the family and the defense of the state, linking the two visually and ideologically.[70] When not shown training, soldiers were shown with their wives or girlfriends, pushing strollers, carrying children, and enjoying family life (the soldier-and-child motif was predominant in NVA propaganda). Through entertainment, the SED "smuggled in" the linkage of the military, the family, defense, and the state; as Jack Zipes notes, it is often through entertainment that the serious work of ideology is done, as it is made to seem unthreatening and playful.[71]

After a long afternoon talking about the aesthetics of militarization in the GDR with Karl-Heinz Freitag, the chief editor of *Armee Rundschau*, he smiled at me slyly and told me what the main purpose of the magazine was:

Yes, *AR* was a military magazine, with a lot of coverage of technology, history, and what not. But the real purpose of the magazine, from my point of view—and I was the chief editor for a very long time—was to prepare boys and men for their service in the NVA, and to prepare women and girls to be good wives and girlfriends, to teach them to love soldiers and be willing to wait for them. We knew we had to convince women to love soldiers. If we didn't, men wouldn't want to go to the NVA.

The militarization of women was of great concern to the East German military and government; the NVA considered it extremely important to direct effort and pressure toward women in order for them to support men to join and remain in the military.[72] Because of the early difficulty in mobilizing women to support its militarization programs, memories of the war, and the reticence of women to date or marry a soldier because of the burdens of family life in the military, the NVA and SED were convinced that men could only be militarized insofar as women were militarized and convinced to support men in the military.[73] A report on a meeting concerning military recruitment on May 26, 1981, states that in order to keep up recruitment, the NVA and other state organs would have to work with girls and women, and it would be necessary to involve the East German women's movement.[74] In a 1985 report to the Ministry of the Interior from the deputy-minister of the interior in Suhl, the necessity of targeting women was made explicit: "The working groups of the German Women's Association are working with increasing intensity with the mothers, wives, brides, and girlfriends of the (military) applicants, but also with all women, to convince them of the necessity (for men) to take up military careers, to educate women about life at the side of an officer, warrant officer, or noncommissioned officer, and to win them over to strengthen the resolve of the applicants."[75]

As Cynthia Enloe has shown, in order for militarized masculinity to "work," women must be militarized as well. Enloe's work shows that in order to entice men to become soldiers, women must be made to accept, love, and support soldiers and their role(s) in the state.[76] Militarization requires a heteronormative family form; the SED and the NVA viewed the family as the "first line" of military socialization, as males were "to be positively influenced for military service by their parents, other relatives, wives, and girlfriends" to insure that youths fulfilled their "duty of honor to the greatest degree possible."[77] Women were consistently portrayed in *Armee Rundschau* as passive, unsure of themselves, apolitical, and interested solely in establishing lasting relationships with men and becoming mothers.[78]

Letter exchanges between soldiers and women were printed in *Armee Rundschau*; these are always examples of relationships surviving the hardships of military service, and always emphasize women's willingness to wait for their "soldiers" to return home. Through letters and articles, women were portrayed as highly respectful and understanding of a man's decision to remain in the army, viewing it as more important than their own careers, and as willing to wait for the soldier, despite the tremendous demands of military service.[79] Women were to be the "hinterland" of soldiers, creating a symbolic link between the defense of the homeland and the defense of women and the family.

An example of this can be found in a letter published in a 1987 issue of *Armee Rundschau*: "Katrin V., Frohburg. Hinterland Katrin. 'I promise that I will remain a safe hinterland for my husband, because the strong and secure love between us will help us to get through his eighteen months of military service.'"[80]

While women's letters contained passages stating a willingness to remain at home, waiting for the soldier to return, men's letters contained poems concerning the stress of being on the "front line of peace." Men's poems celebrated soldiers as heroes, and often utilized a fictive female voice to speak of "waiting for my hero."[81] In this way, letters and poems helped create a "wartime" atmosphere by establishing an artificial war front–home front dichotomy. This "wartime" atmosphere of fear and threat helped maintain the tension necessary to require men to join the military, and to see military service as a proper contribution to national security. A wartime atmosphere served to intensify the feeling for the need of close relationships, something akin to "wartime" romances to solidify familial bonds. It was also to make it seem that the family was threatened and in danger. According to Karl-Heinz Freitag, *Armee Rundschau* paid particular attention to couples in order to insure that soldiers would be able to perform their military service adequately. *Armee Rundschau* served as a means to maintain and enforce traditional patriarchal roles and expectations in men, reconstitute men's position of authority in society, and promote the idea that women also believed in traditional gender roles and values. It also aimed to assuage men's fears that military service would inhibit their chances of finding a girlfriend or wife, or of causing an already existing relationship to fail as a result of military service.[82]

Having established the necessity and primacy of the family for national defense and the reproduction of the party, the SED and the NVA turned to the militarization of children as a way of insuring that new generations of East Germans would see war, defense, the party, and militarization as natural and normal.

FROM CHILDREN TO SOLDIERS

An "effective" militarization program does not simply start with adults; states are interested in shaping the worldviews and mindsets of its citizens from an early age, "catching" them when they are the most impressionable and malleable.

Of primary concern to the SED was the early inculcation of military values and a "military" worldview in children. Through early exposure to military themes and army life, children were to see the military and military service as "natural," as something that was an integral part of their lives and the lives of all proper citizens. Through this exposure, children were interpellated into gender-specific life-courses in sync with militarization policies: men were to become soldiers and protectors, women were to become helpers and supporters of men and the group in need of defense. And all were to become committed communists, party members, and socialist citizens.

In 1975, an East German mother wrote a letter to the women's magazine *Für Dich* (For You), inquiring whether or not it was safe and healthy to allow her son to play with toy soldiers and tanks. Dr. Ulrike Menke, a doctor of education, replied:

Even preschool children know that soldiers protect our Homeland. If the child is prevented from playing war through prohibitions or derogatory remarks, the child will find himself in a conflict situation. From these prohibitions and re-marks, children in this age group can develop negative attitudes toward para-military training and their "duty of honor" in the National People's Army. The child must be made aware of the duties of the armed forces of our state—in the first line by the father and mother. Along with this it is also necessary to develop an age-appropriate "friend-foe" worldview.[83]

Militarization began early. Children between the ages of six and fourteen were expected to join the Young Pioneers, moving on later to the FDJ and GST. Close contacts were established between military units and kinder-gartens and schools, with soldiers making regular visits to classes. Soldiers and other military figures were to serve as role models for young children, especially boys, and "open house" days at military barracks were designed to familiarize children with military equipment, soldiers, and military life. Children were taught that members of the NVA were their guardians and protectors, and East German visual culture stressed the close relationship between soldiers and children by constantly portraying them together.

Beginning in 1969, children in the Young Pioneers were expected to take part in yearly "Pioneer Maneuvers," large-scale military exercises designed to further militarize youths, as well as allow them a chance to display the level of their military knowledge and capabilities. In 1969, 824,000 children participated in the "Snowflake II" war-games (Manouver Schneeflocke II).[84] The use of the term *snowflake* was a means of making the war-games seem less "warlike" or "threatening," and also to imply a recurring temporal dimension. "Snowflake" links it with the winter months, and helps to naturalize it in the seasonal calendar; just as winter comes at a certain period, so too the war-games. And just like the seasons, it is also lent a sense of "naturalness," identifying it with the natural, normal flow of time, fixing it in time and making it seem like a normal part of life. It implied that it would happen again and again, as a naturally recurring phenomenon in the world.

To add to the realism of the exercise, children were issued uniforms, and special scaled-down versions of tanks crewed by children were sometimes used to simulate armored warfare, and to create an interest in the tank corps among young boys. Instead of rifles, children were issued sticks with a red flag tied to the top; they were told that under no circumstances were they to lose their stick. The same type of order is given in basic training in militaries throughout the world regarding a rifle or other personal weapon; to lose one's weapon is one of the cardinal sins of military service, incurring swift and severe punishment. Awards and other citations were given out for those who excelled in tactics, terrain navigation, and other skills. A number of people with whom I spoke considered Manouver Schneeflocke fun and exciting, as they were able to miss school and "play," as well as impress their teachers, NVA personnel, and friends. A description of the war-games from February 24, 1972, stated:

Our class had seven people. A comrade from the People's Police was there as well. After reporting in, everything started. The groups were taken to their areas. Frau P., our leader, had a clipboard, where she recorded the results in meters, minutes, and actions. We took part in the following exercises: ball throwing, swinging [hangeln], club throwing [Keulen werfen], and shooting balloons. . . . We then went back to school, had lunch, and in the afternoon the teachers tabulated the results. . . . The commanders of the classes came forward and presented us with gold, silver, and bronze medals, and certificates.[85]

During "open house" days at NVA barracks, children were allowed to meet and interact with soldiers, play with weapons, crawl on tanks and other equipment, and were presented with a view of military life that made it seem pleasant, noble, and fun. Despite the festive atmosphere of these events, open-house days were viewed with great seriousness by NVA officers and other officials responsible for military-education programs. Open house days were seen as a form of "serious play," and an important component in the political indoctrination and militarization of children. Reports were quickly drafted detailing the events and whether or not officers had been successful in exciting children about the military. The success or failure of an open-house event was often measured by seemingly absurd standards. A report concerning an open house at a base stated in glowing terms that recruiters had achieved immense success in exciting children about military service by serving pea soup (*Erbsenpuree*) from military field kitchens. A number of informants recalled being served pea soup at such outings; contrary to the report, all said that they hated

FIGURE 2.1   Children serving as the crews of specially designed miniature tanks during a children's war-game exercise, *1979*. German Federal Archive, http://commons.wikimedia.org/wiki/File:Bundesarchiv_Bild_183-U0602-047,_Berlin,_Wehrerziehung.jpg

eating the soup and only ate it because they were hungry and it was expected of them.

These sorts of practices show that even the most banal of objects or commodities can be utilized by the state for military purposes; the "social life of things" is not always simply peaceful or predicated on civilian uses. Just as Scarry describes the use of everyday objects by torturers to "unmake" the world,[86] the state can use—and create associations with—mundane, everyday civilian items as a means of carrying out militarization policies and normalizing military service. Military trainers and recruiters can create a link between everyday, nonmilitary items and the military, linking the item with military service, fighting, and killing (Cynthia Enloe describes much the same process with camouflaged baby socks).[87] While arguably similar in certain ways to Scarry's analysis of torture, militarization—as seen by the state—is not to be seen as a form of violence or torture, but as a positive, virtuous process of creating and maintaining a world, not the destruction—or preparation for the destruction—of a world.

INSTRUMENTS OF POWER OF THE RULING CLASS: THE MILITARIZATION OF SCHOOLS AND EDUCATION

Militarization policies rely on "sites" of indoctrination, in the sense that Althusser lays out in his conception of the "ideological state apparatus" (ISA). For Althusser, ISAs are education, schools, the media, and so on.[88] Althusser claims that ISAs play a large role in transmitting the "taken-for-granted" and the commonsensical. Allison, explicating Althusser, states: "Designed and accepted as practices with another purpose—to educate (the school system), entertain (film industry), inform (news media), the ISA serve not only their stated objective but also an unstated one—that of indoctrinating people into seeing the world a certain way and of accepting certain identities as their own within that world."[89]

Following from this, and considering that ideology (in this case, the official Marxist-Leninist ideology of the GDR) defines and shapes what roles and identities are "possible" or "impossible," one can examine the influences that went into creating "soldiers" in the GDR, and the ways in which these men internalized the worldview of the SED as their own. ISAs and ideology create limits on the "possible" while simultaneously appearing as "natural" and value-free. Accordingly, they help create "commonsense" notions of what men and women are to be, and help create notions of "possible" ways of being and acting in society. In the GDR, one possible way of being, and a way of being valorized and heavily promoted by the state, was to be an officer.

Schools and education were key tools in the militarization of East German society, and as the *Machtinstrumente der herrschenden Klasse*—"instruments of power of the ruling class"—were important in the initial military socialization of children.[90] Military education in schools was conducted in subtle and not so subtle ways. As early as the first or second grade, children were required to stand in military-like formations before class, organized around a student chosen as "class leader." A fourth grade grammar text used Border Guards and watch dogs to teach subject-verb agreement, and a math textbook from the tenth grade used artillery firing solutions to teach math equations. And beginning in high school, young men were "tracked" for their eventual service in the NVA. Students who chose a second foreign language in the sixth grade were tracked and marked as potential targets of increased pressure in the eighth grade to choose a military career.[91] Young men who were good at math were sent into the artillery service or became artillery officers, since they were able to do the math required to fire howitzers and rockets. Keeping in mind that the various branches of the NVA were hierarchically coded according to prestige and "manliness" by NVA soldiers, the "math nerds" of high school found themselves highly valued within the army, given the importance of artillery in modern combat.

Beginning in 1978, military education became a required course in the ninth and tenth grades.[92] By introducing military education into schools, "girls and boys were to be provided with a basic knowledge of civil defense, and their willingness to defend the country was to be developed."[93] Additionally, beginning in the seventh grade, pressure was applied by teachers and military recruiters on boys to begin considering a career in the NVA. Although teachers were to begin pressuring boys to consider a career in the military in the seventh grade, archival evidence and interviews show that teachers often began pressuring boys as early as the fifth grade.[94] Teachers were directed to track and identify students they considered prime candidates for military careers. As a report states:

Pedagogical collectives have a great political responsibility: they must come to an understanding as to which suitable students are to be selected [to become career officers or noncommissioned officers], and how to structure concrete work with the individuals to effectively bring about the political and life decision to chose a military career. It is not hard to understand that mere superficial recruitment exercises will do more harm than good.[95]

In this way, children were enmeshed in a system of constant exposure to military themes, and men were placed in a network of military obligations that lasted well into their fifties. As stated in a 1985 premilitary education report from the city council of Plauen, the goal was to "prepare all young men from the 1968 and 1969 age cohorts for active military service through multipronged activities of mass-political work and socialist military education, premilitary training, combat sports, and so on, and to make them aware of what it means to be a soldier in socialism and of all of our defense preparations, and to lead them to see personal responsibility in all of this."[96]

Such measures were necessary, according to the report, because even though many young men "trusted the politics of our party and believed in the political, economic, and military strength of socialism, the party and NVA should not believe that all men feel this way or are firm in their convictions." As proof that some young men did not have a clear "picture of the enemy" (*Feindbild*) and underestimated the growing danger to socialism, sentiments such as the following were listed in the report: "The NATO states will not attack, because they also have fears about surviving, western politicians also state that they believe in peace, and that the soldiers of the West German army, and the 'people over there' also do not want war."[97] The general pattern in these documents seems to indicate that when young men or women did not fully accept the statements of fear and danger presented by the SED, premilitary and ideological training had to be intensified to insure that such opinions did not occur again. Any deviations from official party doctrine concerning fear and danger were considered "false consciousness," and were dealt with through increased education and ideological training.

THE PEACEFUL BATTLEGROUND:
FEAR AND DEFENSE IN THE GDR

One of the founding tropes of the NVA was *Frieden*—peace. The NVA and SED propaganda stressed the need for an armed peace. *Vom Sinn des Soldatenseins* (What It Means to Be a Soldier), a handbook given to all new NVA recruits, put it in these terms:

Peace must be armed, and so well-armed that the aggressor does not stand a chance. We know that threat of war does not come from weapons. Weapons in the hands of aggressors are the real dangers to peace. This forces us to develop and deploy adequate weapons in order to prevent the use of weapons [dass jemals die Waffen sprechen]. . . . The most effective service for peace is service in the National People's Army and the Border Guards of the GDR.[98]

"Wehrdienst im Sozialismus ist Friedensdienst" (Military service in socialism is service for peace) was an often-used slogan to promote the SED's conception of peace. In 1986 at the Eleventh Party Congress, the SED stated that the "meaning of being a soldier in socialism is to maintain peace, and prevent weapons from speaking."[99] Not only was the NVA portrayed and conceptualized as an *Armee des Friedens* (army of peace), but almost all members of the NVA viewed themselves as servants and guardians of peace, rather than members of an aggressive, expansionist military—"a military like our father's," as I heard from a number of officers. As Detlef, a twenty-five-year veteran of the NVA who, after leaving the military, was employed by the civil defense forces, made clear: "We were not the military of our fathers, or the military of the West. We never attacked another country, and we were not interested in attacking another country. Sure, we were armed and ready to fight and die, practiced and practiced for when things got serious [Ernstfall], and ready to attack the West if necessary, but only in order to maintain the peace."

This was a constant theme in all militarization policies in the GDR: soldiers must train to fight in order to maintain peace; as such, these attempts were therefore not "militarization" in the eyes of the SED or

NVA, as I was told again and again, but rather, simply a preparation for "national defense" (*Landesverteidigung*), and the demonstration of their willingness to fight for socialism and the "new" Germany.

The GDR viewed itself as the central "battleground" of the Cold War, and the likeliest site of a war in Europe.[100] In the eyes of the NVA and SED, the GDR was confronted by enemies who were only waiting for an excuse to attack. During the Reagan era, this atmosphere of fear was heightened; SED propaganda played up the fact that NATO, under the sway of the Reagan administration, had become much more aggressive in its stance toward the Soviet Union and other Warsaw Pact states. With the stationing of Pershing missiles in West Germany in 1983 (missiles whose primary targets were Soviet and East German bases within the GDR), the SED began a campaign designed to further incite youths to join the military and develop a willingness to defend the GDR. Although the GDR was the primary target of these missiles, the SED also used this in a cynical fashion; at a time when faults and fissures were beginning to appear in public support for its policies, the SED was able to use the new international situation to attempt to strengthen its grip on the public via militarization policies designed to extend the umbrella of control. By playing up an external threat, the GDR was able to justify the increased militarization of its citizens. Ostensibly a means of defending the GDR from external attack, the SED used it to strengthen its internal hold on power within the GDR at a time when its powerbase was beginning to erode. Paradoxically, "peace" was the means by which society could be militarized.

In what is perhaps one of the clearest statements linking the need to defend "peace" and the desire to use and deploy it as a means of controlling and disciplining the GDR population and bringing them further into the ideological and political control of the SED, Egon Krenz stated in an address to the heads of the departments for security questions at the county (Bezirk) level in 1984:

We cannot reduce military-political propaganda merely to questions of military details. The assertion put forth in the documents of our party and those of other Warsaw Pact states, that a nuclear war would mean the destruction of humanity, should not scare anyone, but rather must be used to mobilize all forces for the defense of peace. Our security policy is focused on preventing war. Therefore, we have to present the peace initiatives of the Soviet Union, GDR, and other socialist states in such a way as to strengthen the conviction that peace can be maintained, and that peace is therefore worth fighting for.[101]

Krenz makes it clear that even though they mean to issue statements concerning the "destruction of humanity," these statements should be used to motivate people, not frighten them. The use of "fear" will be precisely the catalyst that drives young men to join the military willingly. However, this training is not merely to insure that there will be those who are willing to fight, but that the SED would be able to further indoctrinate and subordinate young men to its goals and policies.

EMOTIONS, GENERATIONS, AND DEATH CULTS: THE AESTHETICS OF MILITARIZATION

A key component in turning men into soldiers is to make them feel like soldiers. If one feels like a soldier, one feels like the state, and feels like the fate and future of the state are linked to one's fate and future. Buck-Morss, in a discussion of the work of Benjamin, highlights the importance of understanding the original meaning of *aesthetics—aisthetikos—*in the strict definition of the term: that is, as concerned with the body's sensory capabilities and the reception of the world through tactility, emotion, and experience.[102] In *The Ideology of the Aesthetic,* Eagleton describes the central concern of aesthetics as the "manipulation of the body through "manners"": "What matters in aesthetics is not art, but this whole project in reconstructing the human subject from the inside, informing its subtlest affections and bodily responses with this law which is not a law."[103]

States use both art and ritual as forms of aesthetics and anesthetics to create, manipulate, and control the soldier, to make manipulation and discipline seem natural, as the law which is not a law. Both ritual and manners affect the actions and behavior of the individual by causing him or her to feel a sense of protection, belonging, intensity, urgency, and importance. In a military setting, manners can be considered analogous to drill and ceremony; that is, how the soldier learns to act and hold his or her body in an unthinking, naturalized way, and subsume one's identity to that of the military.

Youths and adults were to feel connected to the state through an appreciation of the seriousness of soldiering, of performing their "duty of honor." Rituals designed to incorporate soldiers into the hallowed grounds of the military and militarized identity were supposed to create a feeling of the importance of being a soldier, to make soldiers feel connected to the state and the fate of the state through their actions and service. They were to "feel" the state in their very beings and emotions. In this sense the "state" is an emotional experience: the term *state* implies emotion, to be in a "state" of commitment, loyalty, anxiety, and love for the state, an emotional state so connected to the state that one is willing to fight and die for the state.

"Aesthetic" and "romantic" means were used to nurture the desire to take part in military service and training. Children were to see military training as an adventure, as fun and exciting, as the possibility to live out fantasies of daring and conquest, of strength and courage, a chance to become a noble defender of the state. A top-secret document on paramilitary training in the GST from 1981 stated: "A portion of the training will be carried out at night. In premilitary training, we are concerned with youthful enthusiasm and romanticism [Jugendfrische und Romantik]."[104] In much the same way that the National Socialists used night marches and events to create an atmosphere of expectation and high emotion, to "awaken" a connection between the soldier and the state,[105] so too did the GST attempt to motivate students through nighttime maneuvers, and all of the paramilitary organizations in the GDR attempted to create the necessary emotional link between the individual and the party/state through mass politics, symbolism, and ritual. "Aesthetic" concerns and "culture" were to intensify the fighting spirit and the will to defend socialism. "With Socialist Culture and Art—for high combat readiness" was one slogan used by political officers to enhance "the development of socialist 'life feeling' [Lebensgefühl] though rich sociality and conversation [Geselligkeit und Unterhaltung]."[106] Ultimately, this "feeling" was to become second-nature, an unreflected physical response, a sort of "aesthetic hegemony" of conditioning, an embodied sense of connection with the GDR.

One of the essential components of East German militarization was the promotion of the "friend/foe" worldview (*Freund/Feindbild*) in which children and youths were to view the "enemy"—that is, West Germany, the United States, and other NATO states—with hatred. Throughout the history of the GDR and the NVA, politicians and military officials feared that NVA soldiers would not fire upon West Germans. A poem contained in the 1983 version of the handbook *Vom Sinn des Soldatenseins* was called "The Song of the Enemy" (Das Lied vom Feind), and was meant to instill hatred and fear toward West Germany and the Bundeswehr:

Soldier, you have a weapon in your hand
And a Worker gave it to you
And you carry that weapon for the Fatherland
And you guarantee the lives of the workers
The Enemy is without pity, and smart
And he's already taken many comrades from us
He doesn't think about love, or child, or wife
Or about tears, shed bitterly

. . .

This is why soldiers must be armed
And ready, when the hour comes
Because when the Enemy fires
The soldier can't cry for help
Yes, then he must hunt down the Enemy.[107]

Poems and propaganda were to shape the way NVA soldiers viewed the Bundeswehr and its soldiers; they were not to be seen as fellow Germans, relatives, or "brothers." Rather, they were the enemy (*Feind*), the class enemy (*Klassenfeind*), the greatest threat to the stability of the GDR, socialism, and the world. Ultimately, the NVA hoped that the successful implementation of this "worldview" would result in the "creation of socialist-military warriors who are ready and able to follow every command of the workers' and peasants' State in an unhesitating manner, and who will fulfill all combat orders with their entire being."[108]

One of the main tropes employed in the attempt to create "socialist military warriors" was the use of exemplary men from the German left—

antifascists, political activists, politicians, and so on. These men were to serve as role models and examples for other men to follow and emulate. A kind of "death cult" arose around Border Guard soldiers and officers who were killed "defending" the Antifascist Protective Barrier. Schools were named after these men, with the intention of motivating young students through both respect for their lives as well as hatred toward the West for having "killed" these soldiers. These men's lives were to become templates of service, honor, duty, and sacrifice, models for how young men were to act and what they were to become. Fallen Border Guards were presented as the martyrs of the GDR and socialism, men who gave their all for the state; their deaths were to be the proof of West German and Western imperialism, aggression, and "banditry." During the naming ceremonies, the life history of the martyr would be read aloud to the participants, who were to make an emotional connection to the dead hero, and desire to identify with this exemplary person.

A report from the Suhl City Council on September 19, 1985, to the Ministry of the Interior concerning "experiences and results in the work of the Socialist Military Education Commission" shows how the various structures and organizations involved in socialist military education were to work together:

As an example of how experiences can be changed into practice, and therefore serve as an example of how better work is possible everywhere, I would like to use the example of one community. In the community of M—— (1,661 inhabitants), in the Neuhaus district, the creation of a Socialist Military Education Commission, under the leadership of the mayor, has conducted military-political work with great results.

Under the leadership of the commission, it has been possible to carry out military-political work in the housing areas, in the factories in the community, and in the polytechnical high school. Sponsorship programs exist between the polytechnical high school and the VEB (Volkseigene Betrieb, or "People's-Owned Company") Messtechnik factory, (military) reserve collectives, and units of the National People's Army. A particularly emotional event was the high school's competition and struggle for the name of the noncommissioned officer Klaus-Peter Seidel, which is being awarded during the thirty-fifth anniversary (of the

GDR) celebrations. The examination of the life and development of Klaus-Peter Seidel, personal contact with his father, and the fact that the double-murderer Weihold is living freely in the FRG, lead to a lasting, positive attitude among the students toward the responsible duty in our armed organs [bewaffnete Organe].[109]

The use of "names of honor" and "emotion" were important aspects in the motivation of young men:

The nurturing of the military-revolutionary traditions of the working class is being used ever more effectively in the motivation of young men. In the Suhl organization of the Society for Sports and Technology, over seventy subsidiary units of the Society for Sports and Technology carry names of honor. The combat traditions of the working class are nurtured in the young men, especially the career military candidates, above all by the appearance of resistance fighters and Activists of the First Hour [Aktivisten der ersten Stunde]. These appearances have a positive effect in the construction of soldier traits such as courage, discipline, and preparedness, especially when the speakers are emotionally effective and speak about their own lives.[110]

The use of resistance fighters and other older men who had taken part in antifascist movements, were part of the *Aufbau* generation, or who had served in the NVA at an earlier period was considered especially useful in motivating younger generations for military service. "Waffen aus Arbeiterhand" (Weapons from Workers' Hands) was a public ritual designed to encourage young soldiers and fill them with a sense of historical purpose. With the families, friends, and girlfriends of the new recruits in attendance, a line of older men, usually resistance fighters or former soldiers, would present the new soldiers with their weapons. The ceremony was intricately staged and designed for maximum emotional effect. Young soldiers were to be immersed in a ceremony of memory, history, and emotion, as they took an oath before their families and friends. It was also a way of instilling "fighting spirit," by using older, respected men as role models for their own behavior, placing them in a natural life-course progression of militarized masculinity and defense of the state. It was to be the practice and ritual of commitment and defense, the solidification of the emotional bond between the soldier and the state.

BECOMING THE STATE

Militarization policies were extremely important to state-formation processes in the GDR; through the net of premilitary and military training, men and women were to be indoctrinated into the goals and achievements of the SED, come to support and uphold SED policies, and become the "new socialist men and women" desired—and designed—by the party. As such, militarization was to promote state formation and party hegemony through a massive program of social engineering, a state-level experiment in social construction. It was the attempt to create a moral universe of watchfulness, sacrifice, preparedness, and dreams of heroism, a moral universe that people were eventually to think of as their own.

While Gramsci saw violence as deeply embedded in social institutions and cultural conceptions of power and identity,[111] militarization is often seen as something else, as somehow removed from this process. Militarization often is not linked directly to hegemony or seen as a cultural form. It is more often seen as the material or logistical preparation for war, rather than the shaping of society for the support of war, military values, and the shaping of cultural forms to support war and conflict.[112] Militarization is much more than the simple production of weapons or the conscription and training of soldiers; it is a cultural form created by the ruling class(es), made to be seen as natural, normal, and commonsensical. Militarization policies are about creating certain types of citizens, certain types of subjects, deemed desirable by the state.

Lears, in his analysis of Gramsci's conception of hegemony, states that the idea of cultural hegemony is to take apart the question "who has power" at both ends, and to problematize both the "who" and "power."[113] The "who" includes parents, preachers, teachers, journalists, "experts," and so on—and here we need to add state and military elites as well—and "power" includes cultural as well as economic and political power. The most powerful form of "power" in this conception is the ability to limit and define common sense and the "taken for granted."[114] Sider states that hegemony is the dominance of a particular class as expressed in and through specific institutions of "civil society": churches, schools, newspapers, public buildings and spaces, systems of status symbols, and so forth.[115] We can add "the military" to this equation as well.

While militarization processes and programs are supposed to join x and y seamlessly, in practice they are fractious and contradictory. We can sketch out ideal types of militarization processes, but the point is to examine how militarization plays out in the everyday lives of citizens, the ways in which the "state" is experienced by people in their daily lives, and the ways in which militarization processes shape the contexts in which people live and act. We can think of militarization as an organizing principle of the state, with actual warfare often being of only secondary importance. The primary goal of militarization is to constantly think about and prepare for war and defense, to create an atmosphere in which soldier-citizens worry about the safety of the state.

The militarization of the East German state was arguably a top-down process, one needed to insure the legitimacy and security of the new East German state and its elites. The SED, despite recourse to repression and secret police, constantly attempted to create a "ground spring" of support for its policies and rule; it was in the interests of those most intimately connected to the party, and those attempting to work their way up through the party ranks, to insure that militarization polices promoted the strengths and legitimacy of the SED. While concerns about the perceptions of external threats by the GDR are not to be discounted, militarization policies were concerned more with disciplining the population of the GDR than defending the GDR from external attack. Although the need for military protection was officially justified as a response to external threats, militarization policies in the GDR were focused on creating disciplined and docile citizens and national defense. To put it another way: the creation of a docile and (correctly) politicized citizen is the first line of "national" defense. By docile citizens, we can think of men who want to become soldiers, women who will willingly marry and support soldiers, couples that will have children and bring them up to worship and respect soldiers, and parents who will willingly sacrifice their children for the good of the state. An NVA military education report from 1983 stated this explicitly: "Parents have a dominating influence (on their children); if we want to win over the young men, we have to have already won over their parents. This is a problem of parents (willingly) sacrificing their children [Problem Opferbereitschaft]."[116]

National defense begins from the inside, as an internal process, as a process of "restructuring" individuals and their worldviews. In the GDR, it was a process designed to create the "new socialist man" who would fight and die for socialism. A population must be made "malleable" and tractable; militarization policies provide the ways and the means to further the ends of state perpetuation. "Threats" provide the impetus, and "peace" provides the reason, the officially stated goal. Peace, however, may not be the actual goal.

CHAPTER 3

Coming of Age in the NVA

THE MASTER NARRATIVES OF MILITARIZATION

"Why did I join the NVA?" Günther said in response to my question. "Why did I join? Well, I joined because I believed in socialism and what it represented, and what it meant in the context of German history. I joined because of the war, and because of what happened as a result of decades of German militarism. I joined because I believed in the new state, the better German state. And I joined because I wanted to make sure nothing happened to our new state and our new experiment. I wasn't going to let that happen."

"Suddenly, I realized that I was completely IN! The system had worked perfectly."

STEFAN,

a three-year volunteer describing his training in the National People's Army

THE ROLE OF THE SOLDIER and the position of the soldier in German society have a long and complicated history, intertwined with questions of class and class mobility, masculinity, hierarchy, domination, aesthetics, and the legitimate use of violence. Beginning with the coalescence of the Prussian state, and the valorization of the military, military values and virtues, and militarized masculinity, the idea of the soldier in German culture and society found a firm anchor. The idea of the strong, brave, loyal, and obedient soldier became the ideal of male identity, the sine qua non of hegemonic masculinity, status, and legitimacy. After World War II, however, soldiers were blamed for the destruction of Germany, and there was a dramatic drop in the appeal of being a soldier and the social standing of soldiers in general, in both East Germany and West Germany. One of the tasks confronting both new German states was how to entice men to join the new military.

As discussed in the last chapter, the GDR employed a vast array of institutions, programs, and policies to entice men and women to learn to love the new NVA and the GDR. The men I worked with did come to love the NVA. Their motives for joining were complicated and diverse; perhaps the most important commonality shared by these men was their class backgrounds, backgrounds which made military service an attractive option—in some cases the best option open to them. These men were very much a product of their times, products of a system—or systems—that made military service politically, economically, and personally attractive. It was also a system that made military service aesthetically attractive, a job that promised power and control, a chance to be an elite. It was also a job that drew upon notions of masculinity, of the "strong" man and soldier who defends the state, the family, women, and children. The officers I worked with grew up in this system, and were ultimately responsible for maintaining the system, for carrying out militarization policies, for making it their life's work. A militarization process is political work carried out by politicized individuals with the intention of politicizing other individuals, of bringing them into the system, of making them embody the system and make it their own: a constitutive—and constituting—part of their lives and identity.[1]

FIGURE 3.1 Three former NVA officers, during an interview in 1999, discussing their experiences after unification. Photograph by the author.

OFFICERS, CLASS, AND COMMITMENT IN THE GDR

One of the first things I noticed during interviews with NVA officers was the role played by class and antifascism in their decisions to join the military. These were men who mostly came from working-class backgrounds, found themselves with very few choices for upward advancement or education in the GDR, and were offered the chance to become officers. Some had lived through the end of World War II, or grown up in and around the devastation and deprivation caused by the war. They also had relatives who had fought in the war, or who told them stories of what it was like to live through the war and fascism.

Prior to and during the Second World War, the military occupied a privileged position in German society, representing order, education, and social status.[2] As historian Jay Lockenour described the traditional status and position of the officer corps in German society:

The officer corps had been a key elite for centuries. . . . They sat at the pinnacle of the social order by the end of the nineteenth century, when merely serving in the reserves meant prestige for the status-conscious bourgeoisie. Under Kaiser Wilhelm II, officers played an important role in the formulation of state policy, both formally, as cabinet ministers, and informally, as the emperor's advisors and confidantes. Despite their apparent isolation in the Weimar Republic and the competition from the paramilitary forces under Hitler's command (the SA and SS), officers remained a privileged elite until 1945, with power, status, and access to wealth denied ordinary citizens.[3]

Historically, the officer corps in the German military was comprised of the aristocracy or landed gentry; there had been a gradual erosion of the "closed" nature of the officer corps by virtue of losses suffered during World War I, and particularly during World War II, as officers were killed and replaced by soldiers and noncommissioned officers from the working classes. After World War II, the status of the military and the idea of soldiering in Germany declined to a great degree,[4] though conceptions of status and class mobility remained. The officer corps still represented a valued class position for some; that a chance to be an officer meant more than just an advancement in monetary security was evident during interviews with those officers who came from "peasant" or unskilled labor backgrounds. For them it represented upward mobility and an increase in personal status and prestige. While this seems to be contradictory in the postwar setting, it appears that in both Germanys of the time, as soon as Cold War tensions began to rise and decisions were made to reformulate armies on both sides of the divide, intense effort was made to rehabilitate the military as an "honorable" career. Even in what was to be a classless society, prewar notions of class, privilege, and honor were still operative, and not so easily eradicated or dismissed. Promises of power and prestige in the new state were key incentives in attracting recruits to the new army.

Officers enjoyed a higher status and standard of living, but in many ways they were literally imprisoned by the NVA, finding their commitment to it to be a burden on themselves and their families.[5] Mary Fulbrook provides an accurate overall description of the status and privileges of the NVA officer corps, although in interviews, officers present a more nuanced and complicated picture of their lives: "The officer corps of NVA . . . [was] of necessity the most isolated from the wider population. They appear to have been compensated for the lack of high, visible public status through privileges in terms of housing, holidays, and schooling for their children, as well as by copious indulgence in titles, medals, awards, ceremonies, and uniforms, in a form of symbolic back-scratching to reward achievement and express mutual esteem."[6]

In terms of recruitment policies, the nascent East German military played on these currents of class envy and upward mobility by actively recruiting among the working class for the officer corps. While the newly formed East German police and later military forces were to be "People's Police" and the "People's Army," recruiters and the SED played on notions of class mobility and status to insure compliance and support for the military. By actively recruiting from the working class, they offered disadvantaged men something that they would never have had in a normal peacetime situation: the chance to join the officer corps and become part of the history and tradition of the German military in a way that only years before had been barred to them by virtue of their class position. They were offered a position in the new society that was to be valued and valorized by the SED; in a very real sense, they were offered positions of power to which they might never have had access. The SED also offered them the chance to be involved in the creation and construction of the East German military from the beginning, an opportunity to take part in the building of something new; this was in keeping with the general spirit of the *Aufbau* (reconstruction) generation in the East, who were motivated by a sense of creating a new Germany.[7] These sentiments arose again and again during interviews with older officers: "We were there from the beginning, we wanted to make something new, a new experiment," was a common theme and opinion. Other officers spoke of joining the early Garrisoned People's Police out of a desire to participate in the "new experiment" of the GDR, to insure that it remained guarded and protected. Gerd, who joined the police in 1951, remarked that "a state needs someone to defend it; all states are like that, and need someone to make sure it isn't attacked, or if it is, that it can be defended. We learned that from the war, and fascist aggression. I thought this new state was worth defending, so I joined." Arthur, who served in the Border Guards, joined for the same reasons: "The GDR was an experiment; it was the first socialist German state, and I wanted to make sure that no one attempted to hinder it. We had been through too much."

For officers like Gerd and Arthur, the *Aufbau*, the antifascist ideology of the new state and the new NVA represented a chance to start over, to reshape Germany in a new, better way, and a way of escaping (or perhaps rectifying) the past. It also offered them positions of power, influence, and status that they would probably never have attained otherwise.

I met Horst in 1999 on a rainy wintry day at his house outside of Berlin. He was in his mid-sixties, a tall, imposing man with thick, gray hair, keen blue eyes, and a very intimidating stare. He had spent his career in the NVA as a tank officer; when an injury prevented him from continuing on in the tank corps, he moved into the motorized infantry, and when he retired, he was placed in the civil defense corps. Horst had spent almost his entire adult life in the NVA and the defense forces, attending military academies in the GDR and the Soviet Union, working in a variety of assignments and command positions, moving around the GDR to different bases (and taking his family with him each time he was reassigned), and eventually retiring as a colonel. He had been a member of the SED both out of conviction and out of necessity; as an officer, he was expected to be a party member, and party membership helped insure a smooth career path. He had spent thousands of hours training, and training soldiers, for the *Ernstfall* (emergency), for war, for when things "got serious." The NVA had been his life, and even though it no longer existed, it was in many ways still his life.

When I first met Horst, I was convinced that he did not like me at all; he was not one of the officers who jokingly referred to me as "*Der Klassenfeind*—"the class enemy"—he seemed to mean it. We met at a veterans group meeting in Berlin during a visit to the group with Rainer Wulf. He seemed somewhat annoyed by my presence at the meetings, and was not exactly sure why I was there. When I first met him, he was cold, distant, and curt. During the next couple of visits to the group, Horst would often look over at me and stare, seemingly trying to figure out what I wanted, and trying to figure out who I was. Over time—and after speaking with other officers I had spoken with—he seemed to get used to my presence, and came to be quite friendly and helpful, eventually agreeing to an interview.

Horst is very involved in the political life of former NVA soldiers, and plays an important role in his veterans group, in which he occupies an elected position. He is very concerned with the well-being and welfare of the members—"of his solders," as he told me one day. This is a carryover from his various command positions, from the time he was in charge of large numbers of soldiers and was responsible for making sure they were well treated and well fed.

As we sat in his study, with the rain beating against the window, we talked about his life and his career in the NVA. He missed it, he said, though he does not want to return to the past, even though the past is with him every day, in more ways than he can explain, and in ways that are not necessarily positive. I asked Horst to describe his life and experiences, and how and why he decided to join the NVA:

I was born in Berlin in 1934; my mother was a housewife and my father a butcher. My grandfather on my father's side was a real capitalist [ein richtiger

Kapitalist], involved in street construction and design. My grandfather on my mother's side was an ordinary worker [ein einfacher Arbeiter] and a member of the German Communist Party, who was arrested in 1933 and imprisoned in the Sachsenhausen concentration camp and at the Brandenburg prison. I had two sides of my family: the bourgeois and the not-so-bourgeois, and I was somewhere in the middle.

Horst, like many other officers who joined the Garrisoned People's Police, and later, the NVA, was born in the years of the Third Reich, and experienced both fascism and World War II. Like many other officers, Horst experienced the advance of the Soviet army into Germany, the final defeat of the Wehrmacht, and the continuous bombing campaigns of the United States and England. Like others, he had spent long periods of time hiding in cellars or bomb shelters, waiting out the bombings, surveying the destruction, looking at the bodies. As I would hear in a number of interviews, former officers were very bitter toward the Allies because of the bombing raids, and in a convergence of personal experience and state discourse, would loudly and angrily curse the "American air pirates" for the destruction of their homes and the deaths of their friends. These experiences, even though they took place when they were young, influenced their later decision to join the new East German military, and also provided a baseline from which to shape—and in some ways justify—their decision to join the NVA.

Since I was born in 1934, I consciously experienced the development of fascism, say, the time between 1940 and 1941 when the war really started up, and up to 1945. I really liked the military prowess of the Germans, and that one was able to join the Hitler Youth at that time [Pfimpfen]. And if you wore the Hitler Youth uniform to school they couldn't beat you or punish you, because at this time there was corporal punishment in schools, and if you wore your uniform they couldn't touch you. This was a conscious decision on their [the Nazi Party's] part, and because of this, a lot of kids wanted to wear the uniform, even if they weren't old enough yet, so that they wouldn't be beaten in school.

While experiences growing up during the Third Reich were mentioned by a number of former officers, none spoke as openly as Horst about their experiences in the Hitler Youth or in the other mass organizations of the Nazi Party. And most did not speak of admiring the "military prowess" of the Wehrmacht, even if they might have felt it.

World War II played a large role in the decisions of some men to join the paramilitary and then the military forces of the GDR. Most of the older officers had experienced the end of the war, or had relatives who had fought. Male relatives who had served in the war made a great impression on a number of officers and played a large role in their decisions to join the military. Horst's father seemed to use his wartime service as a way to shame his son, to "make him a man": "My father, who made it to the rank of a Prussian noncommissioned officer during the Second World War, and who also joined the KPD because of the influence of my grandfather on my mother's side, always said to me, 'The next time it comes to fighting, I'll know how to act and fight as a German noncommissioned officer, and you'll just be serving coffee to the old women behind the front lines.' This always made an impression on me."

Georg, a member of Horst's veterans group, spoke of an uncle who had fought in World War II: "I joined the army because I gave up trying to be a normal civil engineer. But because of my close relationship to my uncle, who had served in the Second World War, I thought about it, and realized that the army paid more, and I could experience more, and that I could still become an engineer. However, I didn't become an engineer, but an artillery officer, but that was how I started thinking about the army."

Ingo, who joined the NVA in the mid-1950s, described his motivations for joining:

I lived through the end of the last war in a basement, waiting for the Allied bombing raids to end, and then waiting for the Soviet army to overrun our town. After the war, and the destruction it brought not only to Germany but to much of the world, I decided that I didn't want to simply sit by and let things happen—I wanted to be a part of something that would make sure there was never a war again. And I remember the Americans and the Russians. The Americans gave us chocolate and chewing gum, and the Russians gave us bread. That's why I joined the National People's Army—I always thought of it as an army of peace, and I served to make sure there was peace. And I think, in my own way, I helped insure there was peace in Europe during the Cold War, and peace during the transition from two states to one.

Felix and Helmut were close friends, both during their service in the NVA and after unification. They were both career NVA officers, and they signed up in the founding phase of the GDR, first in the KVP and later transferring to the new NVA, eventually spending their careers in various posts, and both teaching at the NVA military academy. Like Horst, Felix and Helmut were young at the end of the war; Felix was eleven and Helmut was ten. Felix told me,

For the last six months of the war, there were constant air raids. My family lived in a major city in the East, so we were a target for the Allies. There were raids every day, and it seemed like there was constant thunder from the bombs going off. Because of this, I spent the last six months living in the basement, and didn't come out—there was no reason to come out, because I'd simply have to run right back in because of the bombs. Because of this, when I was old enough, I decided to join the NVA so that there wouldn't be another war. My decision to join the army had nothing to do with "militarism" or military things—it was a desire to help maintain peace, and protect the GDR from outside aggression, because it was our GDR [die DDR war unsere DDR].

Helmut continued where Felix left off. While Felix was fairly detached as he talked about his youth and his experiences during the last months of the war, Helmut was animated, leaning toward me and looking me right in the eye as he told me about his experiences after the war, tearing up as he spoke.

After the war, when I was in high school, every day after school I had to come home and help clear rubble. You have to keep two things in mind when looking at the founding of the GDR: the spirit of a new beginning [Neuanfang], and a refusal to reconcile with West Germany, since the West Germans were simply taking old Nazis and putting them back in to positions of power. The GDR was an experiment that we were determined to carry through, it was a new beginning for us. I had to clear rubble with my hands, a spade, and a wheelbarrow that was only sixty centimeters wide. And no matter what you might think about Karl Marx Strasse architecturally or aesthetically, we created it out of nothing, out of an unimaginable heap of rubble that we thought we'd never be able to clear away. So why did I join the NVA? I'll tell you why I joined the NVA. Like Felix, it had nothing to do with the military, or any interest in the military. I joined the military to help maintain peace, so that if anyone ever, ever tried to take this all away from us, well then—(at this point, Helmut held out his hand and slapped it hard)—This is what we would have done to anyone who tried to take this away from us.

Both Felix and Helmut said that because of the "new beginning" and the desire to rebuild the GDR from the rubble left over from the war, as well as the fear that someone would try to prevent the (re)construction of the GDR, the NVA was seen as a "necessary evil" ("Die Nationale Volksarmee war ein notwendiges Übel"). Because they had lived through the end of the war, they said, and witnessed what war was like, they were determined to prevent anything like it from ever happening again. They were in strong agreement about this point.

These "key experiences [Schlüsselerlebnisse]" of reconstruction, anti-fascism, militarization, and commitment formed the basis for the construction of the life narratives of NVA officers. As Mary Fulbrook discusses, while these kinds of accounts are stylized, they nonetheless are important and valid, as they are also the "fundamental legitimation of all that was to follow" in these men's lives.[8]

The end of the war, and male relatives who had served in the war, made a great impression on a number of officers, and played a large role in their decisions to join the military. The overwhelming defeat of Nazi Germany and its military represented a crisis for German masculinity, as German men caused and lost the war.[9] The GDR officially denied any responsibility for the war, since it was a state founded by antifascists, and was an "antifascist" state. While this may have functioned as a political discourse for state legitimization, at the level of daily life and experience, everyone still knew that Germany had lost the war and that German men were the cause. Horst witnessed the end of the war and knew what had happened, knew that men like his father had fought and lost and were simultaneously damaged and valorized, hero and victim. They had fought and lost, but had become "real" men in the process (at least according to "traditional" notions of what made a man, and because of the continued power of Nazi military indoctrination). The creation of the NVA and the recoupling of the military and masculinity can be seen as an attempt to create a positive (East) German military masculinity; it was to be a "second chance," a chance to serve in an army that was for "peace" and not conquest. Military service seems to have been viewed as both an indication of (male) failure and the source of all of Germany's immediate postwar problems, but also as a way to recuperate and "strengthen" German male identity, and insure that a cadre of men would join the military, in the process protecting and shoring up the new state.

Immediately after the end of the war, the SED created the Free German Youth (FDJ) organization, and a large number of future NVA officers found their way to the military through the FDJ. Even though this organization was similar to the Hitler Youth, and was an instrument of indoctrination, it was viewed by many former officers as an opportunity to escape the anomie and boredom of the immediate postwar era and as an opportunity to take part in social events. One of the main objectives of the FDJ was to organize teenagers' free time in constructive and entertaining ways in order to promote socialism and indoctrinate youths into the tenets of Marxism and Leninism. By providing them with entertainment, it provided the state with a recruitment opportunity, and attempted to mask ideological indoctrination through fun and enjoyment. In this sense, youths were to have no "free" time; rather, all time was to be devoted to the state and the party. As Horst recalled,

The year 1945 and the end of the war and fascism marked the end of a period in our lives, because we had been raised in a certain direction up to then, and then, all of a sudden, everything was gone. At this point, my grandfather, who had been in the Sachsenhausen and Brandenburg concentration camps, began to reshape my life in a new way; this was the time of the slogan "Germans— never again take up arms!" At that time, the Free German Youth organization was founded (in the eastern zone), and we joined, because we wanted to decide ourselves what we wanted to do in our free time, like club evenings and dance evenings. I finished school at this time, and learned a trade as a film technician at the Deutsche Film-Aktiengesellschaft, the East German Film Agency (DEFA).

While in the FDJ, recruiters began asking for volunteers for the People's Police and the Garrisoned People's Police (KVP). Once in the new KVP or NVA, many officers were pressured to stay. Horst's decision to join the People's Police and the Garrisoned People's Police was influenced by his grandfather's experiences in a concentration camp as a political prisoner, as well as his fascination with the military from his time in the Hitler Youth:

I was the Free German Youth secretary of DEFA at that time, and they began to ask for youths to join the KVP or rather, first the VP [Volkspolizei, or People's Police] and then the KVP. I thought about everything that had happened to my grandfather while he was in KZ Sachsenhausen. On October 7, 1952, the first march of units of the People's Police on the Marx-Engels Platz in Berlin took place, and for the first time in the new khaki uniforms (they had always worn blue before that). And this fascinated me so much that I said to myself, "OK, now it's your time to join." I joined on October 9 or 15, and was stationed in K——.

Although he joined the KVP, Horst never intended to make the security forces or the military a career; he simply wanted to serve for a few years and then move on. However, after spending a year as an enlisted member in the KVP, Horst recalled how he was enticed into joining the soon-to-be NVA as an officer:

One Sunday in 1953, I was told to report to a classroom. Suddenly there was an officer standing there, a political-officer, and he asked me how I viewed my prospects in the new armed forces of the future army of the German Democratic Republic. I thought to my self, "What is this man talking about, because no one has talked about an army?" And so I said to him that I didn't want to remain a soldier forever, because I really wanted to become a cameraman at the DEFA studios. I had been the FDJ secretary there, and that's really what I wanted to do and what I wanted as a career. Then he said to me that he could well imagine me as an officer in the future German army. And that settled it.

Max was one of the youngest of the career officers I interviewed, having joined the NVA in the mid-1960s, after the Wall was erected. Unlike officers who joined the NVA in its foundational period, he had no first-hand experience of World War II or of the devastation caused by the war.

At sixty, he was still an imposing presence: very tall, muscular, bald, with an intimidating glance and a voice that went from boom to whisper. Max did not initially have a military career in mind; he first wanted to be an engineer, and then, later, a lawyer. After he was conscripted into the NVA in 1964, he realized that the NVA was not going to let him leave the military, even though he wanted to leave and study law. He seems to have accepted his "fate," and made the best of it:

We were told that when a country exists, then it needs an army, that when one has something, one needs to defend it. That's what Lenin said, but that wasn't the main reason I joined the army; the main reason was that I wanted to become something, and I was successful. That's why I joined the army. It wasn't easy, and I was about to jump ship when I was a lieutenant, because we stayed at one rank for a long time.

I started to do my *Abitur* [high school exams for those wishing to go to the university], and took the test in Berlin for law; I had the possibility of studying law by mail and becoming a lawyer. My idea was to leave the army and become an attorney, but it didn't happen. Lieutenant-General S—— strictly forbid me from doing this, and said to me, "You're going to a military academy. You can complain all you want but you are not going to become a lawyer."

I went to the main military lawyer in Berlin and spoke with him, and he told me that there was nothing he could do; he couldn't even complain to the minister of defense [Heinz Hoffmann], because the minister said that they were trying to build up the rocket forces, and we couldn't simply give away an artillery officer, and then he told me again that there was really nothing he could do. He was a nice, old colonel, a very sympathetic man, but he couldn't help me. Maybe it was for the best. I don't regret it, and later everything worked out well with my professional development, so I really can't complain at all.

As Max and I talked, I finally asked him what it meant for him to have been a soldier and officer in the NVA. At first he seemed taken aback by the question, but after a long silence, he answered,

Now look, I think it's right that an officer has a special place in society, and I think I should say this because of the great burdens he must bear, which the civilian sector doesn't have to do. They just watched, went about their business, and earned enough money. I have the same qualifications as my wife; no, she was more qualified than me because she was teacher, I would say, but she brought in only half of what I brought in. However, it was strictly forbidden for us to talk about what we earned compared to Bundeswehr officers, and we were threatened with dismissal from the army if we did by the political officer of the division. We talked about it a lot, and figured out that we really had a small income if you considered it on an hourly basis.

But our reputation was good. I realized this when I had to go to factories and make certain contacts there. Yes, our reputation was very proper [recht ordentlich]; I would compare it with that of a teacher or an engineer. I never thought of us as anything special or as anything lower. And we were paid well according to the GDR, always in terms of the GDR. Actually, we were very well regarded and respected.

Many of the men I interviewed joined the NVA in the early years of its existence, either joining the Garrisoned People's Police and then moving on to the NVA, or signing up as officers for the NVA in the 1960s or early 1970s. Many signed up for the mandatory twenty-five years and then stayed longer, moving into positions in the civil defense forces, or remaining active in reserve positions. Willingly or not, they had made the military their life while the state imposed it on them. The life of an NVA officer was one of constant work, with very little time off for rest or reflection. Routinely working six-and-a-half days per week, Horst, Max, Georg, and all of the other officers I worked with found themselves immersed in a system of constant readiness, indoctrination, "political-ideological work," and constant preparation for war. Once in, having signed a twenty-five-year commitment to the military and the party, it was very difficult to get out of the NVA: the slightest suggestion that one wanted to leave the military marked one as politically unreliable and suspect— in other words, it ultimately amounted to social, political, and economic suicide. The life of an NVA officer was a Faustian pact of power, prestige, and unquestioning obligation.

As he advanced in rank, the officer was expected to become more and more an example of the "new socialist man," to set the example for lower-ranking officers and soldiers, and to prove to those above him that he was a committed party member and defender of the state (through conviction and coercion, nearly 100 percent of NVA officers were members of the SED).[10] In theory this was possible; in practice, given the ever increasing political, ideological, and military demands on officers, it was impossible. Family life was difficult, as officers were required to spend very long hours on base and in the field, honing and refining their own combat skills as well as the combat capabilities of their soldiers. Life as an NVA officer was very difficult, despite the status and perks, such as trips to the Soviet Union, vacations at NVA resorts (even if only once every five or six years), and, as they advanced in rank, better housing opportunities. Because they were stationed in heavily guarded and restricted barracks, lived in secluded officer communities, and worked very long hours, officers were in many ways cut off from civilians, and were increasingly resented for their perks and their subservience and commitment to the party and the status quo. Over time, a fair amount of distance and distrust grew between the civilian population of the GDR and the NVA officer corps. If not overtly respected, NVA officers were certainly afforded deference because of who they were and what they represented.

As the economic conditions in the GDR improved, and as word spread of the kind of lives officers led, the appeal of a military career as an officer diminished. In the decades following the *Aufbau* and the creation of the GDR, as the GDR became increasingly authoritarian and stagnant, the NVA and its officers were viewed with increasing disdain and mistrust. Among the civilian population, coming of age in the NVA was viewed with fear and trepidation, as something either to exploit for oneself or to get through as quickly and easily as possible. Life as an NVA officer became less and less attractive, and was popularly viewed as something only those with few prospects would consider.

COMING OF AGE IN THE NVA, RELUCTANTLY

A comparison of officers and conscripts from different time periods in the GDR highlights the role played by political-economic and social-cultural factors in attitudes toward military service. Men coming of age in the 1950s and 1960s entered the military for various reasons, but discussions with these men revealed that the NVA represented a secure, stable environment and career choice, as well as a means of climbing the social ladder. By the late 1970s and early 1980s, however, this view had changed. Due to the extreme demands of professional military service in the NVA, particularly in terms of personal time and freedom, as well as the impact of military service on family life, the military no longer represented a viable or attractive career choice for the majority of men. As I was told by men who had served as conscripts in the 1980s, as well as friends and acquaintances who came of age in the GDR in the 1980s, career military service was increasingly looked down upon; it was only for those who had no other options, such as those who had earned poor grades in high school (those with a cumulative average of 4 or 5, with 1 being the highest on the high school grade scale). The romantic notions of self-sacrifice and commitment to a greater good, common during the *Aufbau* years, were over, replaced with more pragmatic and self-interested motivations.[11] Those students who were underachievers, it was commonly held, were the ones to whom the military paid special attention, for they would be the ones most willing to accept what the military offered in terms of a career. And, as mentioned above, the standard of living and overall economic security in the GDR had advanced to a point in which military service was no longer viewed as a means of social advancement. Indeed, career military service, according to my discussions with younger informants, was considered only for "losers" who had no other options. It was also viewed as a sign that one was *Staatsnah* (close to the state), a distinction that many tried to avoid as the GDR aged.

Beginning in the late 1970s, the GDR increased pressure on young men to join the military for longer periods of time or to consider a career in the military. While this can be seen as an increase in the militarization of the GDR, it is not that simple. Yes, there was an increase in militarization and military education in schools. While this could be considered an indication that the GDR was truly and in some essential way a state based on military values, it could also be read in the opposite sense. The increase in militarization policies and military education could be seen as an indication that the majority of GDR citizens did not believe in the necessity of mandatory military service, that the increased pressure to join the military was a reflection that things were beginning to slip. Considering that the military was regarded as one of the primary sites of indoctrination into Marxist-Leninist ideology (consider, once again, Kessler's statement that "it was all about . . . turning men into communists"), and that mandatory military service and extended or career military service allowed the state to "educate" these men and hopefully make them *staatstreu* (loyal to the state), a willingness or desire to take part in military service and support the military was crucial to the SED's maintenance of power. The increases in militarization and military education occurred as a result of the SED's growing realization that they were losing the "hearts and minds" of the citizenry; they were designed as disciplinary measures to insure loyalty and compliance to the state. These increases were also necessary to continue to turn men into better, more loyal communists. By the 1980s, however, as interviews with conscripts show, this campaign was perhaps all too little, too late. Despite myriad policies and structures of militarization programs—or perhaps, because of them—a career in the NVA was increasingly seen as questionable and undesirable.

STEFAN GOES TO THE NVA

Stefan was born in 1965, and entered the NVA in 1983, when he was eighteen. He grew up in a time of relative prosperity for the GDR—when the mutually assured destruction of the Cold War had ossified into a tense, but stable, standoff. By the time Stefan was preparing (and being prepared) for his service in the NVA, militarization programs and policies were in high gear, but it was also a time when the appeal of the NVA was low, and few entered out of the same kind of ideological conviction and love of the new state that characterized the lives of early NVA officers of the *Aufbau* generation. The NVA was seen by the beginning of the 1980s as something that was a part of one's life, yes, but something that one needed to get through in order to move on. And as people learned how to "game" the system, it was seen as something one could use to get something one wanted.

Because military service was seen as a sign of deference and support of the SED and the state, Stefan volunteered for three years in order to secure a better place at the university. Stefan wanted to study automobile engineering after his military service; because this was an extremely difficult and competitive area of study, he decided that his chances would be better if he served three years first. As he told me during out talk, his three years turned out to have been in vain; he was admitted, not to the automobile engineering course, but to industrial engineering. While this was not a bad outcome, it was not his first choice; Stefan added, "But at least I was in the university, so that was something."

I asked Stefan about his time in school, and the role that military education (*Wehrerziehung*) and the pressure to join the NVA as an officer played in his education and his attitude toward the NVA:

It was sometime in either the eighth or ninth grade, I can't remember, but we had to go to a civil defense camp. At least the boys had to go, and the girls, I can't remember really, they had to go away as well and do some sort of cheesecake class. They had to learn how to help during an air raid and become real helpers' helpers. Men were taught how to fight and shoot, with the women in the hinterland learning how to be medics. I got out of going once because of an operation, but they got me the next year. I was really barracked in, just like in a real barracks. It was all targeted for our future, because every boy in the GDR had to go to the army. We had to get up at six in the morning and do exercises, and then shoot machine guns, clean weapons. It was all very paramilitary; it was preparation for life in the NVA. But it was really shitty.

I then asked Stefan if he was pressured to join the military as a career officer when he was still in high school. Stefan paused for a moment, and then continued:

I can remember two times in school, in the seventh or eighth grade. The director came in and cried out, "Stefan, up and out of the classroom." So I left and went to his office, and there was some guy sitting there in civilian clothes, and the director said to me, "Yes, he's from the National People's Army, and he's heard that you've applied to become a career officer, and he wants to know which branch you're interested in." Well, what he was saying was bullshit; I never applied to be a career officer. They would sometimes target you and pick you out, and sometimes not, but would then confront you with it with the school director there and then see how you reacted. And this happened to me twice. Once I said, I don't remember, I was so shocked, and so I said, "Yeah, whatever bullshit you have, how about the tank corps or something." NEVER! I would never do that. And then he said, "Yes, you could do this and this," and the whole thing lasted about half an hour, and I showed a little interest, even though I had no interest whatsoever, but I just felt so run over by the experience and the pressure to sign up for life. I didn't expect anything like this. But nothing came of it, though a few years later it happened again. I told my parents about it, and they were very angry.

This was a warning to me, and then it happened again. This time I immediately told them that it was completely untrue, and that I had no intention of doing anything like that, no intention of joining the NVA as a career officer. The discussion was over after a minute. Of course I had to go the director again, and he asked me the meaning of all this, why I had acted that way. All of this even after I had talked to my parents about it. But that's how they did things in the East. It ruined any trust I had, that I had in my relationship to the state. This made me become even more distant from those communists in the country. We were always not particularly socialist, and this contributed to it.

Despite his experiences and the pressure to become a career officer in school, Stefan decided that he would sign up for three years in the NVA as a way to gain a coveted university position:

I was sitting in school, and the guy next to me knew for sure that he was only going to do eighteen months in the NVA, that he was only going to serve for the required minimum amount of time. He was a member of a church; he was actually Catholic, and the Catholics were always a bit more edgy than the Protestants. So he knew that he was only going to do eighteen months, but he was also much better in school than I was, and didn't have to worry as much about getting what he wanted at the university. I wanted to study automotive engineering, but at that time there were only two seminar groups in the entire GDR, and automotive engineering was a bit more elite and a difficult course of study to get in to. My parents told me to watch out; even though my father had only served eighteen months, my stepfather told me to do three years, because one wouldn't stand out as much that way, and because I would have a better chance of getting what I wanted when I went to the university. I didn't think about it too much really; I just said to myself, "Yeah, I'll do it." And so I went in. For the sake of studying. If I had wanted to be a baker or butcher, I surely would not have done three years.

I wanted to know what the other students in his class did: was he the exception, or did others decide to go in longer or simply serve for eighteen months?

There were eleven boys, and so half of us did three years and half eighteen months. But we did have one officer candidate, and they were always the worst. He did twenty-five years, just like all of those officers you talk to in the *Kameradschaften*, the forever yesterdays at the has-been's club [die Ewiggestrigen beim Klub der Verflossenen], they all did an *Abitur*. They were always the ones with the worst grades, on average something less than a four.

Stefan then spoke of his time in the army. He was sent to the remote (and by all accounts miserable) NVA base at Eggesin in the north of the GDR to attend the noncommissioned officer course, and was then stationed there in a self-propelled artillery unit. While he initially tried to maintain a somewhat detached attitude toward entering the military, he gradually began to feel cut off from the civilian world.

It didn't take very long, not even a year; after a year, I couldn't even imagine life outside of the barracks. I could sort of imagine it, but I was so IN! Maybe I should put it differently. When you join the army at eighteen, you've lived eighteen years. You can't imagine what life will be like in the army. And after one year, it was exactly reversed. Like I had the same feeling, but eighteen years ago. It was like I had already been in the army eighteen years, my entire life. At least that's how it seemed to me. Mornings I put on the same old jacket and boots, everyday. One was so completely in, that I thought that it would be somewhat frightening when the three years were up and I was out—I was frightened about what it would be like to be out of the army after three years and back in normal life. That was a pretty serious revelation for me, because it was just the same thing every day. A human is an individual, but at some point you're so involved in it all—the system functioned PERFECTLY! You got into a rhythm. On the one hand, well, I'm not sure what I want to say. Well, what I want to say is this: one did feel boxed in and confined, like you were locked in. But you didn't really fully understand it, because you were so involved. The army was like a sweater that scratched you all the time. You just got used to it. Like your favorite pair of jeans, you just got used to it. And when I finally made it out, in a short time, say two or three weeks, it was like I had never even been there. It was back to being like it was in the first eighteen years. That just shows you how flexible humans are.

Stefan then talked about his experiences with *Hasserziehung*, or "hate training," in the NVA, and the ways in which NVA officers attempted to motivate soldiers to fight through fear and hatred of "the enemy."

They—the political officers—had opinions that no normal, thinking person could understand. Afternoons were taken up with political education; I don't even remember what the proper term for this was anymore. The political officers were there, and then you came with a group of ten men, and sat around, and they talked and tried to convince you that everything was the way they said it was. Like if a war started, or if you had contact with the West, or that if the enemy was standing across from you, then you would have to shoot your own cousin. That you would have to! Because that's what your own cousin on the other side would do to you. I mean, we just said to ourselves, "What a bunch of shit." We were much more open with the political officers in small groups, and we didn't have any respect for them anyway. But despite all of this, they [the political officers] believed all of this with a conviction that was deep in their souls, and said that this was really how it was. And they kept trying to get us to believe it. They tried to "agitate" us; that was the word for it in the East. They agitated for all of this, and tried to be cool and funny in discussions about this stuff in order to try to make us believe it. No one believed it. The common GDR citizen, not just the NVA, didn't believe this stuff. We were constantly surrounded by slogans like: "Onward to the Tenth Party Conference! Socialism will be victorious!" All sorts of shit like this was plastered up on large signs and posters on the walls, just like you see in advertisements today. You knew that they were there, but you just drove right by them. And when Westerners came over and saw these things and said, "What's going on here?" that's how it was in the NVA as well. We were of the opinion that you simply had to get through this time, and that you had to listen to this stuff from the political officers because we were forced to. But none of this ever really convinced anyone. We were all actually really frightened by the fact that officers, and especially political officers, completely believed all of this stuff.

As the discussion with Stefan progressed, I asked him about officers and the "new socialist man," and the ways in which the SED and NVA attempted to inculcate the virtues and attributes associated with this ideal type of citizen.

OK, so you mean the "soldier personality." Well, I can tell you how it was during the time of the Kaiser, or perhaps even now in America: one was relatively proud to wear a uniform. But I can also tell you how we saw it. When we went on leave, the first thing we did was jump behind a bush and get out of our fucking uniforms and put on a pair of jeans so that we felt normal. That's how we felt about it. There wasn't a second in which we identified with all of that shit. You could keep your car outside of the barracks with civilian clothes in it. We would throw off our uniforms in order to try to get back into normal life, even if only a little bit. So that means we felt nothing of this "soldier personality." On the contrary, you usually felt really sick, just like you did in uniform and when you were outside of the barracks. In the barracks a lot was going on, and that was OK and normal, but when you went out in your uniform, that was really strange—you never felt good about it at all. The reputation of the army was something of a double-edged sword. For example, in the area around Eggesin, who do you think lived there? Officers and officers' families, so they were all in uniform, and they weren't terribly excited to see someone in uniform, not at all. But if you went a few villages away, where life was a bit more normal, women could sense that you were from the army, even in civilian clothes, and in the discos, twenty-one out of twenty guys were from the army. I only tried to meet women in discos a couple of times while I was in the army, and always out of uniform. But I have to say that, at least in my opinion, our reputation wasn't very good.

Stefan was able to speak freely and openly about his time in the NVA, his experiences in militarization programs, and his time in the NVA because he was no longer invested in the NVA. Unlike career officers, who had made the NVA their life, Stefan spent only three years in the military and no longer considered it an important—or constitutive—part of his life. And unlike career officers, the military was not made to represent his life, or to define his identity in the post-unification state. He had simply done his time in the NVA, and that was that. He was not seen as someone who had made the system work, but rather, as one who had been made to go through the system, but kept the system at a distance. Because the NVA was firmly in the past for him, and was not made to be part of his present by the state, he could talk about it and analyze it from the present in a way that most officers could not.

RED RADIATION:

THE MASTER NARRATIVES OF MILITARIZATION

As I sat and listened to Horst, Max, Ingo, Gerd, Felix, Helmut, and the other officers I interviewed, they seemed to be truly committed to the ideals of the SED, to the ideal of maintaining peace through militarization. But I also had the feeling that they were mimicking SED propaganda—propaganda that they had in part helped to perpetuate and maintain. While sincere, their words and phrases sounded very much like the propaganda I had read in SED and NVA documents, magazines, and newspapers. I felt that I was often simply hearing what I had read and researched; however, the important point was that they believed what they were saying. Regardless of how the GDR turned out, they whole heartedly believed in the early experiment and promise of the GDR. In many ways, they took the official state ideology and made it their own, and in the process came to represent the state. As Allison contends, "Ideology is so potent because it becomes not only ours *but us*—the terms and machinery by which we structure ourselves and identify who we are."[12]

This ideologically constructed sense of self is in many ways fragile. During a group meeting with Herbert, Felix, Helmut, and Paula (an NVA sociologist), Helmut, in response to a comment about objectivity and history, said that they had all been *Gläubiger*—believers. They had believed in the system, and believed everything the system told them about the Soviet Union, the West, history, society, politics, and economics. The others nodded their heads in agreement. Herbert said quietly, "I'm reading a book called *Hitler and Stalin*. If I had read this earlier, and known about the crimes committed in the USSR, things would have been very different for me." Helmut looked at Herbert, then said: "What we were taught about the USSR and history was false and one-sided, and because of this, we were all believers. We need to confront our own history, even if it is totally against what we believed and thought about ourselves and our perceptions of ourselves, even if history and our sense of self are at odds."

This was a surprising admission, and was given so willingly as to be disconcerting. It gave me the feeling that these men had somehow been beaten into submission, and were now blaming themselves for what had happened and their roles as "believers." As Borneman explains, master narratives "serve as public matrices for the creation of collective conscience; they give an overarching meaning to a series of experiential tropes, and hence are politically contested frameworks for constructing historical accounts."[13] They had internalized the master narratives of the Federal Republic and the Bundeswehr, internalized what had been said about them since unification (and before). They now seemed to accept their marginalization and inferior position with respect to the West Germans, questioning themselves, their lives, and the state they had served and helped build in the process. "To the extent that the same master narratives are utilized by both citizens and the state," Borneman writes, "they are indices of state legitimacy."[14] It was not a question of reading and learning about the history of the Soviet Union, the GDR, socialism, and so on; it was the impression that through their acceptance of the master narratives of the West and the Federal government, the rug had been pulled out from under them, a sense of anomie and disequilibrium and vertigo and the pressure to rethink their entire lives according to a new paradigm and conception of history and the past that they saw as directly about them and their lives and all they had tried to accomplish. It was like watching a "self" melt before my eyes, dissolved by new conceptions of objectivity, history, and memory. However, this "self"—as representative of soldiers in the state—would not be allowed to dissolve politically.

While the careers of certain officers and soldiers were scrutinized after unification, the reasons for becoming an officer were immaterial. Rather, they were codified and categorized simply by virtue of having been in the NVA, regardless of personal decision or life trajectory. The master narratives of militarization in the GDR determined both how they would shape, see, and describe their lives, and how they would be viewed politically after unification within the post-unification master narratives of proper soldiering, tradition, and military identity.

Political, historical, and cultural contingencies pave the way for the construction of soldiers, not some sort of transcendent "warrior ethos" or inherent masculine nature. Men become soldiers, but not completely of their own free will or under circumstances they would choose; as Mintz writes, the point is to try to understand how people experience their lives under the conditions in which they find themselves.[15] NVA officers were active agents in their own lives, and made choices from options available to them within a system not of their choosing. The acts of these men were "actions taken in specific contexts, but not entirely autonomously or without constraints."[16]

The GDR exercised an incredible amount of sociopolitical force on young men in an effort to turn them into soldiers and socialist citizens, and in the process applied a great amount of pressure on the men's girlfriends or wives and parents. Young men found themselves surrounded by the structures and pressures of militarization, pressures that shaped and warped their life chances and choices. Men who became NVA officers were brought up in the "system," and then became the "system" through their beliefs and actions. Indeed, the "system" continues to define them and impact their lives after unification.

Perhaps the most important aspect in the social construction of soldiers is the role played by the military as a master narrative, how it shapes life narratives, the ways in which individuals remember their lives and see their worlds, past and future. These men adopted the master narratives of peace and defense of the SED as their own, and in the process "became" the GDR. The relationship between state pressure and propaganda about the military and the desirability of a military career elucidates the connection between lived experience and militarization policies. Systems of military representation and signification are directly related to the political-economic circumstances of a state and its time, and it is out of these times, circumstances, and systems that "soldiers" emerge. Broadly stated, men who became officers in the NVA found the messages and statements made by the SED and NVA both convincing and attractive. They joined the military in large part because of the efficacy of these state practices and the material and symbolic opportunities offered by the state for a commitment to military service. In some cases, it was the best "deal" they could hope for.

While Borneman discusses the role of master narratives in the creation of East German identity such as "construction" and "sentimentalization," we also need to consider the role played by "militarization" as a master narrative in framing and shaping life histories. Militarization, while pervasive, was never a smooth, perfect project in the GDR, and East Germans resisted where and when they could. *Rotlichtbestrahlung* (Red radiation) was a term used by East German citizens to protest the militarization of East German society, and the socialization of East German men into "socialist warriors." *Rotlichtbestrahlung* implied that citizens would be "mutated" into good socialist citizens and soldiers, turned into something other-than-human through Communist Party agitprop and coercion. It also implied that those who embraced the military and the party had "mutated." Militarization policies in the Soviet bloc, while often clumsy and never really successful, did play a role in everyday life: even to resist militarization is to be shaped by it. If the East German experience shows us anything, it shows us the effect that a broad and "mass" militarization program can have on a group of people, and the lingering effects of militarization, even when the state and its structures and institutions are gone.

In the eyes of the public in the East and the West, NVA officers were the SED state. The GDR's own militarization policies form both the master narrative of NVA officers' lives and the defining characteristic of West German perceptions of the GDR as a militarized state, a continuation of Nazi-totalitarian militarism. The militarization policies and practices of one state thus became the "defining negative" of military masculinity in the other state—and in the new state after unification as well. Officers were seen on both sides of the border as the men who came closest to this ideal, and made the ideal real.

The ideal of militarized masculinity does not have to be personally obtainable for it to be politically useful. Representations of former officers play a major role in the new state identity of post-unification Germany; they are used as negative examples in order to shore up post-unification notions of proper men and soldiers. In a sense, what was unobtainable in the GDR—the perfectly developed "socialist warrior"—was made obtainable by the Bundeswehr after unification.

PART TWO

Being Militarized

CHAPTER 4

The Writing on the Wall

ON A TYPICALLY COLD, brown-coal-smoggy East Berlin morning in March 1990, NVA Oberstleutnant (lieutenant-colonel) Bernd Klein woke up early. Since the events of November 1989, he had diligently gone about his duties, carefully keeping up the image to his soldiers that all was well, that the NVA had nothing to worry about, even as the GDR was rocked by changes and reforms. Inwardly, however, Klein was nervous; there were all sorts of rumors circulating about the fate of the NVA, what was to happen after unification and what was to happen to its officers; none of the rumors were good, and Klein was worried. He had already spent twenty years in the NVA—as a young man in the GDR he had agreed to sign up to be an officer, which entailed a minimum twenty-five-year enlistment. In other words, it was for life, and in the strict world of the NVA, the military *was* the officers' lives.

On that cold March morning, Klein woke up early, or rather, finally got out of bed, as he hadn't slept at all. He was generally a good sleeper, not prone to sleepless nights or a racing mind. Early on, during his time in the Special Forces, he had trained himself to fall asleep quickly, wherever and whenever he could. But this night had been different, as he was preparing to do something that he never thought he would do, or could even have imagined as a possibility. He got up, carefully put on his dress uniform—something out of the ordinary at that point in time—and quietly slipped out of his apartment in East Berlin. He usually said goodbye to his wife when he left in the morning, but this time he didn't. He just put on his uniform and left. He wasn't sure if he would be coming back.

Even though East Berliners had long grown accustomed to seeing NVA officers, Klein cut a somewhat odd and incongruous figure: an NVA officer in full dress uniform was by now something of a rarity. Five months after the fall of the Berlin Wall, it was clear to most that the NVA was falling apart. There had even been a mutiny in a barracks north of Berlin, after which the minister of defense himself had gone to speak to the angry soldiers and sailors. Now that the Wall was open, the NVA and Border Guards seemed like an anachronism, an army without a mission—or a state. Walking quickly through the crowd, Klein made his was to the S-Bahn train station near his flat. "Everyone looked at me as if I were crazy," he told me. "By this time, people no longer really respected [NVA] officers, and so to see one on the train, in dress uniform, was odd. And to see one heading into West Berlin was even stranger."

Although he tried to present a calm and confident image to his soldiers, Klein was nervous about the future. He had already been in the NVA for twenty years, having started out in the infantry, later moving into the NVA's military intelligence section. He had been to a number of the top Warsaw Pact military academies, both in the GDR and in the Soviet Union, and although the NVA did not have nuclear weapons of its own, he had been trained to calculate the effects of nuclear strikes against major West German cities. As an intelligence officer, he helped maintain a network of informants in West Berlin, and was responsible for spying on the barracks in which I lived when I was stationed in West Berlin from 1986 to 1989.

Klein had joined the army right after high school, and if never the most committed Marxist or member of the SED, he was a very committed soldier. At least until 1985, he told me, when he, like many other NVA officers, began to have secret doubts about the party and the direction of the GDR as a result of Gorbachev's glastnost and perestroika policies. He also began to have doubts about the Wall, and the need for such high security and military preparedness. As he explained to me one day, he was assigned to review a set of contingency plans for security in East Berlin in the event of a war. It was the first time he had noticed, he said, that all of the defenses at the Wall faced in, toward the GDR, rather than out, toward the enemy in the West. He had never doubted the military, but now he began to have his doubts. Regardless, he still did his duty and said nothing about his concerns to his family or friends.

Klein was an experienced officer, quietly skeptical of almost everything and not given to unwarranted optimism. He was deeply concerned about his future, the future of the soldiers under him, and the futures of the families of NVA officers. A few weeks earlier, he had heard disturbing news, news which had shaken him to his core and made him worry about his future for the first time. As a career officer, he expected to simply complete his twenty-five years, maybe spend a few more years in the military or civil defense forces, and then retire with full benefits and a full pension, finally able to spend time with his children and grandchildren at his dacha in a quiet, wooded district on the outskirts of East Berlin. Increasingly, it seemed like this promised (and "reliable") future was not to be. As Klein made his way through the militarized landscape of Cold War Berlin, with its backward-facing Antifascist Protection Barrier—now wide open to fascists, communists, social democrats, conservatives, liberals, atheists, believers, goths, punks, and anyone else who wanted to go through—it was difficult for him to imagine a life outside of the military. The military was his life, and he knew nothing else.

Although everyone knew that the GDR no longer existed as it had for the past forty years, no one was really sure what would come next. East Berlin—the capital of the GDR—was, to the Allies in the West, one of the four sectors of occupied Berlin: Soviet, British, French, and American. Each sector had its own particular "military" feel: the American and Soviet sectors were the most militarized, those where one could see and feel the presence of foreign troops—"friends"—the most. The British and French sectors, with their smaller military presence, had more of a "normal," less militarized, feel. In East Berlin, the capital of the GDR, the NVA was a constant presence, and the yearly parade celebrating the founding of the East German state on October 7 went on for hours and made the streets shake, as it seemed the entire NVA and all of its tanks, armored personnel carriers, motorized artillery, and trucks rumbled down Karl Marx Allee in a demonstration of the GDR's might. It was the stability of the state on parade.

Jostling along in the crowded S-Bahn car with the West Berlin morning commuters and East Berliners and East Germans still exploring West Berlin, Klein made his way toward the French sector, to the French garrison at the Quartier Napoleon. Formerly, seeing an officer in uniform was nothing special; it was such a part of everyday life as to go unnoticed. But by March 1990, to see an NVA officer in full dress uniform on the

S-Bahn, heading into the western part of the city—something that would have resulted in either imprisonment or possibly death for the officer merely six months earlier—was a surreal and somewhat jarring sight. Countless East German civilians had crossed over into West Berlin; NVA officers, on the other hand, were under strict orders to stay in the East, so few had disobeyed and crossed over. And those who did cross over did not come back.

As Klein explained to me in 1999, at an informal meeting of French and NVA officers in January 1990, French officers had warned him that things would not go well for the NVA, despite rumors and promises of full integration or a "second" German army in the east. They had been told by a Danish diplomat with ties to NATO that the West Germans were not going to allow a second German army to exist in the East; there would be one German army, and officers from the Bundeswehr—the West German army—would be in charge and would make up the overwhelming majority of the new German officer corps. In other words, the writing was on the wall for the NVA. With this in mind, Klein had decided that rather than simply sitting by and "letting things happen," he would take matters into his own hands. He would surrender. The Cold War had been a war after all, he reasoned, so he decided that it would be better to surrender and become a prisoner of war—with all of the rights and protections guaranteed to POWs by the Geneva Convention—than to simply wait and see how he and his soldiers would be treated by the West Germans and the Bundeswehr. Given the decades of Cold War propaganda and animosity, most NVA officers, he said, were deeply distrustful of the Bundeswehr, and from what he could tell, and the interactions he had had with them, Bundeswehr officers were suspicious of the NVA as well. There was little love lost between the two armies.

Of all of the Allied armies in Berlin, the French were the least bellicose toward the GDR; they were in Berlin as a result of the Four-Powers Agreement after World War II, and were not a part of NATO. Klein wasn't happy about surrendering, but at least he wasn't surrendering to the Americans or the British; and in any event, the French had a reputation for fairness. Smoothing out the wrinkles and straightening his service cap to making sure his uniform looked proper after the long, crowded S-Bahn ride into

West Berlin, Klein approached the French barracks and requested to meet with the officer who had warned him of the impending fate of the NVA. The guards at the gate were surprised to see an NVA officer approach and ask to be allowed in to the barracks. Confused, they called their officer in charge, and asked what they should do. After a few uncomfortable minutes, Klein was allowed into the barracks and ushered into an office, where he was greeted cordially by the French officer he had met earlier, who offered him a brandy. After pleasantries and military small talk, Klein sat his brandy on a table, came to the position of attention, and said to the officer, "Herr Colonel, I officially surrender myself and my soldiers of the National People's Army of the German Democratic Republic to the French Army of Occupation in Berlin."

The French officer sat down his brandy, and simply gazed up at Klein. Eventually, he gave a sad smile at the NVA officer before him, and then asked him to sit down. The French army and government were sympathetic, he told Klein, but could not accept his surrender, and could not take him up on his offer to surrender his men. Even though the Cold War had been particularly intense, it was, after all, not a "real" war. He was sorry, but his hands were tied; there was nothing he or the French army could do for Klein or the NVA and its soldiers.

It was at this moment that Klein realized the NVA was so irrelevant it wouldn't even be allowed to surrender. Klein thanked him, saluted, walked out, and took the subway back to his apartment in East Berlin.

CHAPTER 5

A War of Signs, Images, and Memories

GERMAN MILITARIES IN THE COLD WAR AND UNIFICATION

On October 2nd, 1990, a *German* army ceased to exist. The National People's
Army of the German Democratic Republic was disbanded following the
unification of Germany according to Article 23 of the Basic Law. There was
no place in the Unification Treaty for the just treatment or the concerns for
the future of the soldiers in this army, like those in the Association of Career
Soldiers. These soldiers believed in the fairness of those who were in charge of
their fate. They also believed in the promises of politicians and representatives
of the Federal Ministry of Defense. And they could not believe that all rights
would be denied them, that all internationally recognized rules and rights
would not apply to them. For them it was unimaginable that rules concerning
human rights as well as the treatment of prisoners would not apply to them as
well. The soldiers of the NVA did not fire their weapons. The majority of NVA
members were not willing to stop the movement for a better GDR with armed
force in 1989 to 1990. This was true for all ranks, from private to general.
Like the rest of the population, they too had lost faith in the political and
military leadership and more or less agreed with the demands of the citizens.

HERBERT BECKER,
Deputy-Chairman of the *Landesverband Ost*, in an open letter demanding the
clarification of the "Status Problem" of former NVA officers.

You can't simply erase someone's biography with a flick of the pen.

MARKO,
NVA tank officer

"WHEN UNIFICATION CAME, and I received my notice that I wouldn't
be able to stay in the military—the Bundeswehr wouldn't have me because I was a lieutenant-colonel and therefore tainted by communism—I
didn't know what to do with my life."

Detlef took another long drag off of his cigarette, and another long gulp of hot, strong, black coffee. Almost all of the officers I knew chain-smoked and drank black coffee, and they insisted that I keep up with them, cup for cup, smoke for smoke, with the result that I would generally leave a meeting shaking and green.

My life had been the military, had been the NVA, had been very long days on the base, away from my family, training, always on alert, training. It was really all I knew. What else was I supposed to do? I had a few friends who had been allowed to join the Bundeswehr, but they weren't sure how it was going to go. Can you imagine joining the army you had trained to fight? It's been OK for them, though they've had a lot of problems in the Bundeswehr as well. Bundeswehr officers—West Germans—look down upon them as "stupid" or as communists who can't be trusted. I miss the military, but when I hear about these sorts of things, I'm sometimes glad I'm no longer a part of it. But I do miss it. It's who I was.

. . .

Unification signaled a radical shift in the symbolic lives and status of former NVA officers. Overnight, their status and "meaning" as soldiers and "defenders of the state" flipped: they went from officially valorized and valued to officially demonized and despised. This reversal highlights the important role played by soldiers in symbolizing and representing the state: while the police may play a more active, daily role in the internal experience of the state, soldiers are the more "visible" representation—and representatives—of the state as the signs of the monopoly on violence claimed by the state. The NVA could not be allowed to symbolize or represent the new German state; despite the rhetoric of the "Army of Unity," no real unification of the two German militaries could occur for the simple reason that NVA officers, as the men seen to have upheld the GDR, could not be allowed to play a leading role in a democratic army. In order to insure that NVA officers would not have influence, the Bundeswehr enacted a series of policies designed to turn NVA officers into the "military other."[1]

In many ways, the dissolution of the NVA and the experiences of the majority of its officers are really not that surprising: the Bundeswehr and the NVA had an intense dislike, distrust, and disdain for one another. The

FRG always considered itself the only legitimate Cold War German state, viewing the GDR as an aberration and a mere continuation of the Third Reich's totalitarian structure. The Bundeswehr followed this trend, seeing itself as the proper and legitimate German military, and its soldiers as the legitimate heirs of German military tradition, as the only men who had the right to call themselves "German soldiers." The Bundeswehr saw no reason to extend legitimacy to the NVA, given the heated nature of the Cold War rivalry. While there were discussions, debates, and rumors about the possibility of the NVA becoming a second German army in the East— a sort of territorial force in the former GDR—this all came to naught.

The Cold War and World War II laid the groundwork for the policies and reception of NVA officers into the newly unified Germany. After unification, former NVA officers found themselves existing in a void: no longer in the military, unable to find jobs, they were left to make sense of their situations as best they could. Like most East Germans, they were "thrown" into a new social and economic system with little preparation; unlike most East Germans, these men were considered "radioactive" because of their service in the NVA.

Stuart Hall's theory of "dominant regimes of representation," and the ways in which the Other is constructed helps to explain the experiences of former NVA officers after unification.[2] Transformed into the "military Other," NVA officers serve as a convenient foil to (West) German constructions of proper soldiers and militarized masculinity, thereby shoring up and naturalizing West German claims to political, cultural, and military legitimacy. They continue to serve as the mirror image—the "negative sign"—of soldiering and militarized masculinity. The dissolution of the GDR and the NVA and the subsequent policies of the Bundeswehr stripped them of their status as "German soldiers"; the *Statusfrage* (status question) is perhaps the most troubling aspect of unification to former NVA officers, as it effectively stripped them of their biographies and life's work. NVA officers do not accept their characterization as the military others of Germany, insisting that they be acknowledged as "German soldiers." This acknowledgment is perhaps their key concern around which all of their other problems revolve. The problem for them lies in their ability to (re)shape history and memory and find a way to "reenter" military tradition. The "Army of Unity" can be seen as a propaganda tool to make it seem that even in the most contested arena of the Cold War—the military—unification had functioned smoothly, that former enemies had come together as Germans among Germans. This was far from the case.

"THE SO-CALLED GERMAN DEMOCRATIC REPUBLIC": IDENTITY, LEGITIMACY, CITIZENSHIP, AND ERASURE

German unification came as something of a shock to the world, and to Germans on both side of the Cold War divide. Despite calls for the Wall to be torn down, Honecker declared it would stand for another "hundred years," and there was little reason to believe he was wrong. Neither side, it seemed, actually believed that the Cold War posturing and claims to legitimacy would ever really be put to the test, or that the rhetoric would necessarily become reality. Each side trained and prepared for war, but war—and the end of each political bloc—seemed an ever more remote possibility. The stasis of the Cold War seemed to prove Honecker right.

Since unification in 1990, German identity has to a great extent been equated with the identity of West Germany. Despite forty years of an economically and historically different experience under socialism, the identity of the GDR and its former citizens has been considered "second class"; some West German intellectuals and politicians went so far as to claim that the East German experience had nothing to contribute to German culture.[3] West Germany claimed to be the "true, the real Germany, presenting itself as the sole power that could represent the German people as a whole," claiming that the "German empire" (*Deutsches Reich*) had never ceased to exist, and that it was identical with it and its juridical successor.[4] East Germany, in contrast, considered itself the "new" Germany, initiating a break with the past and enshrining antifascism as the guiding principle of the state.[5] As Dominic Boyer points out, another distinction made between the two Germanys was that the East German "system" was "dysfunctional, and eventually corrupt," while that of the West was "functional and true to its manifest destiny."[6] As seen from the West, the NVA was a constitutive part of this dysfunctional system.

Prior to unification, West German elites referred to East Germany as the "so-called" German Democratic Republic (*Die sogennante DDR*), the "state without the rule of law" (*Unrechtsregime*), the "totalitarian society" (*totalitäre Gesellschaft*), and the "SED dictatorship" (*SED Diktatur*).[7] After unification, this sort of discourse about the GDR continued. In the first half-decade after unification, the German government conducted two "Enquête [inquest] Commissions" on "understanding" and "overcoming" the "SED Dictatorship."[8] Even sixteen years after unification, the German minister of defense, Dr. Franz Josef Jung, would state in opening remarks at an international military history conference in Potsdam, "No other state in German history was so thoroughly militarized as the GDR; the system of 'Socialist National Defense' was all pervasive."[9]

The obvious result of this sort of historical "marking" is a criminalization of the East German past, delegitimating it within the broader context of a singular "German" history.[10] This delegitimation further serves to promote a singular "German" identity, or rather, by delegitimating the GDR, a renationalization of German identity (read: West German identity) can be accomplished by West German politicians for political ends.

Immediately after unification, in a process similar to the dissolution of the NVA, the purging of East German academic circles reached a fever pitch. It is estimated that by 1992, 70 percent of all East German academics had left or been removed from their positions, a process that easily facilitated the historical effacement of the GDR and effectively narrows any official opposition to the rewriting of history according to West German standards.[11] Jarausch and Geyer note that the stakes in the debate over scholarship on the GDR are high, as they "shape the historical memory of a united Germany."[12] Within some schools of (West) German historiography and political thought, the delegitimation of the GDR continues along these same lines: the GDR is referred to as the "Soviet Protectorate" or the "SED Dictatorship," and the entire history of the GDR is considered "a completely peripheral historical phenomenon." Some West German historians sum up the East German experience with the STASI, reducing East German history and culture to a problem of coercion and terror.[13] In 2005, Hans-Ulrich Wehler, one of (West) Germany's preeminent historians, claimed that "the short-lived GDR was only a 'footnote in world history.'"[14]

German citizenship is based on the notion of *jus sanguinis*, or the "jaw of blood." Only by tracing one's bloodline is one entitled to automatic German citizenship. Following this logic, all former GDR citizens were granted automatic citizenship in the new Federal Republic.[15] According to the West German Basic Law, all East Germans were considered to be West German citizens, making East Germany, in effect, a part of West Germany. This was in keeping with the West German "Two States/One Nation" policy of dealing with the GDR. The Cold War blocs may have produced two German states, but there was only one German nation, an imagined community of Germans separated by politics and a fortified frontier, and represented by West Germans. In its diplomatic relations with the GDR, the FRG refused to recognize the GDR as an independent state; rather, according to its constitution, it held to the position that there was an indivisibly unified German nation, resulting in the permanent denial of the GDR as a sovereign state.[16] As stated in a 2002 press release of the Party for Democratic Socialism (the former East German Socialist Unity Party), "The GDR was not a foreign country for the BRD, and its citizens were German in view of the Basic Law [Grundgesetz]."[17]

Despite the Cold War claims of pan-German equality, East Germans are still to a great degree considered "second-class" Germans. This is a result of the pasts of both East and West Germany, as well as the economic transformation of the GDR. Some arenas—such as the military—are no longer considered "German" as a result of their exposure to forty years of socialism. As Nora Räthzel describes it:

In the course of extended immigration, East Germans seem to have lost their Germanness and become the Other. Now they are not seen as embodying the typical characteristics of the true industrious German, but as possessing a number of negative attributes. . . . All these negative characteristics, however, have to do not with their being "German by blood," but with their being socialized by the Communist system. East Germans are considered as socially and culturally different, not different by nature (by blood).[18]

The overall effect of this stance of political and cultural superiority on the East German experience of unification can perhaps be understood best by listening to two statements, the first by a twenty-eight-year-old

East German writer, who, after unification, stated that the consequences of unification resulted in the "total loss of one's own biography";[19] and the second by the former director of the history section of the East German Academy of Sciences, and a major figure in GDR historiography: "For those who have worked in the GDR, identity will not be created by blanket condemnation of the work and the achievements of more than forty years. The GDR belongs to my identity. I cannot be understood without the hopes and disappointments, the achievements and failures, the expectations and the disillusionment of this country."[20]

The goal of this process has not escaped the notice of many former East German historians and politicians, nor has it escaped the notice of former NVA officers. The East German historian Manfred Kossock wrote, "If East Germany had already paid the bill for the Second World War for the whole of Germany, why should the whitewashing of German history not also be brought about on its back?"[21]

By extension, the experiences and identities of those who lived and worked in the former GDR are also viewed as "illegitimate"; they did not hold up to West German notions of "authentic" German history, which effectively removes any legitimate identity from East Germans.[22] West Germany, according to its constitution, viewed itself as the sole heir to "German" history and identity; the West German constitution, the Basic Law, stated that in addition to West Germans, the document was also drafted "on behalf of those Germans to whom participation was denied."[23] Accordingly, and not wishing to validate the division of Germany, West Germany insisted that there was only one authentic German citizenship, even though from 1967 to 1990 a separate East German citizenship, distinct from that of West Germany, existed.[24] By denying that East German citizenship existed, West Germany further validated its claim to be the only legitimate German state. If there was no separate East German citizenship, there was, in effect, no "real" separate East German state. The denial of the legitimacy of the East German state was also the denial of the legitimacy of the East German military. If the state was illegal, there was no way its military could be "legal" or legitimate, and no way its officers could be seen or perceived as legitimate soldiers, as legitimate members of "German" military tradition. Even before unification had taken place, the ideological stage was set for the eventual marginalization of the NVA, almost insuring that NVA officers would not easily find a place in either the unified state or its military.

A WAR OF SIGNS, IMAGES, AND MEMORIES: GERMAN MILITARIES IN THE COLD WAR

While the Cold War was always a potentially "hot" war, it was also a war of images and representations, of truth claims about proper German history, memory, and military tradition. It was an ideological war between capitalism and communism, about how economic and political life should be structured, how citizens should live and act, and how society should govern itself. The Cold War division of Germany played out with particular intensity in the two German militaries. The two Germanys saw the other as the continuation of a fascist and totalitarian trajectory in German military history, and used the other as a mirror by which to create its own identity. The officers and officials of each state thought that their state had broken with the Nazi past: East Germans highlighting the antifascist activities of the GDR while emphasizing the role of former Nazi officials in the FRG government, and West Germans highlighting the similarities between the totalitarian structures of the GDR and the Third Reich.[25] NVA officers, as products of a system that took them through the Young Pioneers, the Free German Youth, and the Society for Sports and Technology, were seen as products of a totalitarian system that drew heavily on similar institutions in the Third Reich, as well as of the Soviet system of political-military indoctrination.

Both sides of the German divide portrayed the other in the worst light possible, and to a large degree, the propaganda worked. Bill Niven sums up the Cold War stance of each German state toward the other:

The existence of two Germanys as of 1949—here the GDR (East Germany), there the FRG (West Germany)—meant that one Germany could always blame the other, for past as well as present ills. This was made easier by the fact that these two German states were markedly different in economic and political character. The GDR was a communist state. In identifying capitalism as the source of fascism, the GDR was able to draw comparisons between West Germany and the

Third Reich. In identifying totalitarianism as the prime element of fascism and socialism, West Germany was able to vilify East Germany as but the socialist equivalent to National Socialism.[26]

For the majority of West Germans (and many East Germans), the NVA represented an authoritarian, ideologically motivated military serving communism, and, given its Wehrmacht-style uniforms and Prussian discipline, a continuation of the Wehrmacht and Prussian militarism.[27] The Bundeswehr, on the other hand, was officially portrayed as a nonideological defensive army that did not serve the German nation, but the constitution and democratic state. Conversely, the SED and NVA portrayed the Bundeswehr and West Germany as simple continuations of the World War II fascist German state and military, while portraying the NVA as the "new" German military serving an antifascist state which, by virtue of being antifascist, considered itself absolved of the past and all its crimes.[28] Both German states played on the past to create postwar militaries that fit their conceptions of history and their roles in the respective military blocs which they served. Discussions with both Bundeswehr and NVA soldiers and officers showed that during the Cold War, both German armies viewed the other as the largest threat to peace and security. Both sides harbored a special animosity for the other, a stance which has continued after the end of the Cold War and unification.[29]

The kernels of distrust and resentment felt by Bundeswehr officers toward the NVA were sown in the foundational phases of both armies. As both German states began to develop plans for their militaries, the SED drew upon officers from the Nationalkomitee Freies Deutschland (National Committee for a Free Germany; NKFD), a group founded in 1943 in the Soviet Union by captured German officers after the Stalingrad debacle.[30] The NVA was founded by these officers, and drew upon the Nationalkomitee for its tradition.[31] The officers of the NKFD were viewed by the Wehrmacht as traitors. Additionally, the military-theoretical conceptions of Marxism-Leninism and the civil-military relationship to the Soviet Union fundamentally shaped the SED's conception of the military as a new, socialist, "people's army."[32] Given that the Bundeswehr was founded and staffed by former Wehrmacht soldiers with a conservative bent, the NVA was seen as not only a communist military, but as a military founded by traitors to the German homeland and *Volk*.[33] Indeed, as Bald writes, "the NVA and the Bundeswehr were not brothers in uniform. That was true from the first hour. There was always mutual antagonism. Because of this and other factors, there was no unification of the West and East armed forces after unification in 1990."[34]

While both states instituted universal conscription, there were substantial differences in intensity and training. In the GDR, military service and military propaganda were a prominent part of daily life. While not as severe in its approach as the GDR, the FRG maintained (and continues to maintain) a conscription-based military.[35] In terms of training and doctrine, the Bundeswehr stressed its role as an almost nonideological army in order to officially distance itself from the negative legacy of the Third Reich. Soldiers of the Bundeswehr were portrayed as "citizen-soldiers," instilled with *Innere Führung* (inner leadership), which was—theoretically—to prevent them from following illegal and inhumane orders.[36] This was an attempt to distance the West German military from that of the ideological, authoritarian German militaries of the past and the Cold War. Rather than serving the "German nation," Bundeswehr soldiers were to follow *Verfassungspatriotismus* (constitutional patriotism), and wear plain, bland uniforms as a means of preventing the nationalistic fervor and blind discipline of the Nazi military. The concept of "inner leadership," of the German soldier trained to be morally upstanding and ethically principled—and who would not support offensive combat operations outside of the West German border or a totalitarian regime (as prohibited by the postwar West German constitution)—was used by West German elites as proof that the NVA, which did not have this concept, was a continuation of German militarism. The general opinion of Bundeswehr officers was that NVA officers were not "capable" of telling right from wrong, and had in fact been socialized to uphold an unjust, totalitarian regime. A majority of Bundeswehr officers go so far as to say that NVA officers "never had the same profession" as they did, and because of this "fact," there is a vast mental divide between worlds and worldviews.[37] Because of this, former NVA officers did not deserve to be treated as "soldiers."

The delegitimation of the NVA serves to create a new, positive identity for the post-unification German military, particularly as it is now deployed outside of Germany for the first time since World War II.[38] Since 1990, West German historians, politicians, and the press have scrutinized the East German military and its members. In addition to the widely publicized trials and sentencing of former Border Guard troops for crimes and human rights violations, the NVA has come under intense criticism. Meyer and Collmer discuss the fact that in comparison to the Bundeswehr, the NVA was always considered more "battle ready and battle worthy."[39] This is a result of the portrayal of the NVA in West German historiography and in the popular press as the direct descendant of Prussian military traditions, the World War II Wehrmacht, and the Soviet Red Army.

Both Cold War and post–Cold War portrayals of the NVA repeatedly stressed its aggressive nature, portraying it as a military directed solely toward offensive operations, toward conquest. Previously secret NVA documents detail the preparation for and repeated practice of an attack on West Berlin; the most cited example of this is the war-game exercise "Bordkante 86," in which thirty-two thousand NVA soldiers and paramilitaries were to attack West Berlin using, among other things, flamethrowers and chemical weapons.[40] Additionally, plans for the takeover of the Federal Republic of Germany, Denmark, France, and the rest of Western Europe by the NVA were made public.[41] In all of these reports, the NVA is portrayed as a highly trained, combat-ready army, embodying all of the military expertise of the Prussian military tradition, as well as that of the Wehrmacht.[42]

The implied message in the presentation of NVA plans for conquering West Germany has not been lost on former NVA members. It would seem that they are presented solely to represent the NVA as aggressive soldiers, the direct opposite of the Bundeswehr. One former NVA general, Peter Herrich, referring to an article in *Der Spiegel*, stated, "When I read something like this, I get the impression that I became a soldier in order to carry out aggression, to take over foreign lands and peoples."[43] This was a particular point of contention with former NVA officers, who found it hypocritical that they were regarded as militarists and murderers at a time when the post-unification German military has been taking an active part in external military interventions in the Balkans, Iraq, and Afghanistan.

As NVA officers see it, they never fired a shot in anger, did not intervene when the Berlin Wall was opened, and did nothing to stop or hinder unification, while the Bundeswehr is now actively engaged in offensive combat operations outside of Germany in pursuit of what NVA officers consider to be highly questionable or legal goals. The presentation of the NVA as extremely aggressive and combat-ready serves to highlight the "peaceful" nature and attitude of the Bundeswehr. Additionally, the representation of the NVA as highly aggressive and concerned solely with preparations for conquering other countries creates a symbolic link with the Wehrmacht and further reinforces the relationship between the NVA and the Soviet army. Both are considered to have been instruments of "state terror." These comparisons serve to underline the destructive nature of the NVA, unlike the Bundeswehr, which serves to support and protect civil society and democracy.

Ideas, words, and institutions like *NVA*, *GDR*, *German*, *soldier*, *Wehrmacht*, and *SS* are all contested fields of power, memory, and relationships, symbolic markers and identities that have material effects on those involved in refining, defining, and contesting these terms. In many ways, unification can be seen as a dialectical struggle over German soldiers of the past; or rather, a struggle for military legitimacy in the present based on the past. This battle over names—and the power to classify and name—is also a battle over the legitimate naming and codification of unification within a specific version of German history.[44] As Michael Watts comments concerning naming and legitimacy, "it is largely through language that local practices are instituted, but meanings are never fixed and outside forces can often determine what is to be endowed with meaning."[45] The keyword here is "endowed": just what kind of meaning is attached to a name becomes the point of politics, the point at which symbolism coincides with policy and practice. Given that military identity and naming is generally a wrought, contested field of power and practice, post-unification struggles over naming and identity are perhaps overwrought and overcharged. Of course, the GDR Border Guards could be seen as an "illegal" identity, given the role of the Border Guards in the GDR, and their complicity in the deaths of border crossers and the lockdown of the GDR-FRG border. The point here is that "soldiers" and "militaries" are not timeless entities, but rather, institutions and identities intimately linked to history, memory, and politics, in constant flux and constant construction, made to fit a particular political-economic moment in time. Given the tenuousness of German military identity, tradition is used both to give legitimacy to the military and to ensure that military identity remains stable in the face of changing conditions and challenges.

THE HIMMEROD MEMORANDUM, REPRESENTATION, AND THE POLITICS OF MILITARY HONOR

Political expediency drives the perception, representation, and reception of soldiers, regardless, in many instances, of combat and/or war crimes. In 1950, former Wehrmacht generals issued the "Himmerod Memorandum," calling for the public rehabilitation of former Wehrmacht soldiers after World War II.[46] The initial document was conceived of as a planning document for a new West German military, and as a negotiating tool for dealing with the Western Allies.[47] In the memo, former Wehrmacht officers engaged in a rethinking of the "German soldier," working through the ethics and politics of the new soldier, and calling for the "total equality" of a future West German army in any Western military coalition.[48] Most importantly, the Himmerod Memorandum called for the public rehabilitation of Wehrmacht soldiers. Dismayed at what they felt were unfair prosecutions and treatment because of their actions and role in World War II, leading former Wehrmacht generals demanded a public distancing from critical remarks about the Wehrmacht in exchange for their future help in founding a military in the new Federal Republic.[49] Amnesties for former Wehrmacht soldiers were issued in 1949 and 1955 (the year the Bundeswehr was formed), and officers pressed for public statements attesting to the "honor" of Wehrmacht soldiers during the war.[50] In 1951, in order to help secure the support of former Wehrmacht officers for an eventual West German army, Dwight Eisenhower, former commander of Allied forces in Europe during World War II, issued a statement to the effect that: "There is a real difference between the regular German soldier and officer and Hitler and his criminal group. . . . For my part, I do not believe that the German soldier as such has lost his honor. The fact that certain individuals committed what were dishonorable and despicable acts reflects on the individuals concerned and not on the great majority of German soldiers and officers."[51]

This statement was a political necessity; the Adenauer government, as well as the former Wehrmacht generals who were to lead the development of the Bundeswehr, made it clear that they would not cooperate with the Allies unless such a statement was issued.[52] Wehrmacht officers also demanded a cessation to trials and a release of German POWs from Allied prisoner-of-war camps.[53] Considering that a portion of the new German army was to be comprised of soldiers who had experience with the Wehrmacht, it was seen as necessary by the generals and other officers that they start with a "clean" slate, so as to create a distance between the Wehrmacht and Bundeswehr.[54] The new Bundeswehr was to be set apart from the crimes of the Wehrmacht to help assuage concerns about renewed German military violence, among German citizens and around the world.

While the Bundeswehr cannot officially use the Wehrmacht as a source of tradition, it nonetheless continues to find its way into both official discourse and unofficial practice. Following in the footsteps of the Himmerod Memorandum, the Wehrmacht is seen in some circles not necessarily as a perpetrator of a disastrous war of expansion and genocide, but as an army that attempted to defend Germany from the encroaching hoards of the Red Army. A "generally positive" image of the Wehrmacht was present in West German society and political culture by the early and mid-1950s.[55] Seen now as "defenders of the homeland," the crimes and failings of the Wehrmacht could be conveniently forgotten or glossed over due to the contingencies of the Cold War and the fear of communist expansion in the West.

After unification, there was no such memorandum for former NVA officers or soldiers, or any kind of general statement to the effect that only certain individuals were responsible for crimes in the GDR (despite trials holding GDR and NVA officials accountable). Rather, the general opinion of the FRG and the Bundeswehr was that, as members of an institution that upheld an illegitimate, communist, state, all NVA officers were suspect and were no longer "honorable" German soldiers, despite never waging war and despite standing aside as the GDR unraveled.

"MEMBERS OF A FOREIGN MILITARY":
TRADITION, BLOOD, AND CITIZENSHIP

With unification, questions of military tradition, status, honor, and memory took on new importance, and played a major role in the treatment and codification of former NVA officers, and the ways in which the Bundeswehr envisioned and imagined itself and its soldiers. Given thirty-five years of Cold War propaganda concerning the NVA and the Border Guards, as well as the actual deaths caused by the GDR Border Guards, the Bundeswehr deemed it a political necessity to distance itself from the NVA. The new German state and military also needed to solidify its claim on the monopoly of state and military violence, and on conceptions of "real" German soldiers. Fundamentally, if left unchecked, the "Army of Unity" could have seriously undermined the dominance of Bundeswehr officers in both the state and the military. To remedy this, the Bundeswehr developed a series of economic and symbolic policies designed to reinforce their position of dominance. These policies drew on memories of World War II German soldiers to create continuity with the "real" soldiers of German military tradition. The actions taken to strip the NVA of its identity were discursive, bureaucratic, economic, political, and at a distance.

An NVA text from the late 1970s on the creation of its military tradition comes closest to a constructivist conception of how military tradition is created, and how this creation is intimately linked to power and those with the power to create tradition in their own interest. Ironically, the text comes closest to understanding the denial of the NVA as a source of tradition for the Bundeswehr: "In every instance, the construction of tradition means the selection, establishment, and processing of historical facts which are in the interests of specific classes and groups. These are always based on their worldview. The reasons for the maintenance of tradition lay squarely in the demands of the present."[56]

In the runup to unification, and in the following years, the Bundeswehr made it clear that the NVA could not serve as a "tradition model" for the new Bundeswehr, as the NVA had been a "party army" of an illegitimate state, a state that did not follow the rule of law, and whose institutions were seen as similar to those of the Third Reich. According to the Bundeswehr's "Tradition Decree" (*Traditionserlass*), tradition

is the transmission of values and norms. It is constructed through an engagement with the past to produce values. Tradition connects generations, secures identity, and builds a bridge between the past and the future. Tradition is a key component of human culture. It provides a basis for understanding historical, political, and societal relationships.

The history of the German armed forces did not develop without serious failures. During the time of National Socialism, the armed forces were in part criminally complicit, and in part criminally used. A regime without the rule of law [Unrechtsregime], such as the Third Reich, cannot be used for tradition.[57]

The key to this part of the Tradition Decree is the use of the term *Unrechtsregime*—a regime without the rule of law. While National Socialism is explicitly mentioned in the tradition decree, the GDR is also included in the document, as it was continually referred to as an *Unrechtsregime* during the Cold War, and the FRG constantly equated the totalitarianism of the Third Reich with the GDR. The Bundeswehr's position on the use of the NVA as a source of tradition is clear; under the section detailing the use of its own history as a source of tradition, the NVA is explicitly precluded as a tradition source: "Because of its membership in the Warsaw Pact, the National People's Army of the former German Democratic Republic cannot be a part of the tradition of the Bundeswehr."[58]

While "tradition" is a discourse, it is also a practice.[59] Militaries use tradition as a form of identity formation, a way of sublimating the individual to the mass, thereby connecting the individual to the state. Like the silken bandages woven around the Invisible Man, giving him a shape and form, the discourses of tradition presence the soldier while simultaneously entangling him ever tighter in the net of the military and the state. Tradition gives shape to a military and provides it with an operational ethos, a guide to action and a sense of continuity with the past. Tradition provides a military with its heroes and its villains.

After unification, NVA officers were officially coded by the Ministry of Defense as *Gediente in fremden Streitkräften* (veterans of foreign armed forces).[60] In 2005, the designation was modified to "service outside of the Bundeswehr."[61] The ministry's classification of NVA officers as "foreign veterans," or those who served "outside" of the Bundeswehr, makes them, at the symbolic level, "non-German." One of the primary goals of NVA officers is to be recognized as "German soldiers." Not only are they "non-German," but also, as "veterans of foreign armed forces," they are not considered "German soldiers." As such, if they were not "real" German soldiers, then the NVA was never a "real" German army. This classification not only removes them from use in German military tradition, it also removes them from German history and from any claim to being actual German soldiers. It also makes the Bundeswehr the only "real" German army after World War II. Through the creation and practice of tradition in the Bundeswehr, a particular version of German history is valorized, marginalizing certain Germans who become the living measure against which tradition and identity are based.[62]

The "status question" was a topic of constant discussion and concern with NVA officers, a topic that simultaneously engaged and enraged them. In a discussion in his garden in 1999, Max, a former NVA artillery lieutenant colonel, summed up the sense of frustration, marginalization, and disbelief concerning the symbolic status of NVA officers:

First of all I feel, well . . . I live well, but I feel like a second-class person [Mensch zweiter Klasse]; I live well, better than before really, don't have as many burdens. I get sort of an ersatz pension, a minipension, but I can live from it, and since my wife is fully employed, we live very well actually, that's the truth. But what the federal government has done is a bad thing, the CDU [the conservative Christian Democratic Union Party], and in my opinion the FDP [the liberal Free Democratic Party] as well, we are not to be recognized; we can't say "Lieutenant-Colonel or Colonel, retired." This is a question of status and it hasn't been solved. If I had been a Nazi officer, or even an SS officer, then I would be greeted as such, with my SS rank and my name, or as a colonel of the Bundeswehr. When I heard this, I couldn't contain my surprise that this really happens, that this is the way it is done at meetings: these officers are recognized. In mid-March, Poland and Hungary will join NATO; these officers, who were "communist enemies" of NATO, who are lieutenant colonels and captains, both active and retired, they are still officers. It is only we who are no longer officers, and that isn't right. It is unequal treatment of the first degree, and I don't understand it.

Max's narrative expresses the contradictory nature of unification for NVA officers, both their erasure from history and what they see as a misrepresentation of their service. After the dissolution of the Warsaw Pact and Soviet Union, officers of other Warsaw Pact states simply "switched over" into the new militaries of their states, maintaining their positions and rank. East German officers, on the other hand, lost their state, their military, and their status as soldiers, and their service was compared to the atrocities of the Wehrmacht and SS. While Max admits that he is better off materially, it is the lack of status and recognition—and that former Wehrmacht and SS officers are treated with respect—that trouble him (and other officers) most.

THE WEHRMACHT, THE BUNDESWEHR, AND THE NVA: GERMAN MILITARIES IN DISCOURSE AND PRACTICE

While the Bundeswehr stresses the NVA's relationship to the Wehrmacht, its own use and nostalgia for the Wehrmacht remains somewhat hidden. As Niven notes, the Bundeswehr's Museum of Military History in Dresden highlights the relationship between former Wehrmacht officers and the East German Garrisoned People's Police, but makes no mention of Wehrmacht officers helping to found the Bundeswehr: "The NVA's espousal of dubious Prussian military tradition is highlighted, but when the Bundeswehr's nostalgia for the Wehrmacht is conceded, this is attributed to 'individual soldiers,' not the Bundeswehr as an institution. Yet individual soldiers did not name barracks after famous German generals."[63]

While the Wehrmacht influenced the NVA during the Cold War, it is the use of the Wehrmacht—both officially and unofficially—by the Bundeswehr during the Cold War and after unification that is of the most importance here, for it is the influence of the Wehrmacht on the foundational culture and tradition of the Bundeswehr, and the continued reverence of former Wehrmacht soldiers by some in the Bundeswehr, and by the Bundeswehr as an institution, that has impacted the lives, reception, and memory of the NVA after unification. The memory of the Wehrmacht influences how the Bundeswehr as an institution works, and how soldiers in the new Germany are constructed, perceived, conceived, imagined, and received.

The FRG has tried to distance itself from the Wehrmacht as an institution, instead focusing on Wehrmacht soldiers as individuals. In its comparison of the Wehrmacht to the NVA, the FRG always stressed the similarities of the Wehrmacht and NVA as institutions. In this way, the "best" of the Wehrmacht—the bravery of its soldiers, their military prowess, and so on—could be used, while the image of the Wehrmacht as a corrupt political institution was reserved for comparison to the NVA, thereby linking both and absolving the Bundeswehr of its use of the Wehrmacht.[64]

The Bundeswehr's use of individual Wehrmacht soldiers is officially allowed when linking the Bundeswehr to those Wehrmacht officers and soldiers who attempted to resist Hitler and the Nazi Party. In this way, the Bundeswehr can draw upon the Wehrmacht as a way to shape its soldiers; these were men who resisted an illegal regime, unlike NVA officers. During a 1994 speech commemorating the July 20, 1944, attempt on Hitler's life by Wehrmacht officers (the famous Operation Valkyrie), the German minister of defense, Volker Rühe, while discussing how the Bundeswehr was the first democratic German army, went on to discuss the NVA, saying that in relation to tradition, "due to its nature as a party and class army of a communist system, the NVA cannot offer any tradition for the Bundeswehr."[65]

A 1995 study commissioned by the Bundeswehr stated that the Wehrmacht could not be used as an official source of tradition; there was concern that unofficially, the Wehrmacht would be used in the Bundeswehr, and continue to influence its institutional culture.[66] It is the unofficial, "everyday" use and memory of the Wehrmacht and World War II German soldiers in the institutional culture of the Bundeswehr that shapes the reception and representation of NVA officers by influencing policy, perception, and notions of "proper" soldiers. Unofficially, the Bundeswehr has long used the Wehrmacht as a source of tradition, from the naming of barracks and the singing of Wehrmacht songs, to the honoring of both famous and everyday German soldiers from World War II and their military prowess and bravery.[67] As Niven notes, the Bundeswehr used a list of World War I generals—selected by Hitler in 1937 for the Wehrmacht—to name its new barracks, and never shied away from using the names of some World War II generals for barracks names, such as Eduard Dietl, a committed Nazi and commander of the Wehrmacht's mountain troops.[68] Occasionally, this usage comes into the open and causes controversy, such as when the officer in charge of Germany's special forces unit, the Kommando Spezialkräfte der Bundeswehr, declared that the unit's "role model" was the Wehrmacht's "Brandenburg" unit, a unit found guilty of committing war crimes during World War II.[69] More recently, a Bundeswehr unit in Afghanistan created controversy when it used the palm tree symbol—minus the swastika, but nonetheless recognizable as the unit emblem of the World War II Afrika Korps—on its armored vehicles, symbolically linking the Bundeswehr to the Wehrmacht force in North Africa.[70] Despite an official "coming to terms with the past," the Wehrmacht past is in many ways alive and well in the Bundeswehr, providing role models of "proper" soldiering and military prowess. Of course, not all Bundeswehr soldiers look to the Wehrmacht as a role model, or continence its use as an unofficial model of tradition. Nonetheless, the memory of the Wehrmacht is a key component of the Bundeswehr's institutional culture and tradition, its "script" for being a good soldier.

Militarized masculinity in post-unification Germany is bound up with the remembrance of the two Germanys and World War II. Through the negative portrayal of former NVA officers and soldiers, the Wehrmacht and SS of World War II have been rehabilitated in the German cultural imaginary: they "fought" for one Germany, the German nation, and all that is good about Germany. Thus, even though they fought for and served a fascist regime, they were nonetheless "honorable" soldiers engaged in an honorable fight for the "survival" of Germany. Ernst Nolte, a conservative historian in Germany, received a major award for making such a claim about the "honor" of German soldiers and their attempts to save Germany from the "barbaric" Russians.[71]

THE BANALITY OF TRADITION:
THE SEMIOTICS OF RANK AND DEATH

Military hierarchy needs to be explicit; an individual's rank is an expression of where he or she stands in relation to others in the system, of his or her place in the hierarchy. It designates those who "do" and those who have the power to make others "do." Rank is also an expression of the importance and trust the state places in an individual. A further differentiation of importance within the system is the set of awards issued by the military and the state. Awards are given for bravery in combat, technical skills, and for service to the military and the state. Even high-ranking officers can be envious of those who win certain awards or medals: the U.S. general George S. Patton, one of the United State's most famous (and controversial) generals, once said that he "would give his eternal soul" for the U.S. Medal of Honor. Within this symbolic system, some are willing to give all to win a symbolic marker, a signifier of status and prowess. As Napoleon Bonaparte once cynically quipped, "A soldier will fight long and hard for a bit of colored ribbon."

The Bundeswehr could not allow NVA officers to publically use their rank, as that would call their own into question and challenge their position in the hierarchy of the (West) German military and society. Rank is not just for the military: awarded by the state, it makes the bearer visible as the state in society, as the embodiment of the ideals of the state and the personification of the potential for violence by the state. The soldier on the cover of *Paris Match* that Barthes discusses embodies this process: he is France, the French state, the French military, and the potential for French violence, all in one sign of might, power, and legitimacy.[72]

Military rank and medals do not simply constitute public recognition of soldiers; they also comprise a semiotic code among soldiers themselves. By looking at the awards on a soldier's uniform, another soldier can "read" that soldier's career and biography, comparing them to his or her own accomplishments and career. Uniforms are, in a sense, a "concrete," public display of a soldier's life, abilities, and accomplishments. Uniforms are like the armor of the state, the hard shell of might and right that gives the soldier power and in turn provides the "shield" that (theoretically) protects the state. They are a public expression of one's identity within a military hierarchy, demonstrating in no small degree the "manliness" of the person in the uniform. To go by what former NVA officers and conscripts said to me, the more "manly" soldiers were "special forces" soldiers, such as special reconnaissance soldiers or combat swimmers, whereas the least "manly" would be those who served in finance or some

sort of "office" job. All of this would be readily understandable to someone trained to read a uniform. Awards and rank become a sort of talis-
man of male identity and prowess in the military, a shorthand marker of
ability and status in the system.

After unification, the semiotics of rank and medals took on a new
importance in the rivalry between the Bundeswehr and the NVA. While
members of the Wehrmacht and the Waffen SS are legally permitted to
use their rank, contrary to general military courtesies, NVA officers are
officially prohibited from using their military rank, even with the designation "retired."[73] NVA officers cannot officially state "colonel, retired"
on any official documents or in public, nor are they allowed to claim any
academic titles earned in the GDR (this follows a general refusal to recognize GDR academic degrees).[74] In what might seem like a contradiction, they are permitted to wear any medals and awards they received in
the GDR, such as the Order of Lenin or military achievement medals.

The apparent logic of the ban is that NVA officers are not allowed to
mark themselves in a manner that would be ambiguous; that is, by stating
"colonel, retired" it is not clear that they were in the NVA, and they are
officially prohibited from using "colonel, retired, NVA," as this would
amount to a de facto recognition of the NVA. However, if they were to
appear in public wearing the Order of Lenin or other NVA and GDR
medals, it would be immediately clear who they are and where they come
from. As such, their political genealogy is plainly visible; there can be no
ambiguity with regard to their origin, or it would seem, in a conflation
of ideology, essentialized masculinity, and politics, "who" they "really"
are. In his memoir, *Two Armies and One Fatherland*, Jörg Schönbohm,
the Bundeswehr general sent to the East in the months prior to unification
to disband and restructure the NVA, comments that in a discussion with
former NVA generals, they constantly reiterated the fact that as part of
the Warsaw Pact, they had helped maintain peace and stability in Europe.
"Yes, this may have been true," he wrote, "but I had to keep reminding
them that they were still communists."[75]

All of the NVA officers I knew defied this ban, finding it both offensive and belittling. Almost all officers introduced themselves using their
rank, and many had business cards that clearly stated their rank, usually

along the lines of "Oberst a.D., NVA" (Colonel, retired, NVA). Not only were they stripped of their status as "German" soldiers, but by removing their ranks they lost their identities and status as officers as well. Without their biographies, they were rendered "inert" and innocuous by the Bundeswehr, denied the power to signify the state or the military except as negative examples.

The Bundeswehrverband did eventually attempt to work out a compromise: former officers could use their rank, but they would have to place "NVA" in parenthesis at the end of their names. While most NVA officers did not want to use the designation "(NVA)"—seeing it as a way to mark them—some saw it as a way of honoring the NVA, and as a way to distinguish themselves positively from the Bundeswehr. While discussing the intricacies of rank and the status question at a meeting of the Working Group for the History of the NVA, Dietmar—a former combat engineer officer—mentioned that an SPD politician told him, "I was a real [19]68er, and for me, the NVA was a symbol of the new Germany. You should be proud to use the *Klammer* [parentheses] that marks you as an NVA officer." Most officers did not see it this way; they agreed that the NVA was a symbol of the "new Germany," but that rather than identifying them with the progressive side of German history the parenthetical designation marked them as second-class soldiers, somehow "less than" the Bundeswehr and outside of German military history and tradition.

This sort of bureaucratic regulation and banality provides insight into how symbolic systems influence politics and policies, creating systems of inequality. Rainer Wulf recounted an incident illustrating how Wehrmacht officers are symbolically and historically privileged over NVA officers:

A former NVA general, who had been a lieutenant in the Wehrmacht, wrote a letter of complaint to the minister of defense. He signed his letter "Lieutenant, Retired." The minister's office wrote back and did not answer his complaint, but warned him that he was not allowed to use his rank in this manner. The general wrote back, stating that he had been a lieutenant in the Wehrmacht and a general in the NVA. The minister's office wrote back informing him it was permissible to use the Wehrmacht rank, but not the NVA rank, as service in the Wehrmacht was officially recognized and legitimate, whereas that in the NVA was not.

Despite the heated correspondence, in the end, Wulf explained, the general's complaint went unanswered.[76]

NVA officers see their delegitimization extending even into matters of death. While mourning is a private matter for the families of former NVA officers, it is a matter of state importance for Wehrmacht and SS soldiers.[77] Officially, SS and Wehrmacht members who later served in the West German Bundeswehr can receive a state burial because of their service to the West German state, while NVA officers, who never served in the Bundeswehr, are not entitled to this honor.[78] The belief among former NVA officers is that since Wehrmacht and SS soldiers "fought for Germany" (i.e., fascist Germany), they are allowed burials. NVA officers believe that as members of the fascist German military, these officers should not be honored by the state, which claims to have disassociated itself from the Nazi past and its atrocities. Many also believe that the Bundeswehr, as essentially a carryover from the fascist German military, is therefore allowed burials because of its relationship to the Wehrmacht, whereas former NVA officers are denied this because they never "fought" for Germany and served the "antifascist" German state and military. For many officers, this is "proof" that the Federal Republic of Germany is a continuation of the Third Reich, or as put by Willi, a former infantry officer, a "fascist state in democratic clothing." Benno summed up the feelings of many NVA officers when he told me, "Even in death, they want to make sure we know our place."

By refusing official military burials to NVA officers, the German government is publicly stating that these men need not be mourned, and that they are not worthy of mourning or remembrance. They are to be mourned neither by the state nor by the "imagined community" of Germans; declared symbolically "non-German," they are to be swept into the dustbin of history, removed from the military imaginary. Wehrmacht and SS soldiers, however, are worthy of mourning and remembrance because of their "service" to Germany. It is important here to keep in mind Helmut Kohl's visit and wreath laying (along with Ronald Reagan) to a cemetery containing former SS soldiers in 1985.[79] As Jeffrey Herf describes it, Reagan "placed himself in the absurd position of honoring soldiers who had fought for Nazi Germany supposedly in order to help an ally in the Atlantic Alliance."[80] Because the NVA never fought, its soldiers are not men and not worthy of remembrance. And because they never fought for Germany, they are of no importance to the construction of German traditions; coded as non-German, they are no longer a part of the imagined community of Germans.

THE POWER OF MILITARY IDENTITY: DISSOLVING BLOOD AND KINSHIP

In the case of German military unification, political affiliation seemingly negates blood ties, canceling the claim of kinship as a political tool—a claim that West Germany used to good effect during the Cold War.[81] In this sense, politics are thicker than blood, and can serve as a sort of "universal solvent" of *jus sanguinus*. With the designation *members of a foreign military*, the blood bonds of the Cold War were symbolically broken. It is as if service in the NVA were contaminated; former NVA officers, because they are "radioactive," are men to be avoided for fear of contagion. In order to minimize the power of this taboo, NVA officers had to be symbolically removed from both the "German nation" and the German military tradition. In a sense, the fear of communism—or the anticommunist sentiments of the Bundeswehr—generated an intense reaction to the NVA: these men were still dangerous, still "contagious"; because of their political affiliation, they had to be made at least symbolically "non-German." Even with the later designation of "service outside of the Bundeswehr," NVA officers have been marked as someone other than German soldiers, as someone other than "real" Germans, outside the bloodline by virtue of their military service. Of course, NVA officers are still German citizens; their citizenship has not been revoked. Rather, at the symbolic level, they are something less than full citizens or full Germans.

THE "FOREVER-YESTERDAYS AT THE HAS-BEENS' CLUB": TIME AND THE MILITARY OTHER

A military is a register of time: how it sees itself linked to the past, its role in the present, and how it projects the state into the future, as well as how it is seen to be linked to the past or the future all work as a measure of time, marking and signifying history, implying or denying continuity.

Militaries also mark time by marking the soldiers of other militaries as being of a different time. Soldiers are markers of time, as they represent the state, how the state came to be, and how it will continue. Things like tradition, uniforms, technology, strategies, tactics, and the "ethos" of a military mark the "time" of a military, placing it in the imagined chronology and imagined past of the state. But it is a stylized image of the past and future, images of desired pasts and desired futures, a use of stylized time for propaganda, for crafting an image of the military and soldiers that presents the military, soldiers, and the state in the best possible light. Militaries are also presented as timeless, as effacing history while highlighting certain versions of history. Soldiers are both in and out of time: completely dependent on their place in time and history, they can also represent the desired timelessness of the state, the naturalness of the state and violence.

During the Cold War, one of the ways that each side attempted to exert power and influence over the other was to portray the other as "out of time," both literally and figuratively. The West portrayed the East as economically backward, inefficient, and rooted in a worldview suitable for the industrial revolution but not for the "modern" world, and as simply a continuation of the totalitarian institutions of the Third Reich. The East, on the other hand, portrayed the West as the "losers" in the inexorable evolution of society, culture, and economics predicted by Marxism-Leninism, and as a political system riddled with former Nazis and their worldview.[82]

In *Divided in Unity*, Andreas Glaeser discusses the ways in which different conceptions of time were used by West Germans to take East Germans and the GDR "out of time" as a technique of political delegitimation.[83] Following Fabian's discussion of the use of time in ethnographic writing, Glaeser extends this to a consideration of how states use time to create the other—in Glaeser's case, the East German People's Police.[84] In addition to removing people from the bloodline, a state can make the Other by removing those it wishes to exclude from its time register, placing them into another time, one that is behind that of the state. The GDR was always portrayed as being "behind" the Federal Republic and the West, as "lagging," trying to "catch up." All of these phrases imply not quite being in the present.

The GDR, the NVA, and its officers were denied "coevalness" as part of the political project of unification and legitimacy on the part of West German elites. West Germans are able to preserve intact the "organic" nature of what it means to be German by blaming the difference in East Germans on a structural-ideological cause while leaving the "bloodline" intact.[85] This preservation allows for a renationalization of a unified Germany as the *Heimat* (homeland) of all Germans, which reinforces the view that the GDR was a historic aberration, while "Germanness" is constant through time. "Germany" is eternal, or at least the West German claim to it is, while "East Germany" was ephemeral, and somehow out of time and place. NVA officers are seen as literally "out of time"—out of synch with "modern" Germany and the new, post–Cold War, unified Germany. Stefan was on to something when he told me that I hung out with the "forever-yesterdays at the has-beens' club"—the club for those whose time had passed, who no longer fit into the present, and who represented an earlier, totalitarian period in German history.

These sorts of bureaucratic actions and classifications on the part of the state—the "banal practices" of everyday state governance—contribute to feelings and experiences of alienation and marginalization on the part of NVA officers in ways that material marginalization does not. Former officers simply do not understand how the German state can continue to honor men who served illegal, unjust, and genocidal institutions—and who are, in very many cases, war criminals. As NVA officers see it, this sort of privileging of service is a means not only of whitewashing the crimes of the past but of misrepresenting their own service in the NVA. They also see it as a surprisingly strong statement by the Bundeswehr and German government that men who fought, killed, and committed atrocities in World War II are more important to the state and military tradition than men who—despite the human rights violations of Border Guards on the Berlin Wall and intra-German border—did not serve an expansionist and genocidal military regime. This is important, because the Wehrmacht—a military that facilitated Hitler's rise to power and later carried out Germany's war of conquest—is considered worthy of tradition (both officially and unofficially), while the NVA, which never conducted offensive operations, is considered a threat to German military tradition and therefore not "usable" in that tradition.[86] The positions and policies of the Bundeswehr and federal government lead them to believe that they were right in viewing the Federal Republic and the Bundeswehr as mere continuations of the fascist past, a belief that in turn helps perpetuate their marginalization and the popular impression that they are "unrepentant communists" and the "forever-yesterdays."

SOLDIERS, SYSTEMS, AND TRADITION

As detailed by Bald, a "conservative consolidation" of the Bundeswehr occurred after unification, with the result that the much celebrated "Army of Unity" (Armee der Einheit) was a misnomer.[87] The Bundeswehr was in fact not an army of unification, or a unified army, as only a small percentage of former NVA officers and soldiers was taken into its ranks. By limiting the number of NVA officers accepted into the new Bundeswehr, the state appeased West German Bundeswehr officers and assured them that their careers and position in the military would remain safe and unaffected by unification. The general opinion of West German Bundeswehr officers and other West Germans with whom I spoke is that these men were on the wrong side and therefore deserved nothing. Not only were they "on the wrong side," but they chose to stay there, and served in a military and alliance that insured there would indeed be a "side." The German government has seen fit to marginalize these men and their families, not necessarily for what they did, but for what they did not do: they did not leave the GDR, they should have known better than to serve an "illegal" military, and they should have known better than to support a communist government. Fundamentally, because they sided with the Soviets, they were seen as "traitors," and NVA officers could therefore never be seen as "comrades" by West German officers.[88] The memory of World War II set the stage for the marginalization of these men in the present. They are viewed as former servants of an unjust regime; they not only stayed, but they actively believed, and are in a sense blamed for the division of Germany. As Herbert Becker wrote in an appraisal of the "status question": "Surely, the NVA was a different German army from the German armies before it. It was also a different army from the Bundeswehr. But that doesn't seem to be the problem. The problem is this: the NVA served a different social system. Therein lies the reasons for the belittling and discriminatory treatment of those who served in the NVA."[89]

As the Bundeswehr increasingly takes part in military operations around the world, German soldiers look to the past for suitable models upon which to base their actions, models from which to draw "strength"; unfortunately, the only model acceptable for combat troops apparently is the Wehrmacht, even though it was an army of conquest, destruction, and murder. The NVA is disqualified from serving as a model for tradition, not because of its combat history (none), or its role in preventing the unraveling of the GDR from turning into a bloodbath, but because of purely political-symbolic reasons: it was an antifascist, communist military. In this sense, politics is a one-way street: the Wehrmacht can be used, even though it served a fascist state, because it is drained of politics through a comparison with the totalitarian NVA, thus negating the political baggage of the Wehrmacht and leaving its soldiers qua soldiers useful and usable, as ones who "only did their duty" for the fatherland, and who, despite losing the war, are seen as combat role models for the Bundeswehr. In this sense, the Wehrmacht becomes a sign whose signified—its history—is replaced by a myth, a model, a simulation of an epic, honorable past worthy of remembrance and tradition. Much like the soldier on the cover of *Paris Match*, the Wehrmacht soldier becomes an image removed from reality, an idealized version of a romanticized past designed to idealize the present.

In the construction of a new German military tradition and identity, there is no *Vergangenheitsbewältigung* (coming to terms with the past) for the NVA, since the Bundeswehr believes that there is nothing to come to terms with; the NVA would not be a part of the (West) German past or military anyway, so there is no reason to come to terms with it. While the *Wehrmachtausstellung* (the exhibit that examines the role of the Wehrmacht in the crimes of the Third Reich) generates controversy because it is seen in some circles as "too critical" of the Wehrmacht and its soldiers, no such controversy exists around the role and actions of the NVA, even though it never fought in a war.[90] In the opinion of many NVA officers, the NVA is forced to pay for the sins of the Wehrmacht. NVA officers are supposed to negate the legacy of the Wehrmacht, and thus "save" the honor of Wehrmacht soldiers, soldiers who were founding members of the (West) German Bundeswehr; and despite its complicity in crimes and atrocities during World War II, the Wehrmacht nonetheless continues to influence and shape the institutional culture and self-image of the Bundeswehr. By drawing upon a past made safe through a magical transference of taboo and taint to the NVA, the Bundeswehr can resurrect the idea and image of the good, brave, strong, competent German soldier—the German soldier devoid of politics and simply a good "craftsman."[91] It is a kind of political legerdemain that empties the past of problems, transfers them to a substitute, and provides a sign of timeless propriety: the soldier as apolitical paladin.

CHAPTER 6

"Unification Has Ruined My Life"

THE POLITICAL ECONOMY OF THE MILITARY OTHER

Sure, in the GDR, we couldn't criticize our politicians, we weren't allowed to
stand on Alexanderplatz and critique Honecker, but you could go to your boss
and tell him or her that they were stupid, without fear of being fired. Now,
you can protest at Alex and say that the government is stupid, but you can't
say anything critical about your boss. You tell me which system is better.

NORBERT,
NVA infantry officer

We don't want to be millionaires. We just want a little
recognition. But we do need the money.

BASTIAN,
NVA intelligence officer

An educated East German can't trust anything in this democracy.

BERND,
a former NVA rocket officer

NVA OFFICERS experienced unification as a traumatic event; for them,
it represented a sudden and undesired break in their life trajectories, and
for those who were older and had already spent twenty years or more in
the NVA, an enforced and early retirement from the military and their
chosen career paths. Unification represented a giant leap into the unknown for these men and their families: a new social system, unemployment or employment in sectors of which they had little or no knowledge,
and perhaps more distressingly to them, a loss of status or significance
in society, in their communities, and in their families. In the years after
unification, unemployment and underemployment, coupled with illness,

alcoholism, and depression took a toll on former officers. The shock for these men was profound, and in many ways is difficult to comprehend. While they could see the writing on the wall (as it were) in the months prior to unification, the actual dissolution of the GDR and NVA hit them hard. As Hans told me:

The first few years after unification were horrible, really horrible. In some ways, I don't even remember them. I was used to getting up every day, putting on my uniform, and heading off to the base, or if we were on an exercise, staying at the base or in the field. I had respect and responsibility, and I felt like I was doing something useful and productive—remember, we thought of soldiers as workers, so I was working and contributing good work to the state.

Health-wise, I did OK [after unification], but I was very depressed, and I did drink—I drank a lot, actually. But I had a lot of friends who really just couldn't take it, and began to drink heavily, real alcoholics—they drank themselves into a stupor for a long time. And lot of them had heart attacks—they just couldn't take the stress of having nothing to do, and of not feeling useful or needed. There wasn't much for us to do—we tried to get jobs; they were hard to find, but we tried. It's hard for me to think about it, but there were also a lot of suicides as well—they just couldn't take the stress, and put an end to it. But most of all, we sat around, did things around the house, became real house husbands, worked in the garden—something we were not used to, and which are wives weren't used to.

I knew, a few months before October 1990, that I wouldn't be allowed to stay in the military. I was bitter, but I knew there was nothing I could do, so I tried to accept it as best I could. But when that day came, and we lowered the flag and that was that, I was lost. I still have my uniform in the closet, and all of my kit. I look at it, and feel like a part of me—a big part of me, you understand—is hanging in the closest.

Dieter likewise explained to me the difficulties he faced in the years immediately after unification:

There's no other way to say it or explain it other than that our world came crashing down around us. Everything fell apart, including me. We could barely survive on the little pension left to me, and finding a job was impossible. I'd apply for a job, get turned down, apply for another one, get turned down. I'm not sure how many times I applied for a job. I really don't know how my marriage survived, either. I suddenly had nothing and felt nothing, nothing at all. What was I supposed to feel? Everything was taken from me—my career, my rank, my sense of self-worth. It was as if they had just gone into me and ripped me out of myself.

While questions of political symbolism, status, and inclusion in military tradition have played a major role in the lives of former officers after unification, material questions are in many ways first and foremost in their minds, and it is through a combination of symbolic and material policies and practices that NVA officers have been made the "military other" of the new Germany. As the employment futures of many (or most) East German citizens looked uncertain and bleak,[1] NVA officers and career soldiers faced an almost certain end to their military careers. This was particularly true for officers above the rank of lieutenant-colonel, who were deemed ideologically "impure," too close to the former East German government and "state religion" of communism. From an ideological standpoint, there was no place in the new German army for men who had served an "unjust" and "totalitarian" regime, men who had formed the backbone of communism in the East, and who, in terms of the periodization and historical narratives employed by (West) Germany, were seen as a continuation of German totalitarianism.[2] As high-ranking officers (lieutenant-colonels, colonels, and generals), they had spent all of their working lives in the military, forcing them in practice to commit their entire lives to the military and the state. The military was all they knew, and the only skills they had were the ones they had learned in the military, skills that often have no direct application or utility in a civilian labor market. The military is a narrow and exclusive career; managing violence does not have many civilian counterparts. And depending on what kind of violence one manages—or the connection between violence and the state—placement in the civilian market can be difficult or almost impossible.

THE COLD WAR RIVALRY AND THE "SOCIAL DEAD END" OF UNIFICATION

The foundational structures and sentiments of the Bundeswehr, plus the confrontation of the Cold War, set the stage for the uneven treatment of former NVA officers after unification, despite worries and concerns that this would happen in the months running up to unification in October 1990.

In a speech to the German parliament (Bundestag) prior to unification, Social Democrat (SPD) parliament member Walter Kolbow commented on the necessity of fair treatment for NVA soldiers:

The concerns of the military representative about comments by officers of the Bundeswehr, comments which lead one to doubt whether they are approaching the process of German unification with all of the necessary tolerance, fairness, openness, and justice, underscores possible fears. Self-elected discussion leaders cannot be allowed to have a say. We can also not allow the first experiences of these people [NVA soldiers] with the constitutional state [Rechsstaat] to lead to experiences of shock. The GDR must be allowed to bring its contribution to the new defense structure. Naturally, this means that in the transition, a member of the NVA must show that he has the character and can offer the guarantee that he will always support the democratic order as laid out in the constitution.

For the soldiers of the National People's Army—and this has become obvious by statements made in this chamber—the end of their army cannot be allowed to lead them to a social dead end [in das soziale Nichts führen]. We still need a number of ideas to make this possible. But in this regard, it is clear that the only soldiers who can be accepted [into the Bundeswehr] are those who can live with the idea of the citizen-in-uniform. For the others, reschooling and qualification programs must be offered, and they must be shown realistic ways into a new future.[3]

Kolbow's statement makes clear the importance of including former NVA officers in the post-unification military and defense structure: by bringing them into the fold, and giving them the chance to join the new military, they can be enjoined to embrace the constitution and to accept the characteristics of a soldier in a democracy, a "citizen in uniform." He also makes clear that failure to include them can lead to a "social dead end," to anomie, shock, and disillusionment with the new state and system. Kolbow's statement was prescient, in light of the experiences of former NVA officers who were not allowed to join the Bundeswehr, and who experienced unification as a "social dead end."

UNIFICATION AND THE MILITARY LABOR MARKET

Although not usually considered as such, a military is a labor market, and soldiers are workers who worry about their careers, advancement, and their positions and power within that market. Like other types of careers, a military career includes intense competition for positions, billets, commands, and postings. While West German politicians celebrated the idea of the "Army of Unity," Bundeswehr officers worried that their jobs and careers were threatened by the prospect of a flood of NVA officers entering the new military. Accustomed to the security and dominance of their positions, Bundeswehr officers did not welcome the idea of having to compete with NVA officers for positions and billets in the post-unification army. The NVA represented a threat to the dominance of the Bundesewehr, and its claims of legitimacy within the FRG before unification. This was true of the post-unification Bundeswehr as well; NVA officers were seen as a threat to the status quo and to the position of Bundeswehr officers within both the FRG and the NATO military structure. While there were major ideological differences between Bundeswehr and NVA officers, Bundeswehr officers were afraid that an influx of NVA officers would severely impact and damage their careers and material well-being. As Lapp documents, statements by Bundeswehr officers during the run-up to the dissolution of the GDR concerning NVA officers joining the Bundeswehr made clear some of the potential problems of military unification and the overwhelmingly negative opinion held by Bundeswehr officers of their East German counterparts:

- I don't want to have anything to do with members of a party army and traitors.
- I'll never take orders from a former NVA officer.
- They learned to operate under completely different operating principles.
- A lot of informants [Maulwürfe] of the former Ministry of State Security and the KGB were in the NVA. Should we allow ourselves to be infected by those who have gone under cover?
- For every former NVA officer that we do not permanently accept into the Bundeswehr, we can keep an officer of the "old" Bundeswehr in light of the upcoming armed forces reduction.[4]

After unification, the majority of NVA officers found themselves in dire economic straights: removed from their careers, they were forced to contend as best they could with a completely new economic system, learn its tricks and logic, and face policies of symbolic and economic marginalization that complicated matters even further. Officers blamed their experiences on a combination of political, economic, and symbolic factors: they were quick to conceptualize their unemployment as a concerted effort on the part of West German elites to marginalize them because of their membership in the SED and their positions as officers in an antifascist army. In 1995, the Arbeitsgruppe Geschichte der NVA (Working Group for the History of the National People's Army) distributed a series of surveys and questionnaires to over ten thousand former NVA officers. The results of the survey showed that, based on their experiences since unification, a large majority (87.8 percent) considered themselves second-class citizens because of service in the NVA. Additionally, over half (53.4 percent) complained that they were denied jobs specifically by virtue of having served in the NVA. One of the main findings of the report concerning the unification experience of former NVA officers was that "for the overwhelming majority of men of certain age groups, leaving military service meant the premature and permanent removal from a life of employment."[5] Not only was the military closed off to them, but because of their service and rank in the NVA, other areas of employment, such as public service and education, were legally closed to former officers as well.[6] As a result, their living standard declined, placing increased pressure and instability upon themselves and their families. As incomes declined while rents rose, many former officers and their families were forced to move into low-income housing, either on the outskirts of Berlin or in areas they considered unattractive. In many former officers' households, wives bore the brunt of the instability brought about by drastic cuts in pensions, trying to find well-paying jobs to support their families. This was yet another blow to the identity and self-perception of former officers.

In keeping with the ideology of the SED, work and production played a major role in the lives of East German citizens.[7] Since unification, the changes in the East German household have engendered transformations with deep, long-term effects on the political economy of former East Germans. Daphne Berdahl, in her ethnographic study of an East German border village and the changes brought about by unification, discusses questions of consumption and identity among East Germans during and after unification.[8] As Berdahl explains, the political economy of socialism was based on centralized planning, designed to maximize the redistributive power of the state.[9] This meant that East Germans had to rely on social networks to obtain needed and desired goods, and that they were socialized into an economy of hoarding, hiding, and bartering of materials.[10] In the GDR, scarcity was overcome through social networks and personal connections, whether at the level of large-scale industrial production or in the procurement of simple, everyday items.[11] Fundamentally, connections were more important than money in the GDR.[12] The skills needed to survive in a market economy were vastly different than those they had honed in the GDR.

A major point of stress for former East Germans after unification was learning the rules of consumption in a market economy, of figuring out and deciphering the codes, meanings, and logic of commodities, of understanding their production and consumption under capitalism. Like the people with whom Berdahl worked, NVA officers had the same problems and the same learning curve to overcome. Simply put, a population brought up and socialized under socialism was thrown into a capitalist market economy virtually overnight, with very little practical knowledge of how to operate within such a system. Hans-Joachim Maaz, an East German psychoanalyst, describes his encounter with West German consumerism as the "terror of advertising, of oversupply, and the many attractions," and realized that shopping and living in the West required completely different skills than those necessary in the East.[13] I heard again and again from former NVA officers and their families that life in the West forced them to learn new skills, skills which went against their very being and sense of self, and which forced them to act and think in unaccustomed ways with which they were not always morally or ethically comfortable. Some have managed to make due; others, including many former military families, have had a very difficult time getting by.

OUT OF PLACE AND OUT OF THEIR HOMES: THE POLITICS AND SYMBOLISM OF MILITARY HOUSING

In exchange for pledging their lives to the GDR and the SED, NVA officers were often given housing that was considerably better and more attractive than that of the overall East German population. While officers complained about the housing they had early in their careers, they said that as they progressed through the ranks their housing situations improved. When unification came, many mid- and high-ranking officers living in Berlin found that they now lived in prime real estate areas; Cold War–era symbolic and material prestige was about to meet post-unification property speculation head on, and they were in the middle of this collision.

The two greatest worries among East Germans after unification were unemployment and the inability to pay rent, both of which have had a major impact on families and feelings of inclusion in the new state. Indeed, one of the major problems of unification has been affordable housing. Since houses and apartments in the GDR did not have a "capital value," but only use value, they were not considered economic goods but rather entitlements; no one, even those who missed many rent payments, was left without a home.

Former military families were hit hard by the shifts and speculation of the post-unification housing market; during the course of my fieldwork, many former officers lost their homes due to the modernization of the blocks and the gentrification of their neighborhoods, and they were consequently forced to move to outlying and less desirable districts in eastern Berlin, or forced to leave Berlin altogether. In the years immediately after unification, a number of officers and their families were in danger of becoming homeless; it was only by calling on friends and relying on the help of veterans groups that they were able to make ends meet and pay their rent. Collections were taken for families in need, and short-term loans could be procured for extreme cases, particularly in families with an ill officer.

During the years of the GDR, NVA officers and their families were scattered throughout Berlin, but many mid- and high-ranking officers were given apartments in new buildings—the *Plattenbauten* (prefabricated apartment blocks)—which, while seen as inferior to Western standards, were considered luxurious and a sign of privilege in the GDR. Spacious and outfitted with heat, hot water, and modern amenities, apartments in these housing blocks were given to officers who were seen as reliable and dependable. Apartments were a reward for long years of service to the party and the state. The areas of Berlin where many mid- and high-ranking officers lived—such as Mitte, Alexanderplatz, Prenzlauerberg, and Friedrichshain—became very popular after unification, resulting in drastic increases in rent.

Irwin, a former NVA colonel, told me that his apartment, located near the Jannowitzbrücke S-Bahn station near Alexanderplatz, was to be modernized. He said he understood exactly what this meant: he had lived there for almost twenty-five years, and had paid a rent of two hundred East German marks per month (the preunification equivalent of about fifty deutsche marks). Soon after unification, his building was purchased by a West German company, and his rent raised to almost a thousand marks. The purpose of this modernization, he said, was to drive out all of the former East German tenants so that wealthy West German "yuppies" could take over the apartments. Soon after, Irwin was forced to move to much smaller apartment in an outlying area of Berlin.

This was a common occurrence, particularly for those families living in Berlin, both military and nonmilitary. The housing speculation of the immediate post-unification years was in some ways worse for officers, as they had become accustomed to large, modern apartments, and they also had to struggle to find jobs after serving their entire working lives in the military. Officers who lived outside of Berlin had a different problem: while they still lived in former NVA housing blocks, their rents had increased drastically, yet no one wanted to take care of the buildings. This was particularly evident in a small community in Bad Saarow, where a former NVA doctor lived in a dilapidated housing block; apparently the new West German owner had no interest in taking care of the buildings, as he had refused to make any repairs or renovations for over five years. This situation, too, was seen by many officers as an attempt at "forced relocation."

The shifts in the post-unification housing market in Berlin and East Germany were not an overt, concerted effort by the state to remove NVA officers from their homes; it was part and parcel of the overall marketization and commodification of East German real estate and housing after unification. Nonetheless, this is how it was experienced and conceptualized by many officers, particularly those who lived in coveted flats in up-and-coming neighborhoods. The experiences of dislocation and the capriciousness of capitalism and the housing and real estate market led officers to believe that they were in fact the objects of targeted relocations because of their ranks and positions in the GDR and the NVA. It was just one more piece of the puzzle that, when they put it together, constructed a picture of intentional marginalization; it was yet another indicator that they did not belong in the new state. The mysteries of the market, coupled with what they had learned about capitalism in the East, and their own experiences as former NVA officers after unification, produced a profound sense of anomie and dislocation among former officers.

"UNIFICATION RUINED MY LIFE:" COMING TO TERMS WITH THE "PUNISHMENT PENSION"

I interviewed Manfred at his home in an eastern district of Berlin in 1999. At age sixty-three, Manfred was an imposing figure—tall, stern, and possessed of an unwavering gaze and a commanding voice. It was easy to imagine him commanding soldiers, and he was clearly accustomed to commanding respect. Manfred told me about his life in the NVA as a colonel and tank commander until a back injury precipitated a move to a training center, and then about his position in the civil defense forces. He also spoke of his life after unification; he had been able to travel and he had visited the United States. Showing me a map of his travels in the United States, where he logged over twenty thousand miles in a camper, he said: "I was very impressed with the discipline of the police in the United States. They didn't wear earrings like in Germany."

While happy about certain opportunities he now enjoyed, he still felt an overwhelming dissatisfaction and despair about his life after unification:

I'm sixty-three years old and I have spent my entire life working in one form or another. My career in the NVA was work. Since unification, I haven't had a job. I've applied to over 120 positions, but have been turned down for each one. I believe it is because I was a career NVA officer. No one wants to hire us once they see "NVA" on the job application. I've just applied for a job at Tempelhof Airport—it's for a baggage handler job that pays thirteen marks per hour. I'm sixty-three and in poor health, and I'm hoping to be a baggage handler. Unification ruined my life.

As Manfred told me his job history, he began to cry. Upon a return trip to Berlin in 2006, I learned that Manfred had died, still unemployed. His was a narrative I heard from the majority of former officers; based on their age, service, and training in the NVA, they had an extremely difficult time finding employment after unification. If they found jobs, NVA officers often worked as watchmen, security guards, or truck drivers; very few found what they considered to be suitable employment. Hans, whose experiences were similar to Manfred's, spoke with bitter irony about his job search:

I tried for a very long time to find a job, and no one would look at me. Once they saw "NVA" on my application, it was all over. I tried for a couple of years to find a job suited to my qualifications, but I couldn't find anything. As a result, my health declined; I had a heart attack, which kept me from working. I finally did manage to find a job as a security guard at the new Allied Museum in Berlin. I found it ironic that the only job I could get was guarding a museum dedicated to the Allies and their "victory" in the Cold War.

While Germany was forced to come to terms with a second dictatorship in the twentieth century, this was clearly not an easy process, either politically or judicially. While members of the SED Politburo (such as Egon Krenz), high-ranking members of the NVA and the Border Guards (like Klaus-Dieter Baumgarten, the commanding general of the Border Guards), and some lower-ranking members of the Border Guards could be brought to justice for crimes committed in the GDR, there was little legal recourse to a general "punishment" of the NVA, even if the political will was there.

One way the Bundeswehr and the Ministry of Defense could penalize all NVA officers, in addition to symbolic marginalization, was through their pensions. After unification, NVA officers' pensions were cut drastically; the official reason given concerned the number of accumulated "pension points" earned by NVA officers.[14] Economic marginalization is not seen simply as the product of market forces; NVA officers argue that they have been deliberately penalized through reductions in their pensions. This is a serious point of contention for these officers, who have stated publicly that they were mistreated, driven by the political desire to inflict a *Strafrente*—punishment pension—on them for having served in the NVA. For example, in 1999, while West German army officers were legally allowed to earn an additional 120 percent of their pensions after retirement, the pensions of NVA officers were capped, allowing them to only earn 650 marks in addition to their pensions. On average, NVA pensions were between 30 and 65 percent of West German officers' pensions. NVA officers, even though they paid into pension plans in the GDR, did not receive points in the former Federal Republic. Service time in the NVA was declared invalid and not included in the calculation of pensions after unification, leaving former NVA officers entitled only to points gained after unification. This, combined with the very high unemployment rate of former officers, made their economic situations tenuous, creating a great amount of stress for former officers and their families.

While I discussed the *Strafrente* with Arndt, who retired from the NVA as a major after thirty years of service, he quickly sketched out his financial situation. After taxes, he and his wife had approximately fourteen hundred marks per month to cover all of their expenses. His savings had been wiped out, and he had not been able to find a job. It was an embarrassing moment, because he then asked me how much I received per month for my research fellowship. I replied that I received 1,680 marks monthly. This did not go over well:

This is nothing personal, but you're here as a student making more money than I do, even though I was an officer in the NVA and spent thirty years of my life working and contributing to my savings. I have a family, and we have very little to live on—it's hard to make ends meet each month, and we're both getting older, who is going to hire us? We put money into our pension plans (in the GDR), but that was wiped out after unification, and we got nothing. My NVA pension was also dissolved, so like all others officers, all of the money I put in to that was lost. I don't hold this against you—but this—I don't hold it against you, but it's very hard for me to hear this and accept it.

Max, who talked earlier about the "status question," explained why he felt like a second-class citizen in the new state:

I feel like a second-class citizen. . . . The latest example is what the SPD has done. The SPD government has decided on a 3.1 percent pay increase for public service workers. Everybody's happy. But the East only gets 86 percent of what workers in the West get—that means my wife only gets 86 percent of the salary of someone with the same job in the West. The SPD has completely forgotten about Kohl's attempt to slowly bring up the East salaries to 100 percent of that of the West. Yes, it's bad, and it's no wonder that we talk the way we do. Factor in the discrepancies in our pensions, and how we've been the targets of "punishment pensions," and you can start to understand why we feel like we're less than others who aren't even German.

Torsten, who grew up in the GDR, joined the NVA, and later switched to the Border Guards, had this to say about the *Strafrente*:

We grew up in the GDR without complicated needs—most everything was taken care of, so we didn't have to worry about a lot of things. Sure, there were things we wanted like everyone else, but we got used to making do. So our needs were simple. After unification, our standards of living weren't really impacted that badly; our needs were still really the same. What was difficult was the rising costs of rents and food, and our low pensions—this made life very difficult. But we were used to having simple wants, so it wasn't too bad in that way. What we did miss—do miss—is access to culture. That was always accessible and cheap in the GDR. Now, if my wife and I want to see a play, we have to save up for half a year to be able to go. We don't miss the material things, and we're not really interested in the material goods of capitalism. We miss culture and life. We might make more money now than in the GDR, but we can't do much more than live with it, considering the different value and uses of money and prices under capitalism.[15]

As questions of status and symbolism shaped their perceptions of unification, the sheer crush of low incomes and grim employment prospects severely undermined their confidence in the new state. While economic marginalization and insecurity were common experiences among East Germans after unification, the added burden of "The NVA" made unification doubly difficult for former officers.

As of 2006, after years of petitions, complaints, and lobbying, the "pension issue" seems to have been resolved, and pensions for former NVA officers have approached the national average, through the gradual accumulation of pension points after 1990. Even after the gradual leveling off of pensions, Dietmar had this take on why he felt like a second-class citizen in 2006:

You see, I'm not doing too badly at all right now—our pensions are pretty much where they should be, on average with others. So I'm doing OK in that regard. But my children—one of them is a highly trained engineer—are unemployed. So I have to help them out; most of what's left over for me and my wife goes to them so they can pay their rent and make do. Is this what unification was supposed to be about? I'm a forceably retired officer—let me make that clear: I was forced to retire against my will—I'm a forceably retired officer who has to use his pension to pay his children's rent. This is why I feel like I'm a second-class citizen; unemployment is so high in the East and I was forced to give up my career, and I still can't find any kind of work because of my career and training.

Despite the gradual improvement in pensions by 2006, Bastian said to me, as we discussed the *Strafrente* and the "status question," "Sure, the pension problem is cleared up for the most part. It only took them sixteen years to do it. How do you think we feel, and feel about all of the money we lost at the time we needed it the most? We don't want to become millionaires. We just want a little bit of recognition and acknowledgment of our achievements."

As the years went on after unification, NVA officers and their families did better financially than they did in the years immediately after 1990, but in many ways, the point had been made and the damage had been done. By stripping them of their pensions, they were punished financially because of their service in the NVA and to the SED; their "work" was devalued, and their service to their state invalidated both symbolically and materially. While the Bundeswehr and the (West) German government were blamed for pushing through these penalties, NVA officers also blamed "human rights activists" for demanding that they be punished in the same manner as high-ranking members of the SED and the East German Politburo who could not otherwise be punished or sentenced for crimes or human rights violations. NVA officers took this as an indictment of both their careers and their lives, as service in the NVA was made to be seen as both a de facto "human rights violation" and a "crime against humanity."

THE POLITICAL OFFICER AND THE TRAVEL AGENCY

While the majority of officers I interviewed were pensioners (against their will, as they reminded me), trying to make do with small pensions, some officers attempted to start businesses in order to make ends meet, and to try to make the best of the new system. These attempts met with varying success, but the main goal was to continue to feel "useful" and to take an active role in their own lives. Rather than applying again and again for jobs that they felt were beneath their qualifications, they attempted to start out on their own.

Willi, a former political officer, started his own travel agency in Berlin. He was a notable exception—and notable contradiction—to many other officers; he seemed to have thrown himself into "capitalism," not simply to be successful, but in order to preserve his sense of self-worth. Willi spent his entire career in the NVA as a *Politoffizier* (political officer), a position and career of which he was very proud—and unapologetic. There is no equivalent to political officers in Western militaries, though, in some ways, military chaplains come close to holding some of the functions and responsibilities of political officers. *Politoffiziere* were the party whips of the military, and were there to insure the ideological indoctrination and purity of the soldiers—and of the officers as well. Political officers held daily and weekly political lectures and discussions of contemporary topics to insure the correct "worldview" of the military, and to convince them of the justice and correctness of the socialist cause. They also acted as counselors to soldiers (mimicking the role of military chaplains), but their primary role was that of political indoctrination. To this end, all political officers were thoroughly schooled in Marxist dialectics, and were expected to give detailed, on-the-spot analyses of political-economic topics when asked or ordered.

Political officers were in many ways more feared than respected, and the daily lectures for the conscripted soldiers were seen as both a break and a burden. Up until three days before unification, Willi told me, he wore his NVA uniform to and from his home to his base; he was told that he only had to wear it during duty hours, and that he could wear his civilian clothes home. "The thought never entered my mind," he said. "People gave me a hard time about it, but I never had any problems—I don't look like a weakling, do I?" After unification, he did not hide his career as a political officer from anyone:

I let everyone know—I'm proud of it, it's what I did and who I was. I was a real political officer, responsible for political education at both the regimental and the divisional level. Everyone thinks we were bad people, but I don't know why I'm supposed to be a bad person. Of course, I wouldn't put up a sign outside of my shop saying, "Former Political Officer of the National People's Army," but everyone who works with me knows what I did, and they don't have a problem with it.

As the "party whips," political officers were perhaps the most loyal and "convinced" officers of the NVA (and were seen this way as well), since they were the mouthpieces of the SED in the military, charged with promoting the inevitable victory of socialism over capitalism and the indoctrination of soldiers into SED ideology. In a strange twist, political officers were one group of former NVA officers who did fairly well after unification in terms of employment: insurance agencies, in particular, were interested in hiring political officers to work as insurance salesmen. The logic, I was told, was that if they could "sell" Marxism to the troops, they could sell insurance to the masses.

In addition to his travel agency, Willi also sold insurance, and did other odd jobs as well. Willi's business was very close to my apartment in Berlin, and I came to spend a great deal of time with him, and often drove with him to meetings. He was very active in one of the veterans group in eastern Berlin, and conducted veterans group business from his travel agency, which he called his "command post." During our interviews, more often than not he would receive a call concerning the veterans group, or someone would stop by to talk to him about current issues and business. Willi was in his office until midnight most nights, working on veterans groups issues, meeting with other officers, and taking care of his business.

I ran into Willi once at one o'clock in the morning as I was walking home from a bar with two loaves of bread in my pockets; he seemed to find this highly amusing, and proceeded to tease me about it for months. Willi also worked on Saturdays, and seemed to only take Sunday off. He had suffered some serious setbacks, such as being swindled by his parent company, and was sued by a West German couple over a vacation they did not enjoy and felt was his fault. His life was not easy, he told me, but, he was not going to give up or quit. In 2006, however, Willi told me that he had finally been forced to give up his business due to problems with the parent company, and because of the harm it had caused to his health. Never the healthiest person, the long hours required to make the agency a success had finally taken their toll. Willi threw himself into the work of his local veterans group as a way to fill his time; it was also his way of resisting the Bundeswehr, and of staking out his place in the new state. It was his way of not giving in and not giving up.

NVA WIVES:
THE FORGOTTEN HINTERLAND OF THE GDR

While I have focused on the experiences of NVA officers, their wives are very much a forgotten group of unification, a group whose lives in many ways mirrors their lives in the GDR, except for the uncertainty of the economic situations of their lives after unification. As I discussed in Chapter 2, the NVA hoped to "train" wives to be supportive of their husbands, to be the good "helpmeets" of SED and NVA propaganda efforts who would promise to always be a good "hinterland" of support for their husband. The "double burden" of women in socialism—work and the family—was in many ways a triple burden for NVA wives. They were expected to not only work and take care of the family, but support and take care of their soldier-husbands as well, and cope with the overall rigors of military life; this expectation lived on after unification.[16] Although the NVA was gone, NVA wives were still NVA wives, and like other East German women, they had to come to terms with their new lives.

Interviewing NVA wives was not an easy process. After getting to know their husbands, I would ask if it would be possible to sit down and talk to them about the GDR, life in the NVA, and unification. Interviews with NVA wives followed a remarkably similar pattern. I would arrive at their house, and we would sit and have coffee and chat for a few moments. The husband was always present, but somewhere else in the house, puttering about, straightening things up, or vacuuming, but always within

FIGURE 6.1   NVA officers and their wives at a Christmas celebration, December
1999. Photograph by the author.

earshot. We would then start the discussion, and I would ask questions
from my list. After about twenty to thirty minutes, the husband, doing
chores in an adjacent room, would start to interrupt, calling out his opinion, correcting his wife, or simply saying she was wrong. After another
ten to fifteen minutes, the vacuuming or cleaning would get closer and
closer, and the interruptions more frequent and forceful. Soon after, the
husband would sit down with us, and start to answer the questions for
his wife, who would shake her head, look annoyed, and get up and walk
away to make lunch.

In the short amount of time I was able to talk to them, and in discussions with their husbands over the course of my fieldwork, I was able to
get a glimpse of the difficulties faced by NVA wives, both before and after
unification. The life of an NVA wife was not an easy one, given the nature
of the NVA and the strict duty requirements for NVA officers. For both
the officer and his spouse, life in the NVA was one of constant "preparedness" at a level almost unheard of in Western armies. Official doctrine
stated that 85 percent of all soldiers were to be in the barracks at any given
time, and that units were to be in their deployment zones (outside of the

barracks) and ready to fight within two hours of an alarm. Of course, this placed immense pressure on officers and their families. One of the first things I noticed when I visited the homes of former officers who still lived in GDR-era military housing were the small alarm boxes attached to the walls in their living rooms. Whenever an alarm was called, all of the boxes in the housing block would go off, alerting everyone that all officers had to be in the barracks within fifteen minutes. This meant that not only were the officers alerted but their families as well, so officers had to depend on their families to keep up with the pace of readiness and alarms. Paul, an infantry officer whose unit was constantly put on alert, described a typical alarm: "Most of the time the alarms happened at night, say three in the morning. We would be sleeping, and then the alarms would go off and we had to jump into our uniforms and get to the barracks. One time there was an alarm, and I ran out in my uniform, but I still had on my slippers. My wife ran after me with my boots. This was just one of the countless times she saved me from getting in trouble."

While the NVA instrumentalized the family, and saw it as the most important "cell" in the ideological (re)production of the state, it also viewed the family, and particularly wives and girlfriends, with suspicion. Archival materials show an almost paranoid obsession with women and security issues; indeed, many documents maintained that women were the cause of all problems within officer families, and as such, special attention had to be paid to these women. In a report concerning disciplinary dismissals from the military, it was stated that "in many cases, the wives of our officers, who have an indifferent class attitude [klassenindifferente Einstellung] to contact with the West, or who make ultimatum-like demands in regard to the military career of the spouse, are the causes and sources of breaches of discipline."[17]

Ulrich, who served as the head of a weapons depot outside of Berlin for many years, explained to me that in 1982, the STASI (the Staatssicherheitsdient, or State Security Service) began investigating him and his wife for alleged "contact with the enemy." Any contact with relatives (or anyone, for that matter) from West Germany or the "West" in general was strictly prohibited not just for the officer but for his entire family. His wife, Ulrich told me, liked to talk a lot, and still talked to her relatives in

West Germany. Because of this, agents began following him to see if he had any contact with anyone from the West:

I was convinced that I was going to be arrested because of this, because my wife liked to talk to her relatives. I was called in by my commanding officer, and was interrogated by him and two STASI agents. They had followed me for days, and known my exact whereabouts, down to the minute. Because of this, when I came home, I wrote up a letter detailing what had happened in the meeting, and explaining to my wife and children that should I disappear, this is what really happened. I wanted them to know the truth of the matter. All of this because my wife talked to her relatives.

Women were also thought to be a corrupting influence on officers in terms of encouraging the desire for Western commodities. Ulrich told me of the case of an officer who had suggested that NVA officers receive a portion of their pay in Western currency so that they could shop at the fashionable "Intershops." The Intershops were special stores in the GDR that sold Western goods; these goods had to be paid for with Western currency, something that was very difficult to obtain in the GDR unless one had Western relatives. Since NVA officers were prohibited from maintaining contact with friends and relatives in the West, it was theoretically impossible for them to acquire Western currency. Because of his suggestion, he was seen as "subversive" and ideologically "impure." His family was also viewed with suspicion, and his wife was seen as the cause for his desire to obtain Western goods. This desire for goods was then seen as a security risk, for it implied that he was "warming" to the West; the subtext was that no "good" NVA officer would desire such things, and that this desire demonstrated both his ideological "uncertainty" and the "disrupted" nature of the "socialist relationship" in his family. Because of his suggestion, and the suspicion cast upon him and his wife, his family was monitored by the STASI and he was never again promoted.

Officers had very little time for their families, and spent very little time at home. They were required to give notice if they were going to be away from home for longer than two hours, and were expected to stay near their homes when off-duty. Leaves were rare, and were often canceled at the last moment due to some sort of "emergency" at the barracks.

Because of these restrictions and restraints, wives were expected to take care of the family while officers were away and in the field, and generally they were supposed to make due without much help from their husbands. Karl talked about the impact of the military on his family life, and how his wife was really expected to maintain the family:

It was always pretty difficult for us (in the NVA). There were certain periods when we had a lot of alarms, and we were always training so that if a war started we wouldn't be caught off-guard. If a regiment hadn't been combat-ready, that would have been a catastrophe. And so to keep this from happening, we periodically trained very intensively. That's the way it was. But there were times on Sundays or whatever time of the night when the alarm would go off, and then I had two hours and fifteen minutes to have my unit prepared to fight, outside in the concentration area that was located near the barracks. We were always fully loaded with ammunition. We always had to have 85 percent of the soldiers in the barracks, and that naturally meant a lot of work and lots of problems, because many of our soldiers and NCOs were married. To get everything done in the allotted time really wasn't at all easy.

My normal day began at 7:00 A.M., and I was in the barracks by 7:30 A.M. My wife and son usually ate alone, because father had very little time; that really wasn't pleasant at all, but there was nothing I could do about it. And because I usually got home at 5:00, 6:00, 7:00, or even 8:00 P.M., and sometimes later, depending on how serious the situation was in the regiment or division. We had a lot of inspections, and always had additional work to do. Either meetings or some such thing like that, or the day's training wasn't sufficient, like I couldn't get a battery to fire correctly or an exercise hadn't gone as planned, so I would have to do a bit extra.

Dorothee, Karl's wife, described it from her perspective:

People might not know this, but we were always on alert as well, perhaps, in a way, even more than our husbands. Yes, when the alert alarms went off, we were put on alert as well, and had to get out of bed and make sure they made it out in one piece and had all of the things they needed. But we had to stay behind and look after the children and make sure the household ran properly, and we never knew if the alert was real or not, or what was happening, or what would happen to us. I was always on edge, and never really got used to it. I still expect the boxes to go off. I hated those boxes and what they meant for us. I still do.

We moved around a lot, and were dependent on our husbands' careers for our own careers. We really had no say in the matter—we couldn't influence where they would be stationed, so we just had to live with it. When we would get to a new base, it was very hard on me, as I would have to try to find some kind of job, and try to make new friends. My life would feel like limbo for the first year, as I would just be around the house, taking care of things, and working, but not really working. At least my husband was busy, and while it was hard on him, the time passed more quickly for him and he didn't have so much time to think about things like I did. It was very lonely, and I was depressed a lot. But I stuck with it.

Many officers commented that they had no idea how hard life would be in the NVA when they enlisted, especially after they were married. Thomas, who spent his career in the NVA as an intelligence officer, told me, "I had two families: the military and my family." When I asked him which had been more important to him, he hesitated for a moment, and then said slowly, "The military." He later added that it was "good to have a military wife, because they're efficient and help you when you need help." Thomas then told me of a saying in the NVA that for him summed up how military life was experienced by men and women: "The husband changes duty stations, but not his friends." In other words, every time he changed bases, an officer would always know someone at a new base, and expand his connections and network of fellow officers, whereas his wife would normally have to make a completely new set of friends, and was expected to find a new job near the base as well. This dynamic would later have a positive benefit for the officers and a negative effect for their wives after 1990.

After unification, military wives were expected by their husbands to remain good military wives, even though the NVA was gone and their husbands were no longer officers. As the symbolic and material policies of the Bundeswehr made life increasingly difficult for officers, wives, in many instances, were expected to run the family and make sure the family stayed financially afloat, particularly in those families where the husband was not able to find any job or a job with a decent salary. Conversely, NVA wives were in many cases financially dependent and "tied" to their husbands, as they often had very low pensions in comparison to their husbands, and would not be able to make it on their own. Margaret, for example, the wife of an NVA colonel, had a monthly pension of four hundred marks, as compared to the fourteen hundred marks her husband received. In the brief time I was able to speak with her, Irene, who was married to a former lieutenant-colonel in the air defense artillery, told me,

I'm completely dependent on my husband to live, and there's little I can do to change it, even if I wanted to. He still gets fifteen hundred marks per month for being in the NVA, but I only get five hundred marks per month, and there's no way I could live on that. I was a kindergarten teacher, and had to move whenever my husband was transferred to a new base, so I was never able to keep a stable job, and kindergarten teachers didn't make much anyway, and so our pensions are lower. Our rent is over five hundred marks per month, and I just couldn't make it on my own. There's no way I could live on my own with my pension, just no way.

The dependence of the wives on husbands' pensions is a direct carry-over from their lives in the GDR as wives of NVA officers, and the policies directed towards their husbands after unification. NVA officers changed duty stations in the GDR, but not their friends or their jobs; they maintained both a steady, continuous profession and a widespread network of friends and support. Wives were forced to move with their husbands, and so had a fractured and discontinuous work history. As officers age and become ill, their wives are put at risk of becoming homeless, as no one can live on such a small pension; their experiences of life after unification are just as intimately tied to the military as their husbands' experiences are, though with potentially more dire consequences.

Military wives in all modern armies have generally been at an economic disadvantage, expected to maintain the family and see it through difficult times, whether or not the soldier-husband is home or deployed. Cynthia Enloe writes about military marriages and military husbands and wives, and the ways in which a stable marriage is a prerequisite for trust in a security state:

Being a reliable husband and a man the state can trust with its secrets appear to be connected. . . . And yet it is precisely that elevation to a position of state confidence which can shake the foundations of a marriage. Patriotic marriages may serve the husbands, giving them a greater sense of public importance and less of a sense of guilt for damaging the lives of people in other countries. And they serve the national security state. But they don't necessarily provide the women in those marriages with satisfaction or self-esteem. Typically, it is left up to the wife to cope with the tensions and disappointments.[18]

The situations of NVA wives are complicated by the reception, codification, and treatment of their husbands after unification—the marginalization of their husbands has impacted not just the officers, but the entire family, placing them all in precarious positions of dependency. If NVA officers feel like second-class citizens because they were NVA officers, their wives feel the effects of this as well, often having to carry the brunt of economic burdens, particularly in those cases where the husband simply broke down after unification, became ill, alcoholic, or depressed by the loss of status, power, and prestige. Their husbands have their networks and friends in the Deutscher Bundeswehrverband (German Army Veterans Association) to help them weather the problems of unification and integration; for the most part, NVA wives do not have group support. Devalued military marriages, and husbands who lose their elevated positions and the confidence of the state, can shake the foundations of a marriage, just as the foundations of the marriage and the political economy of a military marriage can continue to bind the wife to the husband and compel her to deal with the tensions and disappointments of a military career prematurely ended and publically scorned. As the strain on their families increased, NVA officers felt increasingly threatened; not only was their identity and status as soldiers and officers undermined, but their identity as good husbands and men who could support and protect their families was undermined as well.

THE SWING TO THE RIGHT:
THE UNINTENDED CONSEQUENCES OF POLICY

An officer in the NVA was expected to be a member of the SED, and to always uphold the tenets of both the party and socialism. Officers were required to be the living images and exemplars of the Socialist Warrior, and through their actions, to represent the party and the state. Socialist Internationalism, solidarity, opposition to inequality and racism—these were the attributes and mind sets expected of NVA officers. Whether or not they actually believed in these ideals, NVA officers were expected and required to act as if they did. Most officers considered themselves firmly on the left, antifascist and anticapitalist, and saw themselves as officers of a progressive German military that was wholeheartedly antifascist. After unification, the combination of policies directed toward them—and the overall confusion and humiliation of unification—drove a fair number of officers toward the right and extreme right.

An unintended consequence of the Bundeswehr's policies of symbolic punishment and economic marginalization toward NVA officers has been to push many officers farther and farther to the right, toward parties and political positions that espouse nationalist, nativist, and openly racist policies and platforms. These officers have embraced the xenophobic, anti-immigration, and anti-assimilationist rhetoric of right and far-right parties that, they feel, best represent their frustrations, concerns, and interests.[19] The swing toward right and far-right politics has been a problem for all of the former GDR since unification, but given the additional problems faced by NVA officers, the messages and policies of these parties can be particularly appealing. As of May 2000, the chairman of a local Brandenburg branch of the Nationaldemokratische Partei Deutschlands (National Democratic Party of Germany), a far-right political party, was a former NVA colonel. Some far-right groups dispensed with their anticommunist prejudices in order to attract disenchanted former officers; unlike the federal government, their public statements affirmed both the "Germanness" of East German officers as well as their service as soldiers to the German *Volk*. Unlike the Bundeswehr, far-right parties acknowledged former officers as "German soldiers," stating that even if they served a communist state and party, they were still German soldiers who protected the German nation. This, coupled with the perception that "foreigners" received more benefits and better treatment than they did, pushed many officers to embrace dangerous, and in terms of their backgrounds, seemingly antithetical beliefs, which has only served to marginalize them further.

FIGURE 6.2   Author with Rainer Wulf after attending a veteran's group meeting, Berlin, 2000. Photograph from the author's collection.

Rainer Wulf explained to me that the political affiliation of NVA officers in the late 1990s was overwhelmingly PDS (the Party of Democratic Socialism, the reconstituted SED), followed by the CDU (the Christian Democratic Union) and then the SPD (the Social Democrats). I asked him why the SPD was so hated in the East (this conversation took place during the elections in 1999, in which the SPD was suffering catastrophic defeats in the East) and he said that with the former NVA, the CDU had made some effort to contact them and him personally, whereas the SPD had continually ignored them. He also said that in the GDR, the CDU had already existed (even though as powerless party), so there was more familiarity with it than with the SPD, as the SPD had merged with the KPD (the prewar German Communist Party) in 1946 to form the SED. The SPD had also been aggressive toward the new PDS, which had angered a large number of NVA officers. No matter their affiliation, NVA officers were cynical about the political process and all of the political parties; they came to believe that parties and politicians simply wanted their votes without necessarily having to do anything for them or address their concerns. Since NVA officers were seen as politically radioactive, no one wanted to be seen helping them or working for their benefit. Rolf explained with some bitterness how political parties had approached NVA veterans groups looking for votes and offering support:

As elections near, politicians come looking to us for votes. They promise to do this and that for us, to help us with our problems and address our concerns. But nothing ever happens. They use us for votes, and then just leave us to deal with our problems on our own because it's not really good for them to be seen as actually helping us. We were burned a few times like this, but now we've learned. They still think we're dumb enough to believe them and support them, but we don't. We've learned our lesson about how the system works.

Many veterans group meetings discussed the "problem" of foreigners in Germany; these discussions revolved around the feeling of former officers and their families that they were the "foreigners" and second-class citizens in the new state because of how they had been treated since unification. In many ways, Bundeswehr policies after unification drove these men toward racism and right-wing politics. Before unification, NVA officers conceptualized the differences with the Bundeswehr and the FRG along political and historical terms; after unification, ideas about race came into play. In their eyes, those who immigrated to Germany have been given better treatment than they have had, simply because they are both East German and former NVA officers. Because they have been codified by the Bundeswehr as "members of a foreign military," as the symbolically non-German "real" Germans, they feel they are treated worse than non-Germans who had not served Germany and were not part of the German nation by blood.[20]

UNIFICATION AND DISCONTENT

While many former officers and their families have made do since unification, and live fairly comfortable lives, in my discussions with them there was an overwhelming sense of unease and uncertainty about their futures, and in some cases an almost funereal oppressiveness and gloom in their homes. Most had been forced to move to smaller apartments, and the majority of them were very worried about their ability to pay rent or other bills on time because of the cuts in their pensions. By highlighting and questioning their pasts, unification disrupted and made their present and futures uncertain and unstable; the anticipated rewards of loyal service to the state had been taken from them. Having once lived in a society in which such things were not major life concerns, the shift from economic security to uncertainty played a daily, debilitating role in their lives. They were quick to recognize what they saw as a concerted effort on the part of West German elites to marginalize them because of their membership in the SED and their positions as officers in an antifascist army. Werner commented to me one day, "We were members of the antifascist German military, one that opposed fascism and capitalism, and we stood by our workers. We took this role seriously, we were to stand against capitalism and all that it does to a society, especially how capitalism can lead to fascism. We know why we're being pushed aside. We're still seen as a threat because of who we were and how we think."

The international political and ideological struggles of the Cold War, the confrontation between NATO and the Warsaw Pact, and the rivalry for legitimacy between the Bundeswehr and the NVA play out after unification in officers' pensions, their ability to find a job, their dependence on their wives to keep them and their families together, and in the rising costs and dislocations of the housing market in Berlin. Just because the Cold War is over does not mean that the mindsets or the interpretive frameworks of the era are gone: they continue to shape perceptions on both sides, and in the process, impact unification and the material lives of former officers. Elites—fallen or otherwise—on both sides are in a sense trapped by their histories and understandings of history and memory. This drives policy making as well as the reaction to and reception of policies; NVA officers strongly believe that they were pushed aside because of the side they served and what they represented. To make sense of their lives and what has happened to them after unification, and of the symbolic and material problems they have faced, many NVA officers have turned to forms of memory that link them to the "others" of Germany's recent past, others with whom they believe they can identify as victims of German fascism, whether in the Third Reich or after.

CHAPTER 7

As Germans Among Germans

LIFE IN THE *KAMERADSCHAFT*

We come not as Victors to the Vanquished, but as Germans to Germans.

GENERAL JÖRG SCHÖNBOHM,

Bundeswehr general charged with dismantling the NVA

We want the unity of our people, but with legal equality as Germans among
Germans. We call for the state to recognize us as German soldiers.

GERD RICHTER,

director of the "Kameradschaft Ehemalige Rostock" (Rostock NVA Veterans Group),
in an open address demanding equal recognition for NVA soldiers and officers.

FROM MY FIELD NOTES:

December 3, 1999. At an NVA veterans group meeting in Berlin, Dr. Barst (a
former NVA physician) told the following joke: A Turk, a Wessi (West German),
and an Ossi (East German) die and go to heaven. St. Peter says to the Turk,
"You've sinned a lot, so you'll have to get one hundred lashes on your back, but
you get one wish." So the Turk wishes for a thick blanket to cover himself with
as he is lashed. St. Peter then says to the Wessi, "you've sinned a lot, so you'll
have to get one hundred lashes on your back, but you get one wish." Having
heard how the Turk screamed as he was lashed, he wished for a thick pillow
to be tied to his back. Then St. Peter says to the Ossi, "You've sinned more
than the others on Earth, so you get two hundred lashes, but you also get two
wishes." So the Ossi looks at St. Peter and says, "I wish for double the number
of lashes that I receive, and I want the Wessi tied to my back."

. . .

In 1999, I attended a unique meeting, the first of its kind in postwar
and post-unification Germany: the Sonderversammlung des deutschen

Bundeswehrverbandes (Special Meeting of the German Army Veterans Association). Over four thousand Bundeswehr soldiers and officers converged on Berlin to protest pay cuts, base closures, and outdated equipment. I attended the meeting as a guest of the deputy-director of the former NVA veterans groups, which sent a delegation to the meeting to voice their members' concerns and problems. The NVA delegation was given five to ten minutes to speak about their problems.

As we stood talking and looking at all of the Bundeswehr officers and soldiers in their uniforms in the main foyer of the Berlin Convention Center, where the event was being held, a man in his late sixties walked up to us. He was tall and thin, slightly bald, and had on glasses and civilian clothes of a style worn by older men from East Germany. He was a former NVA colonel; I recognized him from meetings of the Working Group for the History of the NVA. He approached us, smiled a huge grin, and in perfect NVA Deutsch, snapped to attention, ram-rod straight, saluted us, and barked out for all to hear, "Genosse Oberstleutnant, ich melde keine besonderen Vorkommnisse [Comrade Lieutenant-Colonel, I have nothing unusual to report]."

Although this was a military convention, no one was following military "courtesies"—saluting or standing at attention; in fact, the atmosphere was very nonmilitary. The combination of military protocol with former NVA protocol and language made the old officer stand out sharply; all of the Bundeswehr soldiers looked at him disapprovingly, shaking their heads and walking away. The NVA officer I was with looked surprised and shocked; he glowed with guilty pleasure over the former colonel's performance. Both officers felt they had just scored a major point against the Bundeswehr soldiers, whom they made look like second-rate and undisciplined soldiers, and who looked like they had just been slapped.

.   .   .

One of the few avenues of official, state-sanctioned political response open to former NVA officers is the Deutscher Bundeswehrverband (the German Army Veterans Association), the official veterans organization of the Bundeswehr. Founded in 1956, shortly after the formation of the Bundeswehr, the Bundeswehrverband acts as an apolitical and financially independent representative for over 240,000 members. Comprised of four *Landesverbände* (state associations), the Bundeswehrverband has veterans groups and offices throughout Germany. Formed on April 5, 1991, with an initial sixty-five hundred members in Magdeburg, Landesverband Ost (Eastern State Association) is the newest state association, representing the states of the former GDR. *Kameradschaften*—veterans groups—give former East German army officers an official, military forum from which to tell their side of unification and German history. One of the conundrums of unification is the simultaneous embrace and marginalization of the NVA in the *Kameradschaften*. In a seemingly contradictory move, NVA officers were invited and allowed to join the veterans association of the military the NVA opposed, and which still opposes it after unification.

Since the disbanding of the NVA, former NVA officers and soldiers have found themselves bereft of the kinds of social, political, and support networks that they had during the time of the NVA. This was particularly difficult for former officers; their worlds were comprised of the military; their friends, acquaintances, and social spaces were made up of the military, of other soldiers, and their families. After unification, the majority of former NVA officers who were not allowed to join the new Army of Unity found themselves in limbo: they had lost their state, their military, their careers, and seemingly, their ability to make a living, and they found themselves both symbolically linked to the Wehrmacht and excluded from tradition. For men in their late forties and fifties, who had spent their entire lives in the military, this was a serious blow to their identities and sense of self, as well as their self-perception as defenders of the state, as breadwinners, and as good, strong, honorable men who had followed a code of conduct that they believed to be noble and correct. With unification, officers lost their status overnight; when not simply forgotten, they were considered—by both East and West Germans—as pariahs, hard-line communists, or simply anachronisms. No longer considered suitable to represent the German military—in either the past of the present—NVA officers felt cut adrift in the new system.

Dale Herspring, in his history of the end of the NVA, begins a chapter with the quote above from General Jörg Schönbohm, the Bundeswehr general who was sent to the GDR to oversee the dismantling of the NVA, and the transition of former NVA soldiers and officers into the Bundeswehr of the new, unified state.[1] Schönbohm's assertion that the Bundeswehr was not coming to the East as a victor, but merely as Germans to Germans, fell on deaf ears with many former officers, particularly in the years immediately after unification, as Bundeswehr and (West) German policies designed to marginalize former officers came into play. The Bundeswehr in many ways set up a series of contradictory policies, taking some officers into the Bundeswehr, removing others from their careers, and in a move that brought both confusion and opportunity to former officers, welcoming former NVA officers into the official veterans organization of the Bundeswehr, though not necessarily as equal members. In the eyes of NVA officers, theirs was most definitely the relationship of the vanquished to the victors.

This chapter examines life in the *Kameradschaften* and what these groups have provided former officers and their families; the struggles of the former officers to be counted as "Germans among Germans"; and the politics of military signification and honor after unification. In the veterans groups, NVA officers come face to face with the Bundeswehr and its policies, and attempt to come to terms with both. These groups form the space where NVA and Bundeswehr officers come together, and where NVA officers contest the supposed dominance and superiority (as they see it) of the Bundeswehr.

Through the Kameradschaften, NVA officers are able to regain their identities, to become again what they once were, even if only for a while. In the process, they provide a space from which to critique that which they believe was wrong with the past, but also to critique the present. They also provide a forum from which to tell their side of the story, their side of unification and German history, as they attempt to show the Bundeswehr and the new Germany that they—not the Bundeswehr, the Wehrmacht, or the SS—were the most honorable and ethical of German soldiers, and therefore deserve a place in German military tradition as equals and "comrades."

ENGAGEMENT, RESISTANCE, ACCEPTANCE

After unification, the Bundeswehrverband, in the spirit of the "Army of Unity," extended membership to those former NVA officers who were not active members of the STASI (Staatssicherheitsdienst), the East German secret police. In May 2000 there were 12,500 former NVA soldiers affiliated with the Bundeswehrverband. By June 2006, membership had dropped to about 8,000, through a combination of frustration, political exhaustion, protest against German involvement in the war in Kosovo and Serbia, and death.

Many officers viewed the veterans groups as a forum for expressing political discontent and as spaces for "returning" to the NVA and reactivating social and hierarchical networks taken from them after unification. The Bundeswehrverband, however, had another, more practical reason for accepting former NVA officers into its ranks: competition. The Verband der Berufssoldaten (Association of Professional Soldiers) in the GDR had a membership of over fifty thousand. Had it been allowed to continue, it would have represented a serious competitor to the Bundeswehrverband, and undermined the legitimacy of the Bundeswehr and the Bundeswehrverband as the sole representatives of German military legitimacy after unification. Additionally, while NVA officers were not seen as a serious threat to stability after unification, allowing officers into the *Kameradschaften* gave the military a chance to keep an eye on former officers and monitor their assimilation into the new state.

As state-sanctioned spaces of military performance, NVA veterans groups allow men to regain their identities as East Germans and military officers, to become again what they once were, even if only for a limited time in a circumscribed space. The veterans groups function as a space in which to (re-)create their identities as former NVA officers, critique the present, and negotiate their roles in the new German state. In addition to providing NVA officers an outlet to voice political concerns, veterans groups act as "sites of memory" by allowing former soldiers to come together to remember the past and discuss the present and future. As such, they form what Winter and Sivan call "networks of complimentarity," where members remember and share complimentary memories and experiences face to face and re-create past identities.[2] However, through this seemingly benevolent process of identity re-creation and social networking, veterans groups provide the German state and military a convenient "foil" for the creation of new forms of German state and military identity, allowing for the perpetuation of Cold War ideas about the NVA, the legitimation of West Germany as the "true" Germany, and the Bundeswehr as the inheritor of "proper" military identity.

In addition to acting as spaces of military identity, the *Kameradschaften* act as "training grounds" in which to explore the transition from state socialism to market capitalism, to come to terms with unification, and to learn how to become citizens in a completely different social system. The *Kameradschaften* are essential for the project of state building and the creation of new political identities for former NVA officers. The NVA officers who joined the *Kameradschaften* were trying to come to terms with unification and make sense of what it means to be a citizen in a democracy. Unlike many former NVA officers, those who joined the Bundeswehrverband and the veterans groups were making an attempt to embrace the new state.

Some of the most important discussions at veterans group meetings focused on the question of citizenship in a democracy. How can they become good citizens in a democracy, NVA veterans frequently asked, when they feel that there is nothing "democratic" about how they have been treated? Many of these men and their spouses have lived through three social systems—the Nazi dictatorship, the GDR, and now post-unification democ-

FIGURE 7.1   *Kameradschaft* meeting of former officers from an NVA tank division, fall 1999. Photograph by the author.

racy. They have had more experience with "citizenship" than many other people have had, and are particularly sensitive to the ways in which it is expressed, codified, and enacted. They are almost "hyperaware" of the contradictions inherent in the new, post unification system, particularly since they see themselves on the "losing end."

One of the main reasons for participation in the *Kameradschaften* is political representation. As the only officially sanctioned organization representing soldiers' rights, the Bundeswehrverband provides former NVA officers with a forum from which to air their grievances. It has also been an arena for "getting to know" the Bundeswehr—a process that has not been particularly easy for either side. After unification, the Bundeswehrverband was the only organization to offer former officers any form of official, government-sanctioned opportunities to speak out politically. In addition to speaking out for their own rights, many former NVA officers see their role in the *Kameradschaften* as that of being a *Gegenstimme*— a countervoice—to official Bundeswehr and federal government policies and actions. According to a report written in 1995 concerning former NVA officers in the Bundeswehrverband, those officers who joined are somewhat unusual; the report, written by the former NVA colonel who heads the Working Group for the History of the NVA, states that it is uncommon for the an army to open itself up to its former enemies.[3] In this regard, few NVA officers joined the group, presumably because it is the official organization of the Bundeswehr, their former enemy. In comparison, the Initiativgemeinschaft zum Schutz der sozialen Rechte ehemaliger Angehöriger bewaffneter Organe und der Zöllverwaltung der DDR (ISOR; Association for the Protection of the Social Rights of former members of the Armed Forces and Customs Agency of the German Democratic Republic), another organization representing the interests of former NVA officers, STASI members, and police and customs officials, has a membership of over eighty thousand, but does not enjoy any sort of official, governmental recognition.[4] While those former officers who joined the Bundeswehrverband can be viewed as "moderate" in terms of their opinions on the GDR past (something which they themselves like to think), ISOR is considered by many former NVA officers and the public at large to be a "hard-line" organization. Members of ISOR, I was told, are those who have had the hardest time coming to terms with unification and integration into (West) German society. Additionally, ISOR members are deeply suspicious of the Bundeswehrverband; they find it difficult to believe that it is concerned with the best interests of former NVA officers and other members of the GDR armed forces.[5] As Fischer states in his Working Group report on NVA officers' experiences with the Bundeswehr, "Just as it is unbelievable that a western army would open up its professional interest group to members of its former enemy, so too is it unbelievable for many former NVA officers, who simply cannot accept it."[6]

Only a small percentage of career officers who served in the NVA have joined the Bundeswehrverband. Their reasons for joining are many and complicated. Over the course of my fieldwork and interviews with former officers, many stated that they joined the Bundeswehrverband as a way to stay active and to learn how to be "good citizens" in the new state. Some spoke of joining as a way to make sense of capitalism and the new economic system. Primarily, most joined the Bundeswehrverband out of economic necessity and out of fear for their futures. Functioning as a mutual support network, the veterans groups often take up donations for families who cannot pay their rent or other bills, and delegations with flowers are sent to the hospital when officers fall seriously ill.[7] Herbert Becker, the deputy-chairman of the Landesverband Ost, told me that they always try to find money or other support for those officers who are in extreme need or dire circumstances.

Kameradschaft meetings were more than just a chance for NVA veterans to get together to talk about the past; they also provided a way to insure that the present made sense, that it had some sort of form. In a very real sense, it gave members something to live for, to look forward to, to fill their time up in a meaningful way. There was always a sense of sadness present at these meetings, a sense of loss and a sense of people attempting to counter that loss as their identities slipped away. Harry, who joined a local NVA veterans group as soon as it was formed, put it to me this way:

The veterans groups provide us with a sense of purpose again, a sense of belonging. Before we joined, we were lost. It's hard to convey to you the sense of nothingness we felt after unification and the end of the GDR and the NVA. Now we have something to give us direction, and to help us fight and agitate for our rights and recognition. But really, it gives us a focus and structure—lack of structure is very difficult for people who have spent their entire lives in a highly structured environment. It's torture to sit around the house all day, thinking about what was, and feeling like there was nothing we could do about it.

Bernd saw the veterans groups as a chance to meet up with old friends and colleagues, and talk about their lives, situations, and what it meant to live in a capitalist system,

You know, making sense of all of this, of unification and a new economic system, has been difficult and hard to understand. Of course, we knew a lot about it from the critique side, but learning how to live in it on a daily basis has been difficult, particularly when we have to think about paying for things we never had to pay for in the GDR. We talk about rent, insurance, the price of food and other goods, and our pensions and the problems we're having getting the money that is due to us. So yes, it's good that we can meet up and hear different experiences and different ideas and solutions to problems we're all having.

For Martin, the political engagement afforded by membership in the Bundeswehrverband was welcome, but he was fairly cynical about the reasons they were invited to join, or the outcome of their membership:

I'm glad this opportunity exists for us—it's better than nothing. But it is kind of strange that the Bundeswehr, while telling us on the one hand that we don't count as German soldiers, opens up its veterans groups to us and let's us take part, have our own groups, and at least think that we have a voice. Honestly, I'm not sure what this is all about. Sometimes I think they just want to keep an eye on us because they don't really trust us, but who knows. I do always attend the meetings, and think it very important to come and talk and listen, to try to work out our problems. Nothing ever really seems to get done or happen—we talk and talk, but no one seems to listen, and it is really frustrating. If nothing else, it's good to see my friends and talk about the old times. It's good to be a part of a group again, a group of people with similar experiences that I can relate to. Though, I have to admit, I am surprised that I'm allowed to be a part of this.

WRITING COUNTERHISTORIES:
THE "WORKING GROUP FOR THE HISTORY OF THE NVA"

While not a veterans group, one group of NVA officers within the Landesverband Ost played a key role in transmitting the experiences, memories,
biographies, and concerns of former NVA officers. Founded in 1991, the
Working Group for the History of the NVA was dedicated to writing what
its members saw as counterhistories to West German accounts of the Cold
War and unification. The Working Group produced its own journal and
coauthored a number of edited volumes.

The head of the Working Group was an NVA colonel who had a Ph.D.
in history and had been an instructor at the NVA military academy. Other
members included top NVA sociologists, political scientists, economists,
and statisticians. It was a diverse group, representing a cross-section of
NVA academics. The NVA was deeply concerned not only with its own
history—as a way of creating the tradition of the NVA—but with socio-
logical surveys of troop morale as well.

FIGURE 7.2   Author with members of the Working Group for the History of
the National People's Army at their headquarters in Berlin, March 2000. Photograph from the author's collection.

The Working Group is highly successful within NVA circles; its journals always sell out, and its books are in great demand. They provide
an insight into the NVA experience of unification, and the sociologists
and historians in the group produced a survey documenting the experiences of NVA officers in the first five years of unification. Much of their
work deals with the minutia of the NVA, such as command structures,
weapons systems, policies, and so on. Some in the Bundeswehr and the
Bundeswehrverband consider their work controversial, as they question
the claims and statements of the Bundeswehr and the West, and call into
question the standard narratives of "victory" and the smooth running
of unification. The group's 1995 report on the experiences of former
NVA officers in the new state showed the serious problems NVA officers
were dealing with after unification, and the intense feelings of loss that
accompanied their transition into the new state. Many Bundeswehr officers see the Working Group as an attempt by NVA officers to skew and
distort the history of the NVA within the GDR, and are angry that it is
located within the structure of the Bundeswehr's veterans association and
receives funding from it.

THE FEAR OF THE MILITARY OTHER

While NVA officers who have joined the Bundeswehrverband see an advantage in attending veterans group meetings and taking part in the life
of the association, not everyone in the Bundeswehrverband is happy with
their inclusion and membership. Many Bundeswehr officers harbor an
intense dislike for NVA officers, and are overwhelmingly dismissive of
their problems and concerns. At the special meeting of the Bundeswehrverband in Berlin in 1999, NVA officers were given ten minutes to speak
about their concerns and problems after unification. Martin, the leader
of a Berlin veterans group, appeared before the more than four thousand
Bundeswehr officers present at the meeting, and in a tone that was neither
obsequious nor demanding, described the problems with their pensions,
their removal from military tradition, and their status as "members of a
foreign military." Martin did not wear a suit; he wore slacks, a white shirt
without a tie, and suspenders. After the speeches were over, I spoke with
a few Bundeswehr officers about the meeting. In response to my question

about what he thought of Martin's speech, Michael, a Bundeswehr major, commented,

Who really cares how they feel—I could care less. They deserve what they get—they kept the SED running, and helped the Soviet Union in the Cold War. Why should we help them, and give them honors and money they don't deserve? I really don't care what happens to them. I am annoyed by what he wore to the meeting, however—he didn't have any class. He was wearing suspenders, and didn't show us any respect. He should have known better, but maybe he doesn't.

These feelings of animosity and superiority towards NVA officers remain. Encapsulated in this comment are the various layers of disdain toward NVA officers felt by Bundeswehr officers: questions of class, propriety, allegiance, politics, ideology, and expectations and demands of respect and deference. The general opinion of West German Bundeswehr officers and West Germans with whom I spoke is that these men were on the wrong side, and as such deserve nothing. Not only were they "on the wrong side," but they also chose to stay there, and served in a military and alliance that insured there would indeed be a "side." The general opinion of the Bundeswehr toward the NVA was summed up in 1999 by the minister of defense, Rudolph Scharping, who stated publically, "Ten years after unification, it is not in the interest of the majority of Germans to provide former NVA soldiers with rights that would make it seem as if they had served in the Bundeswehr their entire lives."[8]

Almost ten years after unification, many Bundeswehr officers felt it necessary to ban all contact with former NVA officers and NVA veterans groups because of a fear of the "cultivation" of NVA tradition. Some strictly Bundeswehr veterans groups have issued orders instructing their members that under no circumstance are they to speak with or engage in any activities with former NVA officers. In 1999, *Unser Fallschirm* (Our Parachute), the newsletter of a former NVA paratrooper veterans group, reported that the general in charge of a local Bundeswehr base had prevented members of the Bundeswehr veterans group or any soldiers under his command from socializing with members of the NVA group. Despite three years of successful contact between the groups, the new general in charge issued the order without explanation. In the same article, the author of the editorial states that he was invited to a Christmas celebration at a local Bundeswehr veterans group; while there, he was told by a Bundeswehr sergeant that he should leave and that he did not belong there because he served a dictatorship.[9] He then writes: "But this same sergeant has no problem being a member of a group that has a close relationship to a Wehrmacht veterans group, which fought a war on behalf of a dictatorship; but that was the generation of his father and grandfather, who of course one must honor."[10] The honoring of men who fought a war for a dictatorship, and who nonetheless are honored as "German soldiers," is a practice that NVA officers find particularly offensive and problematic.

In a similar situation, the commanding general of the Logistikbrigade 4 (Logistics Brigade 4) issued the Brigadebefehl 01/99 (Brigade Order 01/99) prohibiting contact with former NVA groups and soldiers: "For all units and organizations of Logistics Brigade 4, I hereby prohibit all forms of support for associations, formations, or societies whose purpose is to further comradely solidarity or the cultivation of the traditions by organizations of the armed forces of the former German Democratic Republic. These activities are to be ceased immediately and reported."[11]

Herbert Becker (the deputy-director of the Landesverband Ost, umbrella organization for all NVA veterans groups in the Bundeswehrverband), pressed for an explanation of the order from the Bundeswehrverband. In reply, the office of Association Politics and Law of the Bundeswehrverband responded: "Units of the armed forces of the former German Democratic Republic cannot serve as models of tradition for the Bundeswehr. There is no recourse against this order, because the order prohibits the support of those organizations which promote the tradition of the NVA."[12]

In response, Becker released an open letter to the Bundeswehrverband:

Independent of their membership in the German Army Association, the soldiers of the former NVA feel concerned, because this order has nothing to do with the tradition of the Bundeswehr, but rather, very much to do with all forms of support for those who want to maintain their own tradition. This order is about exclusion rather than integration, and a different measure is being used in comparison to other tradition associations. It seems the concern here is that the Bundeswehr's understanding of tradition should find consensus with the fathers and grandfathers of those who serve in the Bundeswehr [i.e., men who had served in the Wehrmacht].

No one expects that the Bundeswehr should take on or maintain the tradition of the NVA. Despite this, a number of questions remain:

- On October 3, 1990—the "Day of German Unity"—did the Bundeswehr not accept fifty thousand NVA soldiers into the Bundeswehr?
- Is the Bundeswehr not using barracks that were occupied by other soldiers for forty years?
- Did the NVA, or individual soldiers of the NVA, not achieve anything that is at least worthy of local recognition?
- Were there not floods or other catastrophes in the GDR in which soldiers of the NVA did not help with rescues and other forms of assistance?

Is it really the case that in terms of the construction of tradition, what was not worked through with the Wehrmacht is to be worked through with the NVA?[13]

While the majority of Bundeswehr officers look down at NVA officers, not all Bundeswehr officers take a hard-line stance against them, even if they are critical of the role of the NVA in the GDR and the actions of the Border Guards during the Cold War. While the NVA may be of little concern to the Bundeswehr stationed in western Germany, for those Bundeswehr officers stationed in the eastern part of the country, and who have contact with former NVA officers through the administrative structure of the Landesverband Ost, the picture and reality are much more complicated. Younger Bundeswehr officers, while enmeshed in the organizational and "tradition" culture of the Bundeswehr, seem to be more forgiving of NVA officers as well. Kai, a Bundeswehr captain assigned to the Landesverband Ost, was very critical of the way NVA officers were treated after unification:

What exactly are we trying to achieve by pushing former NVA officers aside? I'm not really sure what we get out of it, or what we gain by constantly reminding them that they don't really count or that we don't really care about them or that we "won." They are citizens, and should be treated like citizens, not like something else. Treating them like dirt doesn't help us at all, and just makes them and other East Germans suspicious of us and unification. The side effects [Nebenwirkungen] of our treatment are much more damaging than most members of the Bundewehr understand.

Michael, another Bundeswehr captain active in the Bundeswehrverband, expressed sympathy for the NVA officers: "The Cold War is over, the GDR is gone, so why does the Bundeswehr feel the need to punish these men? They were simply doing the same as us, serving their country as they saw fit. It's a waste of time and energy to continue to punish them. We have bigger problems to worry about right now than the NVA. Really, what do they think they're going to do?"

A TOPOLOGY OF MEMORY: RED FLAGS AND WHITE

Prior to unification, the location of NVA units was a state secret; civilian maps did not show the location of bases. The East German state regarded the location of military units as a secret, as specters on the landscape. But this was something of a public secret: people who lived near a base knew that the NVA was there, and that a base was nearby.

After unification, all of this changed. It was now possible to speak of bases, to talk about who or what had been stationed where, the conditions on the bases, the transition of bases from the NVA to the Bundeswehr, and the renaming of bases. In the period immediately following unification, bases went from public secret to public knowledge. Suddenly, the NVA was everywhere. And nowhere.

On a wall of the Berlin office of the Landesverband Ost, a map shows the location of all of the NVA veterans groups in the former East. The map uses small flags to designate the locations of veterans groups, just as they would have been used on training and exercise maps during military maneuvers to indicate bases or units in the field. The map mirrors the preunification locations of NVA units: it makes it seem as if the NVA and its bases were still there. In a sense, they are: in the mental maps of former officers, who still view and understand the eastern states in terms of where units were stationed, the distances between units, who was stationed where, and the quickest route to and from former bases. A "military template" still overlays the East for former NVA officers, a template based on their lives and experiences.

While the map represents the placement of veterans groups in the present, it is also a map of the past, a map of memory. This sort of "cartographic memory" can be seen as a response to the physical and historical erasure of the NVA after unification.[14] The pins on the map are more than just simple markers: they are ways to keep the memory of the NVA alive in the face of the renaming of barracks and the erasure of the NVA presence in those areas. The small pins keep the memory of the NVA alive, and contest the Bundeswehr through a connection of memory, place, and types of soldiers in these areas. It is a form of geographical-linguistic memory; the place remains, but through renaming, the past in those places is erased and made anew to serve the needs and desires of the new state.

The location of Landesverband Ost, the "headquarters" of the NVA groups situated in what was East Berlin, was marked with a large red flag; that of the main office of the Bundeswehrverband in Nickolaussee, in what was West Berlin, was marked in white. Red versus white, revolution versus reaction: the old tropes of the Cold War marked out clearly in small flags on a map in an obscure office in Berlin, a map that maps out the memory and reality of the Cold War and unification for NVA officers.

AS GERMANS AMONG GERMANS

One evening in early 2000, I received a call from Rainer Wulf. He sounded excited—almost out of breath—as he told me, "I've just received news about one of the upcoming meetings in Rostock. We have to go to this meeting," Rainer told me, "this is going to be a big one. Not just in attendance, but because of what the officer in charge of the Rostock *Kameradschaft* is going to say. They have something really big planned. You can't miss this one. This meeting will get us a lot of attention."

While many meetings of the veterans groups focused on local problems and activities, debates concerning the ongoing process of integration, rights, status, and financial prospects were often contentious and embittered. While the size of each Kameradschaft varied, there were usually anywhere between thirty and a hundred people present. Held mostly in old halls located around Berlin, the meetings generally had an oppressive air to them. Sitting quietly—sometimes sullenly—sipping beers or coffee, and smoking, the leaders of the group would speak and make announcements; an outside speaker on military history or affairs would sometimes follow. Officers would then voice their concerns and problems, and exchange the latest information and directives on their pensions, the "status question," and other points of contention or concern. They would then sit and talk of the GDR and their time in the NVA, reminiscing about their lives in the military; at this point, the atmosphere would become more lively and animated.

Rainer Wulf was right about the meeting of the Rostock NVA Veterans Group. When we arrived, there was an electric atmosphere in the meeting hall, which was large, airy, and well lit. It was at this meeting, held in March 2000, that tensions over the "status question," the symbolic coding of NVA officers as "non-German," and the view of the Ministry of Defense of NVA officers as "foreign veterans" finally boiled over into a public expression of discontent, anger, and frustration.

The meeting was well organized, and the *Kameraschaft* was well connected to the local press, who was present in force, interviewing officers and taking photos. I was interviewed by a reporter from the *Ostsee Zeitung*, which ran an article about my research titled "Former U.S. Sergeant Examines the Feelings of NVA Officers."[15]

At least three hundred officers and their families were in attendance, and a small band played traditional German military marches to rev up the crowd. As the band pointedly played "Ich hatt' einen Kameraden" (I Had a Comrade), a traditional German military song, Gerd Richter, the chairman of the Rostock veterans, took the podium. He stood at the podium for a moment while the crowd slowly calmed down. Reading from an open letter he had written that was to be sent to the West German colonel in charge of the Bundeswehrverband, Richter read in a loud, clear voice:

We want to underline the fact that no one is above or outside the current laws, and German law applies to every German with equal force concerning content and applicability.

We demand the same for ourselves. We are concerned about equality and our equal treatment as German soldiers. We are concerned with the continued project of the internal unity of our German people.

There has to be a stop to the banning of parts of our biographies from the life of our people. No politician will be able to reach our heads or our hearts if, for purely political reasons, he does not recognize us as German soldiers with the same equality as soldiers of the current German army.

Political opportunism is damaging German unity, and we are no longer willing, ten years after the unification of both German states and its people, to put up with discrimination, belittlement, insults, and the limiting of our legal rights.

We declare our strong resistance to these actions. We want the unity of our people, but with legal equality as Germans among Germans. We call for the state to recognize us as German soldiers. In our opinion, it makes no sense that our fathers and grandfathers, who, in the service of a German government that exploited their oath as soldiers, used them to overrun peoples and states, kill or injure people, and destroy property, may call themselves German soldiers, use their ranks and wear their medals and awards. And they are allowed to sit next to us in this organization as German soldiers, while we, German soldiers as well, who never attacked other peoples or countries, are officially denied the right to call ourselves German soldiers.

It is incomprehensible to us that the German government and the Bundeswehr accept soldiers of the Polish, Czech, and Hungarian armies as equals, with their ranks, military diplomas, and state awards, while we, who served and carried out military duties with these same soldiers for decades, went to the same military academies, and in some cases, received the same awards on the same day, are denied this respect as Germans from Germans. This goes against all logic.

We are Germans according to birth, ethnicity, and fatherland. It was not us, but rather, our fathers and grandfathers who led us into wars that were lost. In the end, it was they who gave the victors the possibility to divide our country, which allowed for the political developments in the two halves of Germany.

The East German state was either our place of birth or our new home. We could not choose another one, we belonged to it. Seventeen million Germans could not leave it. The other German state would not have been able to survive it, and German land would have been given up.

We remained true to our homeland; served this separate German state and protected it.

We protected the path of our people. We served the will of our people and the laws of the last freely elected government of the German Democratic Republic, up until the peacefully accomplished unification of the Germans. Without a military revolt.

We were German soldiers aware of our duty, and always acted in the interests of our people, never against it. We performed our military service honorably and with a sense of duty, and we were honored for our service, as is common in all armies on earth. That was our life as German soldiers.[16]

There was a slight pause when Richter finished, as the officers took in what he said. Suddenly, the electric arc of the moment broke, and the officers and their families and friends erupted in cheers and applause that went on for a few minutes, changing from applause to rhythmic clapping. Officers near Richter slapped him on the back, shook his hand, and some hugged him. Officers around me smiled, laughed, shook hands, and shook their heads in delight and disbelief. It was an astonishing sight: officers who generally maintained a very cool, calm, "military" demeanor suddenly cheering and hollering, showing their emotions and letting out the pent-up frustration of the ten years since unification. The officers around me were animated; one said, "Richter got it just right tonight! He said everything that needed to be said in public for all to hear. Now they'll have to listen to us and take us into account!" A former People's Navy officer sitting next to me turned to me and said,

We're Germans, just like they are, and they have to treat us as Germans. We did our duty, we served our state, just like they did. They need to listen, and hopefully now they will. We're tired of being treated like we're second-class citizens because we were in the NVA. We're really sick of this, and we can't take much more of it. We've had all we can stand, and they'll have to listen to us after this. Did they think we would just sit by and take this?

Throughout the speech, and throughout my fieldwork, former officers stated that they wanted to be treated as "Germans among Germans," as equal citizens, and as equally recognized and valued soldiers. This was a call for inclusion; they demanded full acceptance and treatment as German citizens. It was a moment—the only moment—where they openly showed a sense of hope for the future and for redress of their problems. They would share this privately, but I had never seen—and never saw again—such an open display of hope, a collective optimism that, finally, they might get what they want.

But their hopes were short-lived. Richter's letter was forwarded to the Bundeswehrverband, and then sent along to the colonel in charge. There was no reply.

KOSOVO: PROTESTING GERMAN INTERVENTION, AND PROTESTING THE PAST

During the course of my fieldwork, a serious crisis threatened the East German membership of the Bundeswehrverband, and made them question unification and the past: the war in Kosovo. Over three thousand former NVA officers withdrew from the association, citing as their reason their disapproval (to put it mildly) of the NATO "aggression" against Serbia and the participation of the Bundeswehr in the war. The general sentiment among officers was that they had no desire to be members of an organization that supported an army that attacked what they saw as an "innocent" country. This sparked an intense debate within the *Kameradschaften*: one could withdraw in protest, but if one did, that removed yet another voice from the strength of former NVA officers in the Bundeswehrverband to argue and fight for their rights. Rainer Wulf, lobbying continuously for members to stay in the organization despite their opposition to the war, told me:

If they start leaving now, then we lose strength and power in the organization; they need to realize that the only power you have in a democracy is your voice. This is the one small amount of power that we have, and we can't lose it. We need our members to stay in the Bundeswehrverband, and not resign. They have to understand that we need everyone—we can't afford to lose anyone. You can't just walk away if you're unhappy or angry. Many haven't learned that yet.

The war in Kosovo was a severe test for NVA officers in the Bundeswehrverband. For many, it was proof that the Bundeswehr was in fact an aggressive army—like the Wehrmacht—and that the NVA was the real "army of peace" among German militaries. Officers saw the war as a confirmation of their identities and their views of history and the Cold War, as well as a slap in the face in terms of their treatment after unification. They were officers of an army that never attacked another country, yet they were penalized as if they were a criminal army, while the Bundeswehr was taking part in NATO's attack against Serbia. While they had trained repeatedly and extensively for offensive operations, NVA officers were unwavering in their conviction that they had served an army that had helped maintain peace and security in Europe during the Cold War, and had thwarted Western aggression against the GDR and socialism in general because of their service.

As news reports poured in about NATO's bombing campaign against Serbia and Serbian troops in and around Kosovo, outrage and frustration among NVA officers grew. They simply could not accept that Germany was taking part in an attack on a country that many felt had been one of their allies, and they felt frustrated that there was little they could do to stop the fighting and protest Germany's aggression. Letters were written, talks were organized, and almost a quarter of the NVA membership of the Bundeswehrverband renounced their membership. During a particularly heated discussion about the war, Andreas made his position clear:

This is what we always said: the Bundeswehr is just a carry over of the Wehrmacht. And here you see it—they're attacking Serbia again. It's a pure act of aggression and expansion—NATO is attempting to extend itself into the Balkans, and take advantage of the crisis there for its own uses, and as a way to justify itself. This kind of thing could never have happened when the Warsaw Pact was still around, and the NVA still existed. And now look—we're gone, and NATO and the Bundeswehr move in. This is an outrage, it's a war crime, and there should be consequences. We get called criminals, but we didn't attack anyone. I've had enough of this, and I don't want to be part of an organization that supports the Bundeswehr and its war of aggression.

Andreas, like many other NVA officers outraged by the war, resigned from the Bundeswehrverband in protest, and ceased attending veteran group meetings.

The Bundeswehr's participation in the war in Kosovo was seen by some officers as a way to prove that they were in fact the better, more honorable, and ethical German soldiers, members of a German military that did not start or fight in a war, and were therefore not tainted with killing, death, and destruction. While deeply disturbed by the war, some officers also saw it as an opportunity to prove by deed and action that they were the better soldiers and men. Gustav was very concerned about the war, and very upset by the Bundeswehr's deployment to the Balkans. While talking at his house one day, he took a sip of coffee, paused, and then said to me:

You know, I have a plan. We still have our uniforms and our gear—they're in our homes, and we kept as much as we could. It's all hanging up in our closets, ready to go if we need it. I've been thinking about this—I'm sure I could get five to six thousand *Kameraden* from the [veterans] groups together, organize them, get them back in their uniforms and ready to go. We would then march to Kosovo—unarmed—and stand between NATO and the Serbs, and stop this stupid war. We always were an army of peace, you know.

COLD WAR PASTS AND PRESENTS:
AN "AMERICAN BOMBER PILOT" AND THE NVA

Herr Wulf picked me up one evening, and we drove to a meeting of a veterans group in Berlin. As we rode along in the car, talking about the upcoming meeting, Herr Wulf immediately told me about his problems and concerns with this particular group:

"I'm always at war with this group—they're a real thorn in my side. I really don't like how they manage themselves, or how they manage the past."

"What do you mean by 'manage the past?'" I asked him.

"They're slowly coming around to my point of view, but it's taken a lot of work to get them there. It really makes me angry that they can't at least say, 'We're sorry for what happened at the Berlin Wall,' and at least show some remorse."

We were winding along the back streets in the eastern section of the city; Wulf was staring intently, gripping the steering wheel tightly.

All they have to say is yes, we were part of the structure, we were wrapped up in it, and we couldn't see out of it. They just have to say that they didn't know any better, and that what they thought they were doing was right and correct. And now, ten years later, they just need to say that they're sorry, and that they made a mistake. Of course, they don't have to say that everything about the past is wrong, or that everything they did in their pasts is wrong, but they really need to say they are sorry for all of the deaths that occurred along the Wall.

As we pulled up in front of the meeting hall, Wulf looked at me and added,

I know now. I didn't then, but now I do. I'm glad to finally know about how wrong the Wall was, and I'm glad the rest of the world is finally finding out everything that happened. One day, the world will realize this about the United States–Mexico border as well.[17]

At this particular meeting, Herr Wulf used me as a way to chastise the members of the *Kameradschaft*. He wanted to encourage them to act as better "citizens" and to move away from any sort of glorification of their pasts or any tendency toward *Ostalgie* (nostalgia for the former East Germany, which plays on the German word for east, *Ost*). He also wanted them to move away from "Cold War" thinking about the "enemy" and the "hate training" (*Hasserziehung*) they had received—and taught—in the GDR and the NVA.

Herr Wulf told them the story of what happened when I tried to set up an interview with a former officer in Oranienburg, a city directly north of Berlin. The officer initially had agreed to speak with me, but when the war in Kosovo began, he let it be known through a third party that he had no desire to speak to an "American bomber pilot." This, along with "American air pirates," was a common phrase used by the SED and the NVA during the Cold War to imply that all American soldiers were war criminals because of the bombing of Dresden and other cities near the end of World War II. Unlike *Der Klassenfeind*, there was no irony or humor in this phrase. I was later told that the real reason he decided not to talk to me was because he was a former STASI informant in the NVA, and was afraid that I might ask him about his activities (his fears were unfounded, for I had made it very clear at the beginning of my work with former officers that I would not ask them any questions regarding the STASI, nor any personal participation as an informant). Rather than simply saying no, he decided to use me as a way to protest the war and reiterate that the NVA had been right all along about the U.S. military, NATO, and the Bundeswehr.

Herr Wulf reiterated this story to the members of the *Kameradschaft*, and then said to them: "If this is all we are capable of, if we can only live in fear of the past, and call our guest an 'American bomber pilot,' and still think in terms of the Cold War, then we have learned nothing. If all we can do is glorify the past, and not think critically about it and our roles in it—if this is all we can do, we can quit now."

The response of the officers took both of us by surprise. At this point, the room erupted in cheers and clapping, and many officers looked at me, smiled, and nodded. When the meeting was over, many came over to me, pressed business cards into my hand, and offered to be interviewed any time I wanted to speak with them. Wulf thought that the ice surrounding their conception of the past had finally broken up, and that they might actually talk now about their roles in the security structure of the GDR and the injustices of the border. When I asked him why he thought this happened, he said that my presence showed them that others were interested in their problems, and that at least one of their former "enemies" was willing to listen and talk with them, something West Germans in general or the Bundeswehr in particular had shown no interest in doing. Herr Wulf used this story again at other meetings, with much the same results.

"SALON SOLDIERS" AND THE CONFLICTED MEMORIES OF MILITARIZED MASCULINITY

Sitting with Max and Karl in Max's garden one afternoon, the topic turned to a comparison of the NVA and the Bundeswehr, including which military had the better soldiers. Max started to chuckle; then he said:

We never really feared them, no, but we did take them seriously, very seriously, in fact. Fear—fear is for cowards—so we didn't fear them. But we kept an eye on them, and we always stayed at a high level of alert and acted according to what we were told. We stayed alert, and concentrated on that a lot. We always had 85 percent of our soldiers in the barracks, ready to go in case war started. Our motto was "better two drops of sweat than one drop of blood," which meant that we trained and trained for war so that we would be ready. We found out after unification that the Bundeswehr never had that many soldiers on alert, and that they would often only have 5 percent of their soldiers ready during

Christmas. Our jaws dropped when we heard this. What kind of army was this? What were they doing? If we had wanted to attack the West, we could have done it over Christmas and been done with the whole thing in a matter of days.

Yes, believe me when I tell you that I was shocked. We believed that the Bundeswehr was an aggressive enemy, prepared and capable of attacking us at any minute and possibly defeating us. We really believed that during the Cold War. But since 1990, I've seen a lot, and I've been to training areas many times since then. I know where the best places to watch the exercises are here [he is referring to a former NVA training area where he was stationed, which is now used by the Bundeswehr]. They can post twenty guards there and I can still drive in undetected and look at everything. Naturally I covered up my license plate so that no one will know who I am if a guard comes along. I never would have suspected that none of what we believed then was true. This army is somehow nowhere near as battle-worthy as we were, and in my eyes really doesn't have much combat strength.

Karl, who had been looking at the ground and slowly playing with a blade of grass while Max spoke, cut in at this point:

You know, we were lied to about the Bundeswehr. Now that we've had a chance to get to know them, and see how they train, what they think, how they act like soldiers, we aren't impressed. They're nowhere near as strong as we were led to believe. Of course, Max is right, we took them seriously, but we never knew what would happen then, so we had to take them seriously. But now we're in the Bundeswehrverband and can see them close up, and see what they're like. Well, they just don't seem that tough at all. They're more like "salon soldiers" who like to play war than real soldiers who train for war. It does make us think and ask ourselves, how in the hell did these guys beat us? They would never have beaten us on the battlefield, that's for sure.

Staring at me for a moment, Max added:

We weren't sure what to think of you Americans, either. We definitely thought you were better than the Bundeswehr, that's a fact, but we weren't sure what you'd do on the battlefield. We studied Vietnam very closely, and had an idea of how you fought. We knew you had a lot of technology that we didn't have—I saw training films of your depleted uranium rounds, and what they could do to a tank. They were like mininuclear weapons, and we were afraid to show the films to our soldiers because we didn't want to demoralize them. We thought technology was just an example of American cowardice—you used technology for things we would have used men for.

Conceptions of masculinity and technology came up during a discussion with Stefan, the NVA soldier quoted earlier about his experiences in high school. Kerstin, his girlfriend, who was with him during a later discussion, said that she knew all of this from the NVA side. Her father had been an officer in the NVA, and she was raised in an NVA officer community:

My father . . . hadn't been in [the NVA] for long, and he told us that everyone in it was convinced that the NVA would win in a war. We may not have had this technical know-how, but he said they would survive an initial attack, and that we would all stick together, and that the people would stand up and support the NVA, and things like that. We talked about this all of the time. No one doubted this; even when I was a kid I never doubted it. This is how I grew up, and for me the NVA was the greatest thing in the world and was always the best. They may not have had the best technology, but they would have made it through the initial nuclear attack and have won. At least that was always what was said. They were all convinced of this, and it was exactly this conviction that gave them strength. They thought their willpower and belief would allow them to win.

NVA officers believed—like officers of all militaries have to believe in order for militarization to work—that they were superior to soldiers of the West, and in particular, the Bundeswehr. Like all soldiers in all militaries, they had to believe that they were the better, stronger, smarter, braver soldiers. What they might have lacked in technology and advanced weaponry, they made up for through sheer force of will and conviction, a belief that they would prevail, and through "will," were invincible.[18] This sort of thinking is what keeps a military functioning; "will" is a kind of ideological and psychological armor deployed by the state through militarization programs and training that allows soldiers to believe that they will live up to the state's and military's expectations of them as men and soldiers, and actually defeat the enemy and live to talk about their exploits.

Participation in the *Kameradschaften* provides former officers with the chance to contend with Bundeswehr soldiers (as well as NATO and American soldiers); the *Kameradschaften* act as both "sites of militarized masculinity" and "sites of memory." It was at these meetings that former officers could come together with those who had similar experiences (both before and after unification) and similar biographies in order to rethink and relive their pasts, make sense of the present, and think about their futures. As sites of militarized masculinity, meetings allowed them a chance to become, at least for an evening, that which they had been. Although all of the former officers were no longer in the military, military hierarchy still had precedence; higher-ranking members were deferred to and shown respect, proper titles and ranks were used, and everyone seemed to know everyone else's biography and accomplishments. Officers would discuss their training and experiences in the NVA, military history and tactics, and offer their opinions on current global military issues.

Veterans groups are sites of a bitter "coming to terms with the past" as well. Once NVA officers had the chance to "get to know" the Bundeswehr, they had very little respect for it as an army, its soldiers as soldiers, or its officers as officers. They felt betrayed by what they saw as the "weakness" of the Bundeswehr, and there was a feeling of indignation that they were "defeated" by "salon soldiers," the sorts of men Horst's father said would be "serving coffee to old ladies" during wartime. In many ways, this made unification even more painful for them; they felt like they had been defeated by an army that was both militarily and morally inferior to them, by soldiers who were nowhere near as skilled as they were. They felt that they had been beaten by weaklings and cowards.

By taking part in veterans groups meetings, former officers attempt to reinsert themselves into German military history, and into the new social system in general: they were soldiers, and now, as members of a state-sanctioned veterans group for soldiers, they are German soldiers once again, good soldiers and good comrades. By inserting themselves into "positive" history, they are attempting to enter the narrative of the state as equal soldiers and equal citizens. In a somewhat contradictory process, the German government and military have attempted to strip them of their distinction as "German soldiers," yet, by virtue of taking part in these meetings, they are, at least unofficially, recognized as German soldiers. From the point of view of NVA officers, that is the problem: it is unofficial. They demand to be officially recognized as both Germans and soldiers, and as German soldiers who did not start or fight in a war. They want to be recognized as good men, unlike their fathers and grand fathers and other male relatives who fought for an illegal German government. They want to be seen as good men vis-à-vis the Bundeswehr, which they view as a continuation of the fascist military of their fathers and grandfathers, and which the war in Kosovo "proved" to them to be true. Veterans groups are not only sites of memory and performance, but militarized masculinity as well; they can show Germany that they are indeed good, proper men, and perhaps the best German men and soldiers.

While the Bundeswehrverband provides NVA officers a forum to air their concerns, I see it as something else: it allows these officers to come together in order to further marginalize them. Meetings of former NVA officers are exactly that—get-togethers for members of the NVA. These officers are viewed as *still* the NVA: still unreformed communists, still hard-liners, still officers caught up in an NVA "mindset" who think of themselves not as citizens of the new, unified Germany but as NVA officers. Their arguments and opinions are seen as simply a continuation of official GDR antifascism and propaganda.[19] They are seen as merely parroting what they were taught to say and believe because that is all they know how to do.

THE END OF THE NVA REDUX

In 2006, Rainer Wulf seemed defeated—something I had not seen in him in 2000 or 2003. We talked about the future of Landesverband Ost and NVA officers in the veterans groups:

It's really only a matter of time before the NVA is gone from the association. And as you know, there are no replacements; when we're gone, that's it, there'll be no more NVA. I think they'll wait until there are about five thousand or so of us left (in the association), and that's when they'll close down the Landesverband Ost. Once they close it, the only official pipeline and connection we have to the government will be gone, and we will really be on our own. It's hard to think of it being all gone, but that's what will happen. We've worked hard for this—I've worked hard for this—but it's just a matter of time now.

According to the new deputy-director of the Landesverband Ost, as of 2006, the outlook for the NVA veterans groups and the continued presence of the NVA in the association was grim. Given that the NVA no longer exists, there are no new NVA officers or soldiers to join the groups and replenish membership. As of 2006, there were approximately nine thousand NVA officers in the Landesverband Ost, representing a 25 percent drop since 2000. A combination of death, discouragement, disinterest, the deployment of the Bundeswehr outside of Germany, and disgust at the policies of the Bundeswehr and the federal government has depleted the number of NVA officers in the Landesverband Ost. Their numbers have been consistently dropping, and will continue to drop. There is also growing annoyance with the political activities of former NVA officers and the publications of the Working Group for the History of the NVA, which challenge the Bundeswehr's narrative of the Army of Unity and unification. The Landesverband Ost is seen as a financial burden as the budget of the Bundeswehrverband tightens; even though it has the lowest membership, it still receives an equal amount of funding from the Bundeswehrverband, funding that is increasingly called into question because it goes to NVA veterans groups. In many ways, time seems to be running out for the NVA in the Bundeswehrverband, and for the tenuous threads of political representation open to them.

PERFORMING THE PAST TO RESIST THE PRESENT

Militarization, masculinity, and memory: these three concepts, interrelated, play a major role in the lives of former officers. Simply put, each informs and shapes the other, and none is possible without the other. Fluid, these three concepts form the basis for these men's lives, defining who they are, who they were, and who they will be in a future that will call upon the past to make its own present. In a sense, former NVA officers are "prisoners" of memory and history: militarization policies are always predicated upon both the memory of a past war (those who took part in it, experienced it, and how it is "officially" remembered), and the history of a past conflict (who was involved, how that past is written versus oral history and memory; who is writing the history, and whose history is written).

Masculinity as a "discourse," not just simply a lived identity, is dependent on militarization and memory: ways of being a "proper" man, a "good" man, a "good" soldier all stem from the ways in which masculinity is portrayed, codified, desired, and designed. This includes a temporal dimension as well: ways of being in the past impact the present, ways of being in a utopic future impact the present; in a sense, the present is never really "present" except when measured against a past and future. But this is in no way a neutral process, one devoid of intentionality or political agendas; all of these "ways of being" are motivated politically and economically, designed to uphold or further certain ends and projects. It became clear that while masculinity is an important "thing" to study, it cannot be studied in isolation. "Masculinity" in and of itself does not really tell us much. To look at it in isolation only replicates essentialist notions of identity, as if "masculinity" were the starting point, rather than perhaps, to paraphrase Foucault, an "effect."[20] And sometimes, masculinity is not the operative category in play; it may inform a dynamic or situation, but it might not be the most important aspect. A performance may be about something other than gender: a performance of a certain type of history, state identity, opposition, and/or resistance.

The former colonel's actions at the special meeting of the Bundeswehrverband that I described at the beginning of this chapter were not simply a performance of individual identity, but an act of memory: not just the memory of how to act like a man, but the memory of a society, of collective experience, of what it meant to be a proper soldier. It was not simply a gender performance, but a nation-state performance, an enactment of a complex set of signs symbolizing proper ways of being a soldier. It was an act of nostalgia for his past as an officer and for the contexts which allowed him to be recognized as a soldier, a man, as well as a German: the NVA, the GDR, a military base, friends who recognized him as such, and the enemy.

While this may be read as an act of resistance, it was also an act of attempted inclusion: he was attempting to show that he was still a German soldier, part of the German military tradition. By acting like a German soldier and an NVA officer, he challenged the portrayal of the Bundeswehr as an "Army of Unity." Acting like an NVA officer among Bundeswehr soldiers highlighted his absence of identity and called into question the claim of the Bundeswehr to be the legitimate and sole heir of German military tradition. However, by highlighting this absence, his performance overran itself: he became a parody, demonstrating to the Bundeswehr soldiers present that NVA soldiers were "militaristic," not savvy or aware of proper behavior. It confirmed the Bundeswehr officers' suspicion that NVA officers are truly stuck in a different time.

The colonel's performance was done in a space where it would be conspicuous: in a crowd of Bundeswehr officers. It was transgressive because it was "out of place" and designed to mock the West German officers. But it was also an act of resistance and the acknowledgment of his past and that of other NVA officers. While the German government may deny these officers symbolic rights, penalize them financially, and try to strike them from German military tradition and "Germanness," the colonel's performance illustrated what a former political officer said to me: "We're still here."

CHAPTER 8

"We're the Jews of the New Germany"

HEROIC VICTIMHOOD, FALLEN ELITES,
AND THE SLIPPERINESS OF HISTORY AND MEMORY

They want us to simply die and go away fast, and they're
doing all that they can to make sure we do just that.

MICHAEL,

former NVA Colonel, commenting on the Bundeswehr's
policies concerning NVA officers

WHILE GERMAN UNIFICATION can tell us a lot about how a state
sees, codifies, represents, and deals with its own soldiers and with former soldiers of a failed state, it also shows us how the soldiers of a failed
state—the fallen elites of the failed state—see, codify, represent, and
come to terms with their situations and with the policies and practices
of "victory." After unification, many NVA officers felt lost, trapped between the state that had been and the state that was coming in to being.
Having lost the state they had sworn to serve, they were unsure of what
to make of the new state and their loss of power and prestige. They were
also confronted with the fact that they would no longer be able to earn
an income as soldiers, having to rely on the market to find jobs and make
a living. Unable to find jobs, marginalized by the Bundeswehr, many officers had a hard time coming to terms with their lives in the new state,
and began to formulate their own analyses and perceptions of unification.

The responses of NVA officers to unification have been many and
varied, but the policies enacted by the Bundeswehr more often than not
resulted in marginalization, anomie, and the officers' feeling that they
did not fit or belong in the new state, even as they tried to come to terms
with it in veterans group meetings. While the veterans groups provide
NVA officers with the possibility of recognition, resistance, and a political

response to their problems, in practice, many NVA officers have grown increasingly frustrated with the Bundeswehr and the veterans groups; they have developed perceptions of unification and their treatment that reflect their sense of disenfranchisement and anomie. Detlef, a former NVA motorized infantry officer, summed up the experiences and concerns of NVA officers in the new state, and the overwhelming feeling of being both out of time and out of place:

When unification came, and I received my notice that I wouldn't be able to stay in the military—the Bundeswehr wouldn't have me because I was a lieutenant-colonel, and therefore tainted by communism—I didn't know what to do with my life. My life had been the military, had been the NVA, had been very long days on the base, away from my family, training, always on alert, training. It was really all I knew. What else was I supposed to do? I was no longer allowed to use my rank, and I wasn't even considered a "German soldier" any longer because of the *Gediente in fremden Streitkräften* [member of a foreign military] designation we all received for being in the NVA. And what I really can't understand is that Wehrmacht and SS officers are entitled to state burials because they fought for the fascists, but we're not entitled to anything because we were antifascists. It was really hard to find a job—I still haven't—and my pension had been cut as a way to punish me and all NVA officers for having served our state. I had a few friends who had been allowed to join the Bundeswehr, but they weren't sure how it was going to go—can you imagine joining the army you had been trained to fight? It's been OK for them, though they've had a lot of problems in the Bundeswehr as well. Bundeswehr officers—West Germans—look down upon them as "stupid" or as communists who can't be trusted. I miss the military, but when I hear about these sorts of things, I'm sometimes glad I'm no longer a part of it. But I do miss it. It's who I was. I don't feel a part of this state, and I feel like the state doesn't want me to be a part of it. I'm an outsider here. I'm a German citizen and an outsider.

The policies and practices employed by the Bundeswehr after unification have led some NVA officers to move toward extreme positions of memory and understanding, toward the use of forms of historical memory and personal narratives that in many ways skew the past to help them make sense of their present. While many officers try to come to terms with unification in the veterans groups, a fair number of NVA officers take a very hard line against the Bundeswehr and unification. And as they try to come to terms publically with unification, in private, many officers are driven into a dream world of revisionist history, prosthetic memories, and heroic victimhood. In turn, these private conceptions influence their public personas and actions, turning them into the stereotypes deployed by the Bundeswehr. In essence, the practices and forms of resistance employed by NVA officers are an attempt to maintain their identities and their place in the new state and history, as well as to maintain their sense of self in the face of policies which they think are intended to make them disappear, figuratively and literally. As their conceptions of history and memory take often disturbing and troubling turns, these conceptions allow us a chance to see how fallen elites conceptualize and understand their personal histories and the policies and events that resulted in their fall.

Just as the German government and military conflate the dictatorships of the Third Reich and the GDR, so too do some NVA officers conflate the German government and the expansionism, policies, and atrocities of the Third Reich and World War II. Although Richter's speech to the *Kameradschaft* in Rostock can be seen as an official demand for inclusion—as well as a public, political statement of disillusionment and resistance—some NVA officers expressed their frustration and alienation through a disturbing and troubling form of historical memory. The strongest expression of disenchantment and alienation by former officers constructs their experiences as victims not only of post-unification politics, but of the Third Reich as well. Through the use and deployment of Holocaust memories as well as those of German military atrocities, some NVA officers place their experiences after unification squarely within a framework in which the Third Reich, the World War II German military, West Germany, and the postwar Bundeswehr, are conflated, made to blend seamlessly into one another. For many NVA officers, the logic of the new, unified state is the logic of the concentration camp.

THE BIOPOLITICS OF UNIFICATION: "WE'RE THE JEWS OF THE NEW GERMANY"

One afternoon, after about a year of fieldwork, the unexpected happened. Over cigarettes and beers with a group of officers from the local

Kameradschaft at a bar in Hohenschönhausen, a working-class district in eastern Berlin where a large number of former officers live, Uwe, who ended his career in the NVA as a motorized infantry lieutenant-colonel, looked around, and in somewhat hushed tones stated: "We've had ten years of abuse and belittlement at the hands of the government; we can't use our ranks, they've taken our careers and our pensions from us, and we can't get jobs. I tell you—we're the Jews of the new Germany." The other officers nodded in agreement, looking both defiant and sheepish as they shifted their eyes from me to Uwe and to the other patrons of the bar. They seemed to know they were crossing a line, but they also felt that a line had been crossed in their treatment after unification.

This was perhaps the most difficult moment of my work with former officers up to that point. It was a turning point, in the sense that they trusted me enough to say something like this in my presence, and it provided a completely new insight into their view of life after unification and how they saw the past—or multiple pasts wrapped into one bitter present. As Uwe told me how he—and many officers—felt about their experiences of unification and their perception of the policies in place, I bit the sides of my mouth to keep from saying how I felt: outrage and anger at what to me was an offensive claim and a complete distortion of history. I wanted to ask him if he understood the irony of a German officer—even if from an antifascist military—claiming that he and the other officers of the NVA were the "new Jews of Germany."

Instead, I said nothing. Had I expressed my anger, it would have closed off the opening Uwe had created, the "breakthrough" moment all anthropologists hope for while conducting fieldwork, the insight into how people really see and think about their situations, lives, history, memory, and the world. I listened, downed my beer, ordered another, and waited for more talk, as the floodgates seemed to have opened. Uwe continued:

Think about it, think about it, and think about the similarities between the policies and what the government is doing to us, and what the Nazis did to the Jews. Really, it's all very similar to what happened then. We're not allowed to work in our professions, as officers in the military—we're not soldiers anymore—and we have to identify ourselves as something other than a German officer by using "NVA" after our ranks. We're treated as second-class citizens, they cut our pensions so that we can barely live, and we're not even German anymore because we are "members of a foreign military." To me, the parallels are clear.

Again, the other officers nodded in agreement, and Jürgen, who had been fairly quiet throughout the discussion, added:

There's another similarity, and something that really frightens me. We keep fighting to be recognized and accepted as full citizens and as full soldiers— that's why we're in the Bundeswehrverband, among other reasons. And all the government and the Bundeswehr do is say, "We're working on it," or, "It doesn't matter." What they're doing is stalling, and simply waiting for us to die. They're doing to us what they did to the Jews, only this time the Final Solution [Endlösung] is a Biological Solution [biologische Lösung]. Really, what they all want us to do is disappear and be gone. They just want us to die out and want to make sure that we die out.

As they spoke, they shifted in their chairs, fidgeted, played with their beers and cigarettes, and seemed to draw energy from one another as they let out their frustrations and anger. While the other officers spoke, Berthold, rocking back and forth in his seat, looked down at the table. Speaking in a sort of agitated, rasping whisper, he kept saying, "They just want to be rid of us, they just want to be rid of us, they just want us to go away."

THE ARMY THAT DISAPPEARED—OR DIDN'T

The erasure of the GDR and East German identity extended to the military as well, becoming in many ways a directed policy project of the Bundeswehr. In practice, it was a form of "productive erasure"—an erasure that, in a sense, retained the signifier but switched the signified as needed. The new German state and Bundeswehr went to great lengths to delegitimate the NVA and deny it any possible "positive" role in German military identity or tradition. Echoing the comments about their loss of identity as East Germans, NVA officers feel that their situations are "doubly" troubling in the sense that their identities as East Germans are both erased and highlighted because of their service in the NVA; political expediency in the new Germany determines which they are—erased or highlighted—at a given moment.

NVA officers are particularly sensitive about what they see as efforts to "make them disappear"; while they have not been "disappeared" physically, many officers felt that they are victims of the symbolic equivalent. Gerd, a former political officer, became very agitated when I asked him about a documentary that had been made about the NVA after unification, called *Die verschwundende Armee* (The Army That Disappeared). Sitting in his apartment, Gerd took a deep breath, and looked around at the NVA memorabilia that decorated his living room. He paused for a moment, and then, looking directly at me, he slammed his fist on the table, upsetting the coffee cups and water glasses. He shouted: "We're STILL here: the NVA has NOT disappeared." Hartmut, while equally disturbed by what he felt to be a loss of his identity as an NVA officer, seemed in many ways to have taken on and internalized his new "anti-identity" as a former NVA officer in the new state:

The NVA was my life. I spent twenty-five years as an officer, and felt like the DDR and the NVA were in my blood. Now, I don't regret those twenty-five years, but I'm not sure what to make of it. Deep down, I'm still an NVA officer—I always will be. But now, there's no recognition, other than we were an "illegal" army, an army that was totalitarian, like the Wehrmacht, only interested in fighting and dominating our people. I'm here, but not here, if you understand my meaning.

Feeling that they were now "out of time," linked to the totalitarian German past and dismayed that they were seen and portrayed as "militarists," many officers feel that they were being blamed for all that was wrong with the Cold War division of Germany. In 2000, Frank, a former NVA infantry colonel had this interpretation of what he saw as the misrepresentation of the GDR and the NVA:

The West Germans think they won the Cold War. Maybe they did. They think they're the victors, and can write history as they like. By focusing on everything that was wrong with the GDR, by saying it was a dictatorship, and that the

NVA was a "party army" that supported a dictatorship, the West Germans can easily shift all of the blame to us, and draw attention away from all of the problems they've caused with unification, like right-wing radicalism and unemployment. Unification hasn't gone well, but it is easier simply to blame us for the past, and blame us for the present.

Peter, a former artillery officer, expressed the combination of bitterness, resentment, and anger about unification that was common among former officers. His bitterness about unification and the fate of the NVA was equal to the pride he felt about serving in the NVA and his life in the GDR. His home was in many ways a minishrine to the memory of the NVA. He and his wife still lived in an apartment near his former base; in the living room, the white alarm box for alerts was still on the wall, a reminder of the time when at the push of a button, the NVA base commander could signal an alert, requiring all officers to be in uniform, on base, and at their battle stations. I had the distinct impression that Peter still hoped it would go off again one day: an alarm that would fill the void of civilian life and make him whole again.

Peter's home was decorated with a number of small statues and commemorative plates of the Prussian king Frederick the Great (1712–86), the man responsible for setting the stage for the later model of German military prowess and military culture. After sitting down and engaging in small talk about how I liked Berlin, I ate *Eierkuchen* [German pancakes] with Peter and his wife at their home, while Peter talked about how West Germans have been able to move in and make millions or billions of marks in the East. He said that a common theme heard from West Germans is, "What have you East Germans done to deserve better treatment?" His answer, he said, was "simply forty years of my biography and our work in the GDR, for which we now receive nothing—East Germans cannot realize the fruits of their own labor." The West Germans, Peter said, are able to make money on the reconstruction and work that was done by East Germans while at the same time belittling East Germans for being lazy. Both he and his wife mentioned that the Bundeswehr and the police were able to take over brand new NVA and People's Police buildings and barracks without having to pay for them, and that West Germans were able to get a lot of other free things from the GDR. I asked him if he thought that unification was in fact more like colonization, and if so, what he thought of "West German colonization," a phrase I heard from a number of officers:

I don't want to say this too harshly, but East Germans are now the "white nig-gers" [Weisse Neger] of Germany. I'm embarrassed to say this, but there's a lot behind it—it is colonialism by the West Germans, just like other countries colo-nized by the West in general, and I'm saying this as a way to express solidarity with those people and show what's been going on here with unification. It's in the way they think about us. For example, Bundeswehr soldiers sent to the GDR to help dissolve the NVA before unification were given *Buschgeld* [bush money] because they were being sent into the wild, unknown bush country of the dark and dangerous East, just like the colonizers sent to conquer and plunder Africa. That's really all we are to them.

As he said this, he laughed a laugh of disgust and defiance. His wife sim-ply sat still and stirred her coffee, and said nothing.

THE SECRET MUSEUM

To counter the sense that they were being "disappeared," some officers took steps to insure that the NVA would remain, even if clandestinely, or in ways not necessarily open or accessible to the public. After uni-fication, Eduard, a career air defense officer, seemed to have made an easy transition into the new system. Despite his seemingly wholehearted embrace of capitalism and apparent distancing from his NVA past, Edu-ard maintained a "secret" museum dedicated to the NVA and its tradi-tions. Located in an outbuilding on the property he owned, the museum was known only within former NVA circles, and could only be visited with an invitation from Eduard. Inside was a "treasure trove" of NVA memorabilia: the limousines that carried the minister of defense and his deputy while they reviewed the troops, ceremonial swords and daggers, and the uniforms of the minister of defense and the chief of staff of the NVA. Perhaps the most striking and somehow most quixotic of dis-plays were the more than two thousand tin soldiers perfectly arranged to represent an NVA parade. All of the various military branches were painted accurately, and the spacing between soldiers had been calculated to represent that of real life. All of the key players in the parade were painted and represented. The entire "parade" stretched over nine feet along one of the side walls of the museum. "I'm only waiting for the navy to be finished, and it will be perfect," Eduard told me with a large, proud smile on his face.

Stepping into this museum felt like stepping back into an idealized version of the NVA; it was, in a very real way, an attempt to (re-)create the "tradition" and memory of the NVA.[1] Within the museum, tables and a bar were set up in order to celebrate holidays, anniversaries, and special occasions. Unlike the meetings at veterans groups, I had the feeling that the museum did not serve as a critical space, or place in which to help integrate them into post-unification society; it was a place that celebrated a certain mythologized past, and was far removed from the problems and "null-time" of the present. In many ways, it was a theater space.

As we left, Hartmut, who had come along to the museum as well, commented to me that he disliked such attempts to glorify and mythologize the NVA. He did not feel that it was productive in any way, that it only served to heighten the sense that former NVA officers were "crazy" or indeed "militarists." He said that a large number of officers shared his opinion. A few months later, I was told that Eduard had been part of a group that celebrated the birthday of another former officer at the museum. At the party, all of the officers arrived in their NVA dress uniforms and "pretended" that they were back in the GDR and the NVA. The other officers involved in the conversation shook their heads in apparent embarrassment, commenting that the "old hard-liners" were giving them a bad name. Despite this, they all seemed to respect Eduard for his success in business. Regardless of what they felt about him as a hard-liner, many officers were happy that he had set up the museum as a way to maintain the memory of the NVA, at least unofficially, and even if in ways that ran counter to inclusion in the state. The dress-up parties may have been an embarrassment, but it was still seen as a kind of opposition and resistance. While small and secret, at least there was a space where the NVA and its traditions lived on.

OVER THE WALL AND IN AND OUT OF THE COLD: COFFEE, CAKE, AND REVISIONIST HISTORY WITH THE RED GENERAL

Trials for crimes committed by the East German Border Guards along the Berlin Wall and the GDR-FRG border began in the mid-1990s. Both high- and low-ranking soldiers and officers were charged, and many were convicted of human rights abuses for the deaths and injuries they caused while preventing "illegal" border crossings. Though many understood the trials as a way of coming to terms with the abuses of the East German government in the West, many NVA officers saw the trials as yet another attempt to discredit the GDR, its leadership, and its military.

Klaus-Dieter Baumgarten was the highest-ranking Border Guard officer convicted, sentenced to six years in prison for his role in the deaths along the Wall and the border.[2] As the commanding general of the Border Guards and the deputy-minister of defense of the GDR, it was Baumgarten who reportedly signed the yearly *Schiessbefehl* (order to fire) on *Grenzgänger* (border crossers), people attempting to cross the border "illegally" from east to west.[3]

I had heard about his recent trial from a number of officers during meetings and interviews. By all accounts, his trial was angry and contentious. He was not about to accept his punishment or the perpetuation of the GDR's image as a totalitarian and oppressive state without a fight; to have done so would have been to condemn his own life and career. Baumgarten's sentence, in the eyes of many NVA officers, was a political act, an effort to punish the leadership of the NVA and the East German Communist Party. Despite what they saw as a "sham" trial with a predetermined outcome, many thought Baumgarten acquitted himself well. "General Baumgarten showed his worth and honor," Peter, a former Border Guard officer, told me. "When he told the court that they could do what they wanted to him, but that they should leave his soldiers alone since they were following his orders, he showed real soldierly virtue and self-sacrifice." His concern for his soldiers, Peter told me, showed that he was more honorable than the court officials, the Bundeswehr, or the new state. According to Dietmar, another NVA officer, "He sacrificed himself by looking after his troops at his own expense and future, and took the brunt of the punishment."

Because his wife was ill, the court allowed Baumgarten to return home three days a week. In many ways, his sentence was more symbolic than punitive. It was during one of these weekly breaks from prison that he agreed to meet with me. After Baumgarten picked me up at the S-Bahn station in Erkner, we sped off to his house. He took a circuitous route, seemingly to prevent me from knowing exactly where he lived (it worked—all I could tell was that we were in a typical Berlin suburb). Baumgarten ushered me into his home, which was full of fresh flowers. Unlike most of the officers' homes I had visited, there were no military objects or knickknacks; it was the most "unmilitary" space I had visited. It was a very bourgeois home, something I found somewhat unsettling, given his position and role in the East German military and security apparatus. Baumgarten had risen quickly through the ranks of the NVA and the Border Guards, eventually becoming both the commanding general of the Border Guards and a deputy-minister of defense. He had been a very powerful and feared man in the GDR, and was now, in his words, "serving prison time because of my political and military biography."

Baumgarten's wife had prepared lunch, and we sat down, ate, and drank a beer, moving on to coffee and strudel afterward, all the while talking about the NVA and unification, and about Baumgarten's life in the Border Guards. Baumgarten was extremely proud of his position and role in the GDR. He joined the early People's Police, switching later to the NVA and the Border Guards. While serving as a tank commander, the hatch of his tank had slammed down on his hands, severing the tips of both index fingers. His missing finger tips, plus the fact that he had been convicted of murder for the deaths on the border, lent him an air of menace as we talked about the experiences and treatment of former officers after unification. "The German Democratic Republic," Baumgarten said, "was the better German state, and the National People's Army the more honorable—actually, the most honorable—German military that has existed, but look how they treat us after unification. We never started a war or attacked another country. I'm proud of how the Border Guards acted during a potentially very dangerous situation when the Wall was stormed. They averted a war because they didn't fire. We should be treated differently because of this, but we're not."

As we talked, the conversation turned to his trial and the trials of other Border Guard officers and soldiers. Up to this point, Baumgarten had been unexpectedly friendly, charming, and charismatic, but the subject of the trial seemed to flip a switch in him. His tipless index finger waving in the air, Baumgarten's voice began to rise and sputter, as his face became increasingly flushed:

I've been sentenced to six years in prison for doing my duty and following the lawful and legal laws of the German Democratic Republic. I served my country and party loyally and honorably for thirty years, and always did my duty to the utmost of my abilities. Our laws were very clear. While I'm sorry for every death that occurred along the border, those people who tried to cross the border knew the laws, and knew they were breaking the law when they tried to cross illegally. They put us in a position to have to open fire to stop them—they knew what they were doing and they knew the laws. They made us fire; we are the victims here, not them. But now a number of us have to go to jail because we followed the law and were true to our state. It's pure injustice, but it's victors' justice—they think they can do what they want to us.

As I sat listening to Baumgarten defend his position and role in the GDR, raging against his trial and conviction and the people who broke the law and made him a victim, I felt myself sliding into a different time, Berlin in the 1980s, when the Wall and shoot-to-kill orders were very much a part of the everyday experience of the city.[4] For Baumgarten, the Cold War and its prerogatives were still very much alive. As he spoke, he seemed to be there.

Baumgarten then took a breath, composed himself, and became very serious. An air of proud defiance welled up in him:

The real reason—the real reason, no matter what they do or what they say— that they want to punish us is very simple: we prevented the capitalists in the West from making forty years of profit in the East, and they're angry about it, and they want to make sure that the NVA and the Border Guards pay dearly for this. We kept them out, we protected the state and made sure socialism had a chance without the interference of the fascists or industrialists. We kept them from making money, and they want revenge.

I've been sentenced to six years in prison for following legitimate orders and giving legitimate orders. Keep this in mind: I was a Red general. If they (the Bundeswehr) could have used the Wehrmacht's Commissar Order to simply march me out and shoot me, execution-style, they would have, believe me.

When he mentioned the Wehrmacht's Commissar Order (the order, issued to the Wehrmacht in 1941, to execute all Soviet commissars immediately upon capture), he began to shake with rage. For Baumgarten, as for the other officers, there was little difference between the Federal Republic and the Third Reich, or between the Bundeswehr and the Wehrmacht. He was a victim, he said, not only of West German justice, but of fascist justice as well. As a "Red general," Baumgarten believed he was targeted because he had served a system that opposed capitalism and the accumulation of capital. The only thing stopping them from executing him, he went on, was the fact that "the Allies still control the Federal Republic and its politicians and military leaders and keep their overt fascist tendencies in check." Otherwise, as a representative of communism, he would be dead. "They couldn't defeat us militarily, in a war, so they had to defeat us after the fact, "legally," when we were not able to fight back effectively in a system that we don't fully understand," Baumgarten said. At no point in the conversation did Baumgarten connect his trial and conviction to his role in the deaths along the border. He had followed orders and issued orders in accordance with GDR law, and was therefore not guilty of any wrongdoing. The real criminals were those who tried to cross the border, those who "made" the Border Guards apply deadly force.

The remainder of my meeting with General Baumgarten consisted in variations on a theme: he and other officers were victims of political repression, and had been punished simply to appease "human rights activists." They were targets in a witch hunt. Baumgarten was angry, bitter, defiant. We sat for a few hours more—Baumgarten talking, I listening—and then he took me back to Erkner in his Trabant. He took a different route.

TIME SHIFTS AND THE SHIFTING OF GUILT

As I came in from the cold—the cold of the day, and the emotional cold I felt from meeting with Baumgarten—I realized that he was the most hard-line officer I had yet encountered, probably the most hard-line of any I would encounter during my fieldwork. Baumgarten, for better or worse, lived in the past. I felt that when I entered Baumgarten's Trabant, I had climbed over a wall into the GDR, crossing into an alternate reality of death, defense, and justification. When I got out of his Trabant at the station, it was with relief, as though I had made it back over a wall.

Baumgarten was unrepentant in his conviction that he had done nothing wrong. He was, in fact, a cliché: the officer who explains away violence by claiming he was "just following orders." In his opinion, death at the hands of the state is justifiable when committed according to the laws of the state, regardless of the morality of the laws used to justify the deaths. Even the flowers, the strudel, and the bourgeois furnishings of his home seemed to be ways to distract him and others from what he had done; they illustrated that he was an "ordinary man," himself a victim of state violence. In reality, he was far from ordinary. He was highly intelligent and extremely charismatic. He had risen to the level of general and deputy–defense minister, which took an uncommon set of skills and instincts, as well as a willingness to submit oneself to the party and the military. He had to be willing to implement and carry out orders that most "ordinary" people would not.

Perhaps the most chilling aspect of my meeting with the general was the fact that he seemed to truly believe that what he had done was honorable and correct. In his eyes, he had committed no crimes. On the contrary: he had prevented crimes from occurring. For this reason, his trial and sentencing made no sense to him. It was an inversion of his vision of the world and his ideas of law and justice. Baumgarten so thoroughly believed in the legitimacy of violence along the former border that he thought the "real" reason for his conviction was not the shoot-to-kill orders or the deaths of "border crossers," but the fact that the Border Guards had prevented West Germany from exploiting "the East" (as Nazi Germany had, in a conflation of the GDR, the Soviet Union, and socialism). In his eyes, how could using "legal" force to protect one's border—even if the "threat" came from both the inside and the outside—be illegal or wrong? Therefore, the only logical reason for his trail was his resistance to exploitation. Because he had prevented profit he had to pay—like a "Red general" in World War II. Profit was what counted in the West, and profit was the measure by which he had been tried and convicted.

While NVA officers are in some ways denied coevality,[5] many often seem to seek out this sort of time displacement by continuing to see their roles and actions in the GDR as untainted by crime or controversy. By living the memory of their pasts, they remove themselves from the cultural, political, and ethical working-through of the present. Their inability to see that their actions in the GDR were human rights violations all but insured that they would be seen as firmly anchored in a past—their own, and that of the GDR—that prevented them from feeling remorse. Baumgarten—and the other officers who said they "regretted" every life lost along the Wall—may have come close to an apology, but they were nowhere near actual atonement or regret.

When I asked other officers about Baumgarten, they described him as a "hard-liner" and a "real workers' and farmers' general"; that is, a peasant who became an officer and is therefore uneducated (this characterization plays off the official GDR motto, *Der Arbeiter und Bauern Staat*, "the workers' and peasants' state"). I mentioned that some officers had compared themselves to Jews in the Third Reich. These sorts of extreme views were not to be taken seriously, I was told. Egbert Fischer, chairman of the Working Group for the History of the NVA, said that while he had heard some officers claim that they were the "Jews of the new Germany," he found it "an offensive and preposterous statement, a statement of ignorance and desperation." Despite these protestations, a fairly high number of officers said they could understand why someone would make such a statement—they simply found it "exaggerated."

The majority of NVA officers may be the "victims" of a certain kind of bureaucratic victor's justice, but in refusing to reflect critically on their past or present, officers and fallen elites like Baumgarten are in many ways their own unwitting judge and jury. Klaus-Dieter Baumgarten died in 2008, convinced until the end that he had committed no crimes and had served his state and party honorably. "I never gave an order that I have to be ashamed of, never," he said as we talked about the Berlin Wall and the Cold War. Baumgarten saw himself as a victim of unification and as a victim of an imagined memory of the fascist past in the present. For this, he saw himself as a hero.

PROSTHETIC MEMORIES OF FASCISM:
THE HUBRIS OF FALLEN ELITES

Given that the GDR was officially an "antifascist" state, NVA officers were trained and served in an atmosphere heavily influenced by anti-fascist and Soviet experiences during World War II, historical memories which served to frame memories and points of reference in regard to the Bundeswehr and their treatment after unification. For some NVA officers, the anti-Semitism and anticommunism of the Third Reich, and the World War II "specter of Judeo-Bolshevism" that framed the Wehrmacht and SS eradication of Jews and communists, are conflated into the Bundeswehr's policies toward them.[6] By considering themselves the objects of "Judeo-Bolshevism," and because they were communists, NVA officers perceive themselves as victims; they see similarities in their treatment and that of Jews in the Third Reich. As they frame their memories and experiences, the narratives of these officers slip, moving seamlessly from a "loser" to a "victim" narrative.[7] They relate the Cold War and their experiences after unification to the Holocaust and the actions and atrocities of the World War II German military, conflating the Bundeswehr, the Wehrmacht, and the SS, and seeing themselves as the victims of all three. They draw upon what Alison Landsberg calls "prosthetic memories," imagined experiences of past traumas—such as the Holocaust and the treatment of Jews in the Third Reich—which they themselves never directly experienced but which shape their experiences of trauma in the present.[8] Given their perceptions of their treatment, this is simply further proof for them that (West) Germany is a continuation of Nazi Germany and the Bundeswehr a continuation of the Wehrmacht and the SS, and that what they were trained to believe in the GDR and NVA is true. For this reason, Baumgarten was able to speak without any sort of irony about the "Commissar Order," and other officers could equate themselves with both communist *and* Jewish victims of Nazi Germany *and* post-unification Germany. As Bartov, Grossman, and Nolan write, the Holocaust has become the universal symbol for inhumanity, atrocity, and trauma.[9] Only by invoking the memory of the Holocaust can some officers register and make sense of their experiences, condemning the German government and military in the strongest way they know.

As became clear through discussions around these points, these same officers see a further similarity in the symbolic marking of Jews and NVA officers. Both groups are coded as "non-German," and removed from the German "bloodline," thus removing them from inclusion in the "family" of the nation by virtue of blood, and thereby making them "foreign." As they see it, both are denied certain economic and civil rights, assigned symbols to mark them as something outside of civil society (the Star of David for Jews and former medals and awards for NVA officers), and assigned a certain "essential" quality to their identities. Many officers—like Jürgen—also believed that the German government was attempting to achieve a "biological solution" (*biologische Lösung*) or "biological Final Solution" (*biologische Endlösung*) to the "NVA problem"; that is, refusing to listen to their concerns, and in the process, waiting for them to die of old age and illness. As such, many connected this "biological solution" to the "Final Solution" (*Endlösung*). This sort of thinking and "theorizing" is similiar to Boyer's discussion of conspiracy theories among former East German citizens as a way of uncovering the "truth" behind the political and historical events leading up to, and shaping, unification.[10]

While some NVA officers may perceive and construct certain symbolic similarities to Jewish victims of the Third Reich, the lived experiences of victimization are in no way similar. Despite their feelings of victimhood, they are in no danger of physical violence by the state. They can choose not to wear medals (few if any actually do), and even if they have a difficult time finding work, they are not legally prohibited from doing so. While they may be—at least in the eyes of the military—symbolically "non-German," this coding does not in any way have the same impact or level of violence as the coding of "non-German" that Jews and other minorities in Germany faced during the Third Reich. Simply put, they do not need to fear being disappeared, taken from their homes and forced to work to death in concentration camps, or being murdered by the state. While the Bundeswehr's policies are troubling in their use of historical memory, they are ultimately a way for the Bundeswehr and the German state to claim an essential legitimacy in the face of historical competition, to remind NVA officers that they lost the Cold War, and that they were, in effect, "traitors" to the German nation. They may be policies of symbolic exclusion, policies based on different ideas of what it means to be a proper soldier and a proper man, policies designed to emphasize strength over weakness, and a kind of Cold War "needling" over victory. They are not policies of extermination.

The linkage of the Holocaust, Cold War rivalries, and post-unification experience by some NVA officers fits well with Todorov's observation concerning the "usurpation of the narrative of heroism by the narrative of victimhood."[11] Many NVA officers see themselves as heroes for their service in an antifascist military, and for the fact that they never attacked another country—and as victims of a state and military that to many is a continuation of the Third Reich. They also see themselves as heroes for not preventing German unification, for allowing the GDR to dissolve peacefully. They see themselves as heroes, not because they used their training as soldiers to fight, but because they used their training to know that fighting would have started a world war. As a number of officers made clear to me, they "could have stopped unification if they had wanted to." It is also an attempt to lend themselves a certain historical importance by equating themselves with victims of fascism, which lends legitimacy to their service and duty in the NVA: in their eyes, it is proof that West Germany was, and is, a fascist state. From their perspective, the only way to make sense of unification, and of their treatment after unification, is to fit it within a narrative that they already know, one that explains both the "inherent" fascism of the Federal Republic and their own roles as the defenders of a new type of German state and military created to counter fascism.

HOPING TO BE *HOMO SACER*: IMAGINING A STATE OF EXCEPTION IN ORDER TO MAKE THEMSELVES EXCEPTIONAL

Of all of the twists and turns of unification, and the often confusing ways in which both the NVA and the Bundeswehr imagine and reimagine the German military past, perhaps the most surprising is how NVA officers— as fallen elites—fall back on a kind of fantasy of victimhood, a sort of masochism of memory intended to reestablish their status as elites of victimization, as they call upon what they see as the ultimate victim—Jews in the Third Reich—and equate their experiences and suffering with theirs to effect a transformation of themselves into the victims of the same kind of murderous policies employed by the Third Reich to eliminate its enemies. By constructing their experiences of victimhood in this way, NVA officers hope to be *homo sacer*—one who can be killed but not sacrificed by the state, one who represents the extreme limits of the state—in order to give their experiences meaning and value.[12] As Agamben describes in his book on this topic, those reduced to "bare life" are stripped of political life (*Bios*), and reduced to Zoë, or bare life, life without protection or rights.[13] Those reduced to bare life can be killed without repercussions, and their deaths are not seen as homicide.

By constructing victimhood narratives of their experiences after unification that link them to the Holocaust and victims of Nazi aggression, NVA officers create identities for themselves that draw upon the abject others of the Third Reich as a way to emphasize the injustice of their treatment and highlight the connections they see between the post-unification state and the Third Reich. In other words, everything they learned in the GDR about West Germany is true, and their worldview is correct; in a time of upheaval and political-economic change, there is a constant they can count on, and that is their own interpretive framework. Part of this framework is a construction and conception of themselves not only as the victims of unification but as the victims of a kind of lingering fascism. NVA officers are on to something, however: while they cannot be killed and are not rounded up and imprisoned en masse, their treatment does highlight a certain limit to the German state and a willingness to exclude people from symbolically full citizenship as a way to shape the identity of the new state. While overplaying their hand, NVA officers highlight the logic of the politics of inclusion and exclusion as a technique of governance in the modern state.

NVA officers are both inside the state and outside of it; as such, they are in a sort of modified "state of exception."[14] The FRG engages in a form of "limited exception" in their policies against NVA officers; the officers are not entirely "in" the state, but neither are they entirely "outside" of the state in the ways they imagine themselves to be. They are outside of the state in the sense that they are portrayed as non-German soldiers and the abject men of German military history. They are inside the state in the sense that despite their views, they are still citizens, and even though the Bundeswehr treats them as second-class citizens, they are still allowed to join the Bundeswehrverband. While they are in some ways "outside," some NVA officers overemphasize their exclusion to create new identities as victims of unification; they understand their predicament, and hope to push the logic of it to extremes.

The exclusion of NVA officers from the German military does not mean that they are necessarily fully excluded from the German state as a whole. They are denied full inclusion as a way of creating an overall sense of inclusion for East Germans as a whole, and as a way to demonstrate a willingness to "punish" those who upheld the SED. This is also a way to placate West German concerns; the NVA cannot be allowed to be fully within the new state because these were the men who opposed the FRG during the Cold War. They are too closely related to a willingness to violence that would have been used to bring down the West German state for them to be fully included in the new state; their partial removal from the state is a way to bring all Germans together. While they cannot be killed, they can, at least symbolically, be sacrificed for the good of German unity. For NVA officers, their sacrifice—and dreams of self-sacrifice—to the unification process is a kind of death, a death they try to link to the Holocaust in order to give it and themselves some kind of meaning and importance, a kind of anti-identity through an imagined death.

As they make themselves into the victims of unification and the Third Reich, they engage in a fantasy of victimhood in which they really are the Jewish and communist victims of the Third Reich, made into noncitizens and nonhumans by the post-unification state. NVA officers are victims of unification in the sense that the policies employed by the Bundeswehr and Ministry of Defense are punitive and unproductive in terms of the overall goal of unification, but they are not the victims of Nazi genocide. They see themselves as the men who can be killed but not sacrificed for the good of the state because they are the "new Jews of Germany" and "Red officers"—and in their eyes, they would be killed by the West Germans, if West Germans could only figure out a means to get away with it; rather than "really" doing it, they do it through backhanded means or by simply ignoring them, by letting the "biological solution" run its course. By identifying themselves as the victims of the Third Reich, NVA officers reinforce their conceptions of the FRG as a fascist state and reinforce their identities as antifascist victims deprived of their humanity. As fallen elites, they attempt to regain a certain valorized position by making themselves into the ultimate form of valorized identity: victims of fascism. If they cannot regain their status as elites in the state, then they can gain a certain valorized status as the martyrs of unification, the ultimate counterpoints to the "legality" of the new state. They may not have had the opportunity to sacrifice themselves for the GDR during the Cold War, but they can make themselves into the honorably sacrificial and sacrificed soldiers of the East German experience of unification— and therefore be worthy of honor and respect. By making themselves into the *homines sacri* of unification, they hope to make themselves into elites again. As officers of the National People's Army, in their minds, they die for their people and sacrifice themselves for their state, even if their state no longer exists, and even if their people do not necessarily want the sacrifice.

THE SPIRAL OF LOSS AND PRESTIGE:
FALLEN ELITES AND THE MILITARY OTHER

NVA officers claim they suffered a significant loss in symbolic prestige, and feel as if their identities have been taken from them. Symbolic loss equals a loss of identity, but also an *excess* of identity. As they counter this loss, they become more and more the "NVA" of stereotype and the imagination—a dangerous spiral, politically: the more they try to keep their identity or address the "absence" of their identity, the more their identity outruns and defines them, further marginalizing them. The more they attempt to redress or counter their "loss," the more they become the NVA of the (West) German imaginary, evidence that they are not fully integrated because *they* do not seek full integration but, rather, a return to the past. According to this logic, their marginalization is their own fault: they are victims by their own doing.

As Borneman remarks in his discussion of the practices of state formation, "as a device of power, democracy is as dependent on the externaliza-
tion or creation of negative others as on the internal dynamics of citizen
formation."[15] National and state identities come into conflict in the new
cultural, political, and military imaginary of Germany. East Germans were
always considered part of the "German nation" by West Germany during
the Cold War, but now that Germany is unified, former NVA officers are
the "bad Germans" because they served a different German state. In this
instance, *jus sanguinas* (the "law of blood," or citizenship based on ances-
try), is replaced by *jus soli* (the "law of soil," or citizenship by birthright).[16]
NVA officers are denied their "Germanness" because they lived in and
served the "other" Germany and are thus symbolically no longer part of
the German nation. The unified German state appears to find it necessary
to symbolically dismiss NVA officers because of prior state allegiance in
order to construct a new state identity; they are no longer German because they served a state that was counter to West Germany, while former
SS and Wehrmacht soldiers, who are seen as having served the German
nation—and a state that did not rival the preunification Federal Republic—are afforded full rights and status. The sense of disillusionment and
anomie that former NVA officers feel is caused by this tension between
national and state identity: they thought they were serving Germany and
were part of the German nation, regardless of political system. In the new
Germany, the construction of state and military identity seems to require
the negation of the national identity and biographies of certain Germans
based, not only on their own pasts, but on Germany's contentious and
tortured past of the twentieth century.

CHAPTER 9

Death and Allegiance

When I asked him if he missed his life in the military, Max, a former artillery
officer, paused for a moment, and then told me that he still thinks and
feels like a soldier. "Whenever I go on vacation, I still study the lay of the
land, where the hills and trees are, and try to decide where I would place
my artillery battery, where I would place my observation post, and where I
would place my command post. I still think this way, and I can't help it."

THERE ARE MANY WAYS one can study the military: as an institution,
as an instrument of power and oppression, as an economic engine or drain
on the economy, as a collection of weapons systems, as an archipelago of
bases crisscrossing a country or the world. A military can also be studied
through the people in it, through a consideration of what it means to be a
soldier in a military. An anthropology of soldiering looks at the military
as an institution through the experiences of the members of the institution, and the ways in which they are made into soldiers. Perhaps most important, an anthropology of soldiering examines what it means for those
involved to be soldiers, and what they mean to the state that makes them.
People are born into certain contexts, and one aspect of these contexts is
the military-security context of the state.

As a political tool, militarization is something done by certain people
to other people, people with an interest in creating what Catherine Lutz
calls "the military normal."[1] Militarization entails a series of questions
that state actors—politicians, bureaucrats, members of the military—
must ask themselves: How exactly do we want our soldiers to look? Want
kinds of soldiers do we want? How should they act and think? How
should they think of the state and the nation? How should they think of
themselves? How should they view the enemy? How should they view
the use of violence, as the perpetrators of violence on behalf of the state?

These are all questions that states—and the bearers of power and policy who make these decisions on behalf of the "state"—must confront when building up a military. It is this array of decisions that brings soldiers into being. This is particularly significant when the military is not intended just for the defense of the state, but also as a key tool in the building of the state and the creation of a bond between the individual and the state, the construction of the citizen-soldier. After deciding how soldiers and the military should be and what they should represent, state actors, with the power to make these conceptions "stick," must decide how to bring these ends into being, how actually to bring about and implement militarization policies, create a positive military identity and simultaneously create the "military other" of improper-inferior military masculinity. Militarization is both a process of representation and concrete political action. Cynthia Enloe's work on militarization and gender is instructive here: state actors draw upon preexisting cultural forms for militarization, and in the process, change them to fit current needs, desires, and requirements.[2]

Soldiers are never just soldiers, and a military is never just a military. While they may in some ways be cut off from the civilian world, both soldiers and the military are intimately tied to the civilian world, both for support and for—at least nominally—their raison d'être. Without a civilian population to protect (or at least use as an excuse to claim the task of protection), militaries and soldiers in modern nation-states would have no reason for being. It is also from the civilian world that militaries draw and create soldiers; soldiers are always first civilians. In order to make soldiering palatable, the military must begin early on with the process of convincing people to believe in and support the military, and make the military an appealing job choice. German unification shows us that soldiers are never just simply soldiers: they must be the right kinds of soldiers with the right opinions, mindsets, and feelings toward the state. Militarization is a process designed to create feelings of love, support, and sacrifice toward the state in citizens, feelings so intense that citizens will become soldiers. Without these attributes, the soldier is no longer a soldier, and becomes a mercenary, a contractor, or a potential threat to the stability of the state.

Soldiers represent the end point of a vast array of structures, processes, systems, and desires, and the congealed imaginative work of designing humans who will willingly kill other humans in order to protect the state. All sorts of metaphysical categories, such as "honor," "courage," "duty," and "loyalty" come into play in the construction and continued existence of soldiers, categories used to shore up their identities, bind them to the state and one another, and create a state of acceptance. Soldiers are expected to embody and represent these ideals, ideals which, by extension, are to represent the state and all that is good in the state. Like Zen koans, soldiers are compelled to contemplate these ideals, and through contemplation, continuously take shape and ignore all but the state and the military. By internalizing these ideals, soldiers are to internalize the state. And having internalized certain versions of these "truths," soldiers might find it difficult to internalize new ideas of the truth, and a state might find previously socialized soldiers suspect.

But even these seemingly "eternal" categories are shaped and conditioned by the state; one state's loyalty and commitment is not necessarily compatible with another's, and loyalty in one is treason in the other. Only soldiers socialized into the "right" sorts of eternal attributes are acceptable to the state, and may call themselves "soldiers." To insure that soldiers will willingly fire on other soldiers, states attempt to insure that other soldiers are seen as "less than," dangerous, dishonorable, murderers, and generally, something not quite human.

A military is a vast exercise in signification, and a vast repository of signs, meaning, and representation. From the performativity of uniforms, with their myriad meanings, the codes they transmit, and the messages of strength (or weakness) they send, to the state theater of parades, a military is an attempt first and foremost to intimidate and impress both friend and potential foe visually, to make the former think of war as desirable and the latter to see it as something to be avoided. Soldiers represent how the state came into being, and what it is prepared to do to continue to exist.

None of this is to take away from the real violence required of soldiers by the state and often committed by soldiers, violence demanded and expected by states in order for soldiers to retain their status, and for state elites to retain and maintain the state. What unification allows us to see is how states make soldiers and make soldiers signify death and violence and allegiance. This is a side of soldiering and a perspective on the role of the soldier—and former soldiers—that often goes unexplored.

MILITARIZATION AND HEGEMONY

Militarization requires the structuring—or restructuring—not only of everyday life, but of how people experience and conceptualize life itself. While an understanding of the processes that make up militarization is important, a mere focus on process excludes a consideration of what it actually means to be a soldier in a state, what it means to be militarized, to go through the process (knowingly or not), to be the focus of state power and attention, to be shaped in such a way that one is willing and prepared to give one's life for the state and the nation, and to accept these ideas of sacrifice as natural, normal, and good. As a tactic of hegemony, militarization is the "saturation" of everyday life, culture, and politics with military values and norms, values and norms that support and uphold the political projects and success of the state and those in power. It is perhaps *the* tactic of hegemony, of creating a well-spring of spontaneous support based on fear and defense, as it is literally an attempt to convince people to give up their lives and take lives for the good of the state, to make them believe that the goals of the state are commensurate with their own well-being, survival, and social reproduction.

Militarization must seem like spontaneous consent, a kind of nonviolent dominance of a group through "peace" that brings about the acceptance of violence and military values as a natural good unto itself, and through this acceptance, acceptance of the state and its policies and goals. Soldiers are supposed to act from conviction rather than compulsion, and be ready to willingly give their lives. As Sheehan notes, it is important that the soldier feel a part of the nation, that he or she be an active citizen rather than a passive object.[3] An attention to the interplay between militarization and hegemony goes a long way toward understanding and explaining how states can train and convince someone to kill or otherwise subordinate another human being simply because they wear a different uniform or represent a different vision or way of seeing the world.[4]

The amount of time, energy, and resources devoted to such a project are immense—perhaps, from the state's point of view, necessarily so. But this also says something about what it means to be a "soldier." Contrary to essentialist claims about innate male aggression, that "soldiers are born," an examination of state militarization programs in the GDR—and the FRG as well—shows otherwise. States must invest so much time and energy into "making" soldiers because the overwhelming majority of men (and, increasingly, women) do not in fact wish to become soldiers, and must be convinced that it is something one should do. This highlights a very important point: states must make men into soldiers because men do not come ready-made as soldiers, and do not come as ready-made defenders of the nation-state. Soldiering has to be made attractive to them, made "natural." By "making it natural," it has to be made to seem like a natural course of events, a normal part of a man's life, the uncovering or valorization of something that was already in him from the beginning.

MILITARIZATION IN THE GDR

Militarization in the GDR was a process designed to create certain types of citizens, citizens who were to embody the state, become the state, who through their lives—and potentially at the cost of their lives—would perpetuate the party and the state. Militarization policies in the GDR show how a state imagines and makes a soldier, and why. While the NVA's stated goal was to provide the GDR with soldiers ready, willing, and able to defend the GDR, the end result was to make men compliant and active socialist citizens. Militarization was a form of social and political reproduction designed to insure the state would continue.

The first line of "national" defense is the nation itself, and the necessity of turning men and women into "citizens" with an emotional and personal stake in the perpetuation of the nation. Simply making men into soldiers is not enough to insure the defense of the nation; this only creates, in a sense, a group of mercenaries. The real goal involves much higher stakes: creating men who feel they are the nation, that their families, as a part of them, are microcosms of that nation: defend the family and you defend the nation, and vice versa. Soldiers must be made to make an automatic connection between the family and the nation-state. However, the way soldiers experience this connection must also be somewhat blind, unreflective, and uncritical: it cannot go any further than that, it cannot recognize inequalities or ambiguities in the system.

Essentialist conceptions of military masculinity elide the political desires and "necessities" of creating soldiers. In these conceptions, men are already soldiers; the rest is just a sort of "additive" effect, an enhancement of an intrinsic nature. But this "addition" is much more than that: it is the active development of men into soldiers, of turning men into political actors who incorporate the needs and goals of the state into their being, and who "become" the state. Perhaps it is this process which essentialists see as the indication of an "always-already" nature to soldiering. But if this were the case, why would the state take such pains to insure that men would become soldiers? Indeed, there would be no need to "combat pacifism," as NVA documents mention over and over, if men were always-already soldiers. Men must be made "enthusiastic" about military service: keep in mind the original meaning of the Greek *enthusiasmos*—to be possessed or inspired by a god (which is to stand outside of one's self and make oneself selfless). By becoming selfless for the state, they become the state, become the stand in—the metonym—of the state. They are to become "selfless" in this seemingly "natural" desire to die for the protection of the nation and state. And it is always coded as dying for the nation—as the metaphor of the family, community, and the self—rather than for the state, the political structure(s) that make it all possible, which set it all in motion. This selflessness must be for the nation, the "body politic," the fatherland or motherland, for it is there that the emotional attachments are most easily made, rather than for the cold, bureaucratic structures of the state, even though in fact this selflessness serves, protects, and reproduces the state, state elites, and structures of power and inequality.

The East German experience, while more pronounced and encompassing, is not that different from militarization policies enacted by many states—the United States included. States "need" soldiers and a military, and the most effective way to insure this form of militarized social reproduction is to begin with children and young adults, exploiting their "youthfulness" and "romanticism," influencing them while they are still impressionable and malleable. The glorification of soldiers through the media, songs, cartoons, and so on; visits to "open house" days at bases; public displays of military technology, prowess, and might; youth groups, whether party-based or akin to the Boy Scouts; the use of "dashing" uniforms to set soldiers apart from the quotidian and "weak" civilians; promises of power, prestige, and respect: all are strategies employed by states and militaries to entice the young to honor and emulate the military and soldiers, and to make them willing to give their lives.

GERMAN UNIFICATION:
THE PRISM OF MILITARIZED CONSTRUCTIONISM

German unification is a prism through which we can see the ways in which history and memory coalesce in the cultural politics of the military. It is also a way to analyze the construction and deconstruction of soldiers in the modern nation-state. Unification strips away the supposed "natural" quality of military masculinity and soldiering, and shows it to be an explicit project of the state. The "magic" of militarization—the smoke and mirrors of state propaganda about defense and duty—is unmasked, showing militarization programs to be concerned, not only with making certain types of soldiers, but with making certain types of citizens who will uphold the state.[5] The experiences of former NVA officers allow us to examine how soldiers are imagined and represented, how these representations work in conjunction with state and military legitimation, and how these representations affect real people in real situations. It is an insight into how a state celebrates victory and treats its military "has-beens."

The practices and policies enacted by the post-unification German state and military serve as a model for understanding how states make soldiers and deal with former soldiers, particularly if these soldiers have been seen as the "enemy" or "losers" of a war, whether hot or cold. This model could prove useful when analyzing the situations and experiences of former soldiers in states such as Iraq, where the dissolution of the Iraqi army and the Baath Party has had disastrous consequences, or possibly even North and South Korea, should they ever unify. Stripping professional soldiers of their status and identity and penalizing them economically is a formula for potential—or very real—disaster. The German experience serves as a cautionary tale of how state actors should and should not design "reunification" or reintegration strategies for former soldiers, unless, of course, the desired goal is social and political marginalization. Integration strategies for fallen elites have to attend to their sense of identity, self-worth, status, and careers as soldiers, as well as to the fact that these might be men who know little more than soldiering and working for the state. These sorts of programs require that close attention be paid to the politics of military masculinity and military othering.

Unification shows us more than just the political merging of two states. It shows us not only what happens when the military of one state is subsumed into that of another, but how militaries and soldiers are made in the first place. Through its unraveling, the NVA shows us how soldiers come into being, how people experience these categories, and how states imagine soldiers. Unification can be seen as a sort of "reverse engineering" of military identity and the "hard poetics" of soldiering, a snapshot of how a state thinks about its soldiers and how people experience the making of soldiers. Through their unmaking, NVA officers give us an insight into the construction of soldiers and their worlds, how they come to signify and are made to signify, and how soldiering impacts their everyday lives. It also allows us to see how the structures and systems of militarization work, and how these structures and systems draw on the past to create a militarized present iteration of the state. We can also see what happens when soldiers lose their identity as soldiers, even if they never fired a shot. NVA officers see themselves as having lost a bloodless war, even as they discount the deaths along the border. And as fallen elites, NVA officers show us how those who formerly held power and were seen as the backbone of the state try to make sense of their loss of identity and of the state which gave them structure. Having grown up in, embraced, and become the soldierly ideal of the GDR, NVA officers found their pasts a heavy burden in unified Germany.

When the two Germanys unified, the dominant German state—West Germany—was forced to confront the fact that the new, unified state would contain its former enemy, a military predicated on its possible destruction and overthrow. Of course, the NVA, without Soviet political and logistical support, was never in a position to seriously undermine the security of the FRG. Regardless, NVA officers represented a symbolic threat and problem that demanded resolution: seen as the "pillar" of the party and the state, NVA officers could not simply be left to their own devices, or left "undealt" with.

In terms of a purely military integration of the Bundeswehr and the NVA, the Bundeswehr had very few options when it came to taking on former NVA officers, particularly higher-ranking officers who had spent most of their careers in the NVA and had been socialized and trained to think of the Bundeswehr as the enemy. Additionally, an outright absorption of the entire NVA into the Bundeswehr was not possible, for both political and economic reasons. Despite this, the policies enacted by the Bundeswehr after unification did little to convince NVA officers denied service in the Army of Unity that unification was not a West German take over of the GDR, and that the Bundeswehr was in fact and deed little more than a watered-down Wehrmacht, with all of the anticommunist and fascist tendencies one would expect from such an army.

The failure to integrate NVA officers as symbolically full citizens was, I believe, a mistake, a mistake based on Cold War rivalries and conceptions of soldiering, and the need for political-military legitimacy in the present. It was also a failure based on constructions of military masculinity and military "machismo." It begs the following questions: Even while soldiers and officers connected to killings and deaths along the Wall and border have been and should be prosecuted (I should add that the NVA was an instrument of state repression, control, and coercion, and not a very "pleasant" army to be in), what was the ultimate political utility of symbolically and materially marginalizing the vast majority of NVA officers in terms of unification? Did the NVA as a whole need to be punished in a way that the Wehrmacht was not after World War II? While the Bundeswehr may have been able to celebrate a kind of victory, has the ultimate result been a contribution to the continued animosity and uneven experience of unification?

DEATH AND ALLEGIANCE

A soldier's meaning in many ways has nothing to do with the soldier's life or biography: the meanings attached to a soldier by the state are strangely detached from the life and actions of the soldier. In much the same way that militaries attempt to make soldiers anonymous, to strip away their individuality as they are forced into the collective identity (and fate) of the military, the identity of the person is stripped away publicly. The soldier becomes a vessel of meaning for the state to fill as needed and when necessary, and by agreement with the military for a position in the state hierarchy. Of course, individual action can—and does—play a role in the creation of military identities: through bravery in combat, in a positive sense, and through crimes, misdeeds, and cowardice, in a negative sense. A state must portray its soldiers in the best possible light, while portraying those of other states as somehow inferior, whether through prowess, politics, technology, or simply by virtue of being soldiers of a state seen as illegitimate.

Perhaps more than any other profession, the military hangs its fate on the same peg as that of the state: if the state falls, so too does the military, in particular, the officer corps. The creation of military identity is a political act on the part of the state, as soldiers represent not only the military but the state as well. In many ways, it is the "state" making its own image as it sees fit, and as it sees necessary. Of course, the "state" here is comprised of countless actors who have an investment in making the state work, and of maintaining their own positions in the state; "the state" for them is their own imagined, objectified lives and futures. This identity comes with benefits and possibilities: to subsume one's own identity to that of the state results in a payoff by the state, the possibility for economic and social advancement, the possibility for the powerless to gain power. Or, as unification shows, for the powerful to become powerless.

In exchange for yoking one's life to the fate of the state, of being willing to die for it, the soldier receives certain symbolic and material rewards and rights. NVA officers were willing to fight and die for the GDR and socialism (just as Bundeswehr soldiers were willing to fight and die for the Federal Republic and capitalism) because they had pledged twenty-five years of their lives to the NVA. After unification, and in the eyes of the Bundeswehr, how could those officers who had served a considerable number of years in the NVA be trusted to fight and die willingly for the new Germany and capitalism, the very system they had sworn to destroy?

From a military standpoint, German unification was a metadebate about death and allegiance. It was about the willingness to fight and die for certain ideals, for a certain worldview or belief in a material or symbolic order. Unlike conscripts, these were men on both sides who volunteered to serve their respective systems, systems which drew on the other to give purpose to the other. Bundeswehr and NVA officers represented the pinnacle of commitment in the Cold War struggle between capitalism and communism, between certain types of world orders; rather than simply being soldiers from different ethnic groups or states, they were Germans who found themselves in two different state systems. The willingness to die—and the willingness to kill—for a system or a state made these men both similar and different. After unification, NVA officers were the men who would have died for the GDR as well as those now trying to integrate into the state they would have fought against.

After unification, NVA officers' individual biographies or their experiences in the GDR no longer mattered. Symbolically, they were simply "the NVA," and because of the Cold War rivalry over death and allegiance, had to be marginalized and "othered." Otherwise, the role of the Bundeswehr in the Cold War, and the individual biographies of Bundeswehr officers, would have counted for little, both in their own eyes and in the eyes of the public. If they were shown to have been in any way "equal" during the Cold War, the entire Cold War would have been in vain for Bundeswehr officers, and their sacrifices and struggles all for naught, at least according to the logic of military masculinity and identity formation. Despite their inaction in November 1989, it was this question of allegiance and the threat of death and violence that tarnished them, erasing their biographies, nullifying their decision to stand aside and let the GDR fall. This resulted in a kind of living death after unification: they were demonized by the FRG and the Bundeswehr as the bad, illegal, improper, and ultimately irrelevant soldiers of German military history.

Soldiers are myths we tell ourselves about ourselves, that states tell its citizens about how we would like to think (and how we should think) about duty, honor, allegiance, violence, killing, and death. We make soldiers into an idealized version of ourselves, our pasts, and our futures, an idealized version that masks the unpleasant reality of state formation and legitimacy. Because soldiers come from us, we have to think of them as—and we have to make them represent—a positive image of violence, as it reflects back on us. Our soldiers—"we"—would never commit the types of violence and killing that "their" soldiers would commit, or that "they" would allow their soldiers to commit. We tell ourselves these things about our soldiers and their soldiers because we're really talking to ourselves about ourselves, about the values we place on life and death; we have to make killing seem noble and legitimate, because ultimately, we are the ones doing it. And the only way to really make it seem legitimate is to make it seem that the illegal and unlawful violence is wielded by other soldiers, not our own.

A soldier is a vessel that we fill with all sorts of metaphysical problems and conundrums about death and killing, problems and ethical dilemmas we think we have solved in the very being of the soldier, a being brought about by the state itself. States make soldiers into an image of acceptable, honorable death—of either the soldier or those killed by the soldier. Soldiers are the answer to the state's tautological questions about death: anything less calls the bluff on the state's claim to its monopoly on violence.

Reference Matter

Notes

PART ONE: MY BROTHER, MY ENEMY

1. Anonymous East German poem intended to make NVA soldiers think of Bundeswehr soldiers not as potential "brothers," or Germans, but as enemies who they should fight and kill without compunction. Translation by the author. Originally broadcast on the East German radio station "Berliner Rundfunk" as part of a propaganda effort in March 1978. Source: Sabine Dengel, *Untertan, Volksgenosse, Sozialistische Persönlichkeit: Politische Erziehung im Deutschen Kaiserreich, dem NS-Staat, und der DDR* (Frankfurt am Main: Campus Forschung, 2005).

CHAPTER 1: THE MILITARY IMAGINARY

1. See Charles S. Maier, *Dissolution: The Crisis of Communism and the End of East Germany* (Princeton, NJ: Princeton University Press, 1999), p. 290.

2. Nina Leonhard, "Biographische Lebenskonstruktionen ehemaliger NVA-Soldaten," in *Militär, Staat, und Gesellschaft in der DDR: Forschungsfelder, Ergebnisse, Perspektiven*, ed. Hans Ehlert and Matthias Rogg (Berlin: Christoph Links Verlag, 2004), p. 717.

3. Deutscher Bundestag, Drucksache 14/8920, 25 Apr. PDS Antrag: Deutsche Einheit in der Bundeswehr herstellen, press release, 2002.

4. Oberst a.D. Dieter Müller, Landesverband Ost, personal communication, 2006.

5. See John Borneman, *Belonging in the Two Berlins: Kin, State, Nation* (New York: Cambridge University Press, 1992); John Borneman, "Uniting the German Nation: Law, Narrative, and Historicity," *American Ethnologist* 20, no. 2 (1993): 288–311; Dominic Boyer, *Spirit and System: Media, Intellectuals, and the Dialectic in Modern German Culture* (Chicago: University of Chicago Press, 2005); see also Andreas Glaeser, *Divided in Unity: Identity, Germany, and the Berlin Police* (Chicago: University of Chicago Press, 2000).

6. See Borneman 1992.

7. Jonas Frykman and Orvar Lofgren, *The Culture Builders: A Historical Anthropology of Middle Class Life* (New Brunswick, NJ: Rutgers University Press, 1987).

8. Georg-Maria Meyer and Sabine Collmer, *Kolonisierung oder Integration: Bundeswehr und Deutsche Einheit: Eine Bestandaufnahme* (Opladen: Westdeutscher Verlag, 1993).

9. Lesley Gill, "Creating Citizens, Making Men: The Military and Masculinity in Bolivia," *Cultural Anthropology* 12, no. 4 (1997): 527–50; Cynthia Enloe, *The Morning After: Sexual Politics and the End of the Cold War* (Berkeley: University of California Press, 1993); Ruth Seifert, *Militär—Kultur—Identität: Individualisierung, Geschlechtsverhältnisse und die soziale Konstruktion des Soldaten* (Bremen: Edition Themen, 1996).

10. See Maier 1999, p. 332; and James A. McAdams, *Judging the Past in Unified Germany* (Cambridge: Cambridge University Press, 2001).

11. McAdams 2001.

12. McAdams 2001.

13. Peter Joachim Lapp, *Ein Staat—eine Armee. Von der NVA zur Bundeswehr* (Bonn-Bad Godesberg: Friedrich-Ebert Stiftung, 1992).

14. Eric Wolf, *Envisioning Power: Ideologies of Dominance and Resistance* (Berkeley: University of California Press, 1999), p. 275.

15. See Brian Ladd, *The Ghosts of Berlin: Confronting German History in the Urban Landscape* (Chicago: University of Chicago Press, 1997); and Peter Carrier, *Holocaust Monuments and National Memory: France and Germany Since 1989* (New York: Berghahn Books, 2005), for their discussions of the interplay between the physical landscape, history, memory, national identity, and violence in Berlin.

16. See Konrad Jarausch and Michael Geyer, *Shattered Past: Reconstructing German Histories*, (Princeton, NJ: Princeton University Press, 2003), p. 63, for the efforts of former East German scholars to write counternarratives and counterhistories of unification.

17. Michael Herzfeld, *Anthropology: Theoretical Practice in Culture and Society* (Malden, MA: Blackwell Publishing, 2001), p. 1.

18. John R. Gillis, ed., *The Militarization of the Western World* (New Brunswick, NJ: Rutgers University Press, 1989), p. 1.

19. Catherine Lutz, "Making War at Home and in the United States: Militarization and the Current Crisis," *American Anthropologist* 104, no. 3 (2002): 723–35.

20. Aradhana Sharma and Akhil Gupta, eds., *The Anthropology of the State: A Reader* (Malden, MA: Blackwell Publishing, 2006), p. 11.

21. Charles Tilly, "War Making and State Making as Organized Crime," in *Bringing the State Back In*, ed. Peter B. Evans, Dietrich Rueschemeyer, and Theda Skocpol (Cambridge: Cambridge University Press, 1999), pp. 169–91.

22. Dietrich Rueschemeyer and Peter B. Evans. "The State and Economic Transformation: Toward an Analysis of the Conditions Underlying Effective Intervention," in Evans, Rueschemeyer, and Skocpol 1999, pp. 46–47.

23. Rueschemeyer and Evans 1999, p. 47.

24. Sharma and Gupta 2006, p. 11.

25. Phillip Corrigan and Derek Sayer, *The Great Arch: English State Formation as Cultural Revolution* (Oxford: Basil Blackwell, 1985), p. 3.

26. Tilly 1999; Wolf 1999; Philip Abrams, "Notes on the Difficulty of Studying the State," *Journal of Historical Sociology* 1, no. 1 (March 1988): 58–89; Eric Wolf, *Europe and the People Without History* (Berkeley: University of California Press, 1982).

27. Herzfeld 2001: 12; see also, Katherine Verdery, *What Was Socialism, and What Comes Next?* (Princeton, NJ: Princeton University Press, 1996), for a discussion of an "anthropology of the state."

28. Linda Green, *Fear as a Way of Life* (New York: Columbia University Press, 1999).

29. Detlef Bald, *Die Bundeswehr: Eine kritische Geschichte, 1955–2005* (Munich: C. H. Beck, 2005), p. 132.

30. George Mosse, *Fallen Soldiers: Reshaping the Memory of the World Wars* (New York: Oxford University Press, 1990), pp. 20–21.

31. Charles Taylor, *Modern Social Imaginaries* (Durham, NC: Duke University Press, 2004).

32. Roger Lancaster, *The Trouble with Nature: Sex in Science and Popular Culture* (Berkeley: University of California Press, 2003).

33. Lutz 2002; Hugh Gusterson, "Anthropology and Militarism," *Annual Review of*

Anthropology 36 (2007): 155–75; James J. Sheehan, *Where Have All the Soldiers Gone? The Transformation of Modern Europe* (Boston: Houghton Mifflin, 2008).

34. Enloe 1993; Gill 1997, Seifert 1996; William Arkin and Lynne R. Dobrovsky, "Military Socialization and Masculinity," *Journal of Social Issues* 34, no. 1 (Winter 1978): 151–68; Sabine Frühstuck, *Uneasy Warriors: Gender, Memory, and Popular Culture in the Japanese Army* (Berkeley: University of California Press, 2007); Lesley Gill, *The School of the Americas: Military Training and Political Violence in the Americas* (Durham, NC: Duke University Press, 2004); Paul Higate et al., *Military Masculinities: Identity and the State* (Santa Barbara, CA: Praeger Press, 2003); Morris Janowitz, *The Professional Soldier: A Social and Political Portrait* (New York: Free Press, 1960); Rhoda Kanaaneh, "Boys or Men? Duped or 'Made'? Palestinian Soldiers in the Israeli Military," *American Ethnologist* 32, no. 2 (2005): 260–75; Catherine Lutz, *Homefront: A Military City and the American 20th Century* (Boston: Beacon Press, 2001); Catherine Lutz, "Militarization," in *A Companion to the Anthropology of Politics*, ed. David Nugent and Joan Vincent (Malden, MA: Blackwell Publishing, 2007), pp. 318–31; Seungsook Moon, *Militarized Modernity and Gendered Citizenship in South Korea* (Durham, NC: Duke University Press, 2005).

35. Frank Biess, *Homecomings: Returning POWs and the Legacies of Defeat in Postwar Germany* (Princeton, NJ: Princeton University Press, 2006).

36. Biess 2006, p. 13.

37. In 1995, the Bundesverfassungsgericht (Federal Constitutional Court of Germany) passed legislation which, in effect, made it illegal to openly state that "soldiers are Murderers" (*Soldaten sind Mörder*) or "soldiers are potential murderers" (*Soldaten sind potentielle Mörder*) (BverfG Beschl. v 10.10.1995—1 BvR 1476191, 1 BvR 1980191, 1 BvR 102192, 1 BvR 221192). This decision is the result of four separate cases from various areas in Germany (FRG), in which individuals openly expressed their opinions that "soldiers are murderers." In 1995, after much debate, the Federal Court issued a decision stating that it is permissible to state that all soldiers in the world are murderers, but that it is still punishable to state that soldiers of the Bundeswehr are murderers. Lt. Col. Bernd Albers, Assistant Military Attaché, German Embassy, Washington, DC, personal communication, July 2, 2002.

38. See Michael J. Shapiro, *Violent Cartographies: Mapping Cultures of War* (Anne Arbor: University of Michigan Press, 1997), for an analysis of "cartographic" imaginaries and war.

39. David I. Kertzer, *Ritual, Power, and Politics* (New Haven, CT: Yale University Press, 1989); Taylor 2004; Benedict Anderson, *Imagined Communities* (London: Verso, 1991).

40. See also Mosse 1990; and George Mosse, *The Image of Man: The Creation of Modern Masculinity* (New York: Oxford University Press, 1996).

41. Taylor 2004, p. 23.

42. Michael Walzer, "On the Role of Symbolism in Political Thought," *Political Science Quarterly* 82 (1967): 191–205, as quoted in Kertzer 1989, p. 6.

43. Kerzer 1989, p. 96; see also Wolf 1999, pp. 3–8.

44. V. I. Voloshinov, *Marxism and the Philosophy of Language* (Cambridge, MA: Harvard University Press, 1973 [1929]).

45. Voloshinov 1973; Martyn J. Lee, *Consumer Culture Reborn: The Cultural Politics of Consumption* (New York: Routledge, 1993).

46. Lee 1993, p. 45.

47. Lee 1993, p. 46.

48. See Wolf 1982.

49. Shapiro 1997, p. 27.

50. Roland Barthes, *Mythologies* (New York: Hill and Wang, 1972).

51. Kertzer 1989, p. 2.

52. Sam Keen, *Faces of the Enemy: Reflections of the Hostile Imagination* (San Francisco: Harper and Row, 1991).

53. Sheehan 2008, p. 16.

54. George E. Marcus and Michael M. J. Fisher, *Anthropology as Cultural Critique: An Experimental Moment in the Human Sciences* (Chicago: University of Chicago Press, 1986), p. 25.

55. Scott 1987.

56. Laura Nader, "Up the Anthropologist: Perspectives Gained from Studying Up," in *Reinventing Anthropology*, ed. Dell Hymes (New York: Vintage Books, 1974), pp. 284–311.

57. Antonius Robben, "The Politics of Truth and Emotion Among Victims and Perpetrators of Violence," in *Fieldwork Under Fire: Contemporary Studies of Violence and Survival*, ed. Carolyn Nordstrom and Antonius Robben (Berkeley: University of California Press, 1995), pp. 81–104.

58. See George Mosse, *The Nationalization of the Masses: Political Symbolism and Mass Movements in Germany from the Napoleonic Wars through the Third Reich* (Ithaca, NY: Cornell University Press, 1975); Klaus Theweleit, *Male Fantasies*, 2 vols. (Minneapolis: University of Minnesota Press, 1987–89).

CHAPTER 2: EMOTIONS, GENERATIONS, AND DEATH CULTS

1. BA-MA DVW 1/55636:000019.

2. See Hope Harrison, *Driving the Soviets Up the Wall: Soviet-East German Relations, 1953–1961* (Princeton, NJ: Princeton University Press, 2003), for Harrison's discussion of the GDR as a "super ally" in the Soviet ideological contest for prestige and influence with China.

3. Detlef Bald, *Militär und Gesellschaft, 1945–1990: Die Bundeswehr in Bonner Republik* (Baden-Baden: Nomos Verlag, 1994), p. 149.

4. Bald 1994, p. 148.

5. Eric Wolf, *Pathways of Power: Building an Anthropology of the Modern World* (Berkeley: University of California Press), 2001, p. 60; see also Andrew Bickford, "Male Identity, the Military, and the Family in the former German Democratic Republic," *Anthropology of East Europe Review* 19, no. 1 (Spring 2001): 1–11.

6. Eugen Weber, *Peasants into Frenchmen: The Modernization of Rural France, 1870–1914* (Stanford, CA: Stanford University Press), 1976.

7. Benedict Anderson, *Imagined Communities* (London: Verson), 1991; Catherine Lutz, "Militarization," in *A Companion to the Anthropology of Politics*, ed. David Nugent and Joan Vincent (Malden, MA: Blackwell Publishing, 2007), p. 323.

8. See Weber 1976; Omer Bartov, Atina Grossmann, and Mary Nolan, introduction to *Crimes of War: Guilt and Denial in the Twentieth Century* (New York: New Press, 2002), pp. xi–xxxiv; James J. Sheehan, *Where Have All the Soldiers Gone? The Transformation of Modern Europe* (Boston: Houghton Mifflin), 2008.

9. Leo Braudy, *From Chivalry to Terrorism: War and the Changing Nature of Masculinity* (New York: Vintage Books, 2005), p. 246.

10. Bartov, Grossmann, and Nolan 2002, p. xvi.

11. Frank Biess, *Homecomings: Returning POWs and the Legacies of Defeat in Postwar Germany* (Princeton, NJ: Princeton University Press, 2006); Heide Fehrenbach,

"Rehabilitating Fatherland: Race and German Remasculinization," *Signs: The Journal of Women in Culture and Society* 24, no. 1 (Autumn 1998): 107–28; Mark Fenemore, *Sex, Thugs, and Rock 'n Roll: Teenage Rebels in Cold War East Germany* (New York: Berghahn Books, 2009); Karen Hagemann, *Home/Front: The Military, War, and Gender in Twentieth Century Germany* (Oxford: Berg, 2002), p. 30; Susan Jeffords, "The Remasculinization of Germany in the 1950s: Discussion," *Signs: The Journal of Women in Culture and Society* 24, no. 1 (Autumn 1998): 163–70; Robert Moeller, "The Remasculinization of Germany in the 1950s: An Introduction," *Signs: The Journal of Women in Culture and Society* 24, no. 1 (Autumn 1998): 101–6; see also Ute Poiger, "A New, 'Western' Hero? Reconstructing German Masculinity in the 1950s," *Signs: The Journal of Women in Culture and Society* 24, no. 1 (Autumn 1998): 147–62.

12. Robert Moeller, *War Stories: The Search for a Usable Past in the Federal Republic of Germany* (Berkeley: University of California Press, 2003).

13. Braudy 2005, p. xi.

14. Arkin and Dobrovsky 1978; Frühstuck 2007; Gill 1997; Enloe 1993; Gill 2004; Higate et al. 2003; Gusterson 2007; Janowitz 1960; Kanaaneh 2005; Lutz 2001, 2007; Moon 2005; Seifert 1996; Thomas Künhe, "'. . . Aus diesem Krieg werden nicht nur harte Männer heimkehren': Kriegskameradschaft und Männlichkeit im 20. Jahrhundert, in *Männergeschichte-Geschlechtergeschichte: Männlichkeit im Wandel der Moderne*, ed. Thomas Künhe (Frankfurt am Main: Campus Verlag, 1996), pp. 174–92.

15. George Mosse, *Nationalism and Sexuality: Middle-Class Morality and Sexual Norms in Modern Europe* (Madison: University of Wisconsin Press, 1985); Mosse 1996.

16. Enloe 1993; Gill 1997; Mosse 1985, 1996; R. W. Connell, *Masculinities* (Berkeley: University of California Press, 1995); see also Kühne 1996a.

17. Andrea Cornwall and Nancy Lindisfarne, *Dislocating Masculinity: Comparative Ethnographies* (New York: Routledge, 1994), p. 3.

18. Matthew Gutmann, "Trafficking in Men: The Anthropology of Masculinity," *Annual Review of Anthropology* 26 (1997): 385–409; *The Meaning of Macho: Being a Man in Mexico City* (Berkeley: University of California Press, 2006); Roger Lancaster, *Life is Hard: Machismo, Danger, and the Intimacy of Power in Nicaragua* (Berkeley: University of California Press, 1994).

19. Tim Carrigan et al., "Towards a New Sociology of Masculinity," *Theory and Society* 14, no. 5 (1985): 551–603.

20. Cornwall and Lindisfarne, 1994.

21. Dorothy Hodgson, *Once Intrepid Warriors: Gender, Ethnicity, and the Cultural Politics of Maasai Development* (Bloomington: Indiana University Press, 2004), p. 11.

22. Cornwall and Lindisfarne 1994.

23. J. Collier and S. Yanagisako, eds., *Gender and Kinship: Essays Toward a Unified Analysis* (Stanford, CA: Stanford University Press, 1987).

24. Gutmann 1997.

25. Volker Berghahn, *Modern Germany: Society, Economy, and Politics in the Twentieth Century* (Cambridge: Cambridge University Press, 1987), p. 208.

26. Tony Judt, *Postwar: A History of Europe Since 1945* (New York: Penguin Books, 2005), p. 243.

27. Judt 2005, p. 243.

28. Harrison 2003, p. 9; Detlef Bald, *Die Bundeswehr: Eine kritische Geschichte, 1955–2005* (Munich: C. H. Beck, 2005), p. 39.

29. Harrison 2003; Judt 2005.

30. Berghahn 1987, p. 211; David Clay Large, *Germans to the Front: West German Rearmament in the Adenauer Era* (Chapel Hill: University of North Carolina Press, 1996).

31. Harrison 2003, p. 54.

32. Harrison 2003, p. 54; Judt 2005; Large 1996.

33. Dale Herspring, *Requiem for an Army: The Demise of the East German Military* (Lanham, MD: Rowman and Littlefield, 1998), p. 21.

34. Harrison 2003, p. 7.

35. Herspring 1998, p. 6.

36. Harrison 2003, p. 5.

37. Harrison 2003; Herspring 1998; John Borneman, *Belonging in the Two Berlins: Kin, State, Nation* (New York: Cambridge University Press, 1992); Mary Fulbrook, *The People's State: East German Society from Hitler to Honecker* (New Haven, CT: Yale University Press, 2005); Mary Fulbrook, *Anatomy of a Dictatorship: Inside the GDR 1949–1989* (Oxford: Oxford University Press, 1995).

38. T. M. Foster, *The East German Army* (London: George Allen and Unwin, 1980).

39. Fulbrook 1995, p. 260.

40. Torsten Diedrich, Hans Ehlert, and Rüdiger Wenzke, eds., *Im Dienste der Partei: Handbuch der bewaffneten Organe der DDR* (Berlin: Christoph Links Verlag, 1998).

41. Fulbrook 2005, p. 123.

42. Hans Ehlert and Matthias Rogg, eds., *Militär, Staat, und Gesellschaft in der DDR: Forschungsfelder, Ergebnisse, Perspektiven* (Berlin: Christoph Links Verlag, 2004), p. 1.

43. Paul Heider, "Ideologische Indoktrination und Traditionspflege in der Nationalen Volksarmee," in *Militär, Staat, und Gesellschaft in der DDR: Forschungsfelder, Ergebnisse, Perspektiven*, ed. Hans Ehlert and Matthias Rogg (Berlin: Christoph Links Verlag, 2004), p. 170.

44. Heider 2004, p. 170.

45. Konrad Jarausch, *After Hitler: Recivilizing Germans, 1945–1995* (Oxford: Oxford University Press, 2006), p. 40.

46. Foster 1980, p. 28; Ulrich Mählert and Gerd-Rüdiger Stephan, *Blaue Hemden, Rote Fahnen: Die Geschichte der Freien Deutschen Jugend* (Opladen: Leske und Budrich, 1996), p. 140.

47. Manfred Backerra, *NVA: Ein Ruckblick für die Zukunft- Zeitzeugen berichten über ein Stuck deutscher Militärgeschichte* (Köln: Markus Verlag, 1992); Holger Jens Karlson and Jörg Judersleben, "Die Soldatensprache der NVA: Eine Wortschatzbetrachtung," *Muttersprache* 104 (1994): 143–65.

48. Werner Hübner, "Zur Rolle der Partei in der Nationalen Volksarmee," in *Rührt Euch! Zur Geschichte der NVA*, ed. Wolfgang Wünsche (Berlin: Edition Ost, 1998), p. 451.

49. SAPMO DY 30/IV/2/2039/182:97.

50. Corey Ross, "What About Peace and Bread? East Germans and the Remilitarization of the GDR, 1952–1962," *Militärgeschichtliche Zeitschrift* 58, no. 1 (1999): 111–35 (Munich: Oldenburg).

51. Carol Cohn, "Sex and Death in the Rational World of Defense Intellectuals," in *Violence in War and Peace*, ed. Nancy Scheper-Hughes and Philippe Bourgois (Malden, MA: Blackwell Publishing, 2004), pp. 354–61.

52. Fulbrook 1995; Georg-Maria Meyer and Sabine Collmer, *Kolonisierung oder*

Integration: Bundeswehr und Deutsche Einheit: Eine Bestandaufnahme (Opladen: Westdeutscher Verlag, 1993); T. Beck, *Liebe zum Sozialismus-Hass auf dem Klassenfeind: Sozialistisches Wehrmotiv und Wehrerziehung in der DDR* (Luneburg: n.p., 1983); Gunther Böhme and Wolfgang Spitzner, "Schutz des Sozialismus- Recht und Ehrenpflicht," *Einheit* (May), Ministerium f. nationale Verteidigung der DDR, Berlin.

53. Daphne Berdahl, *Where the World Ended: Re-Unification and Identity in the German Borderland* (Berkeley: University of California Press, 1999), p. 48.

54. Heider 1998; Diedrich, Ehlert, and Wenzke 1998: 51; Heinz Marks, *Gesellschaft für Sport und Technik: Vormilitärische Ausbildung in der DDR* (Köln: Markus Verlag, 1970), p. 8.

55. SAPMO DY 30 864:43; see also Maria Elisabeth Müller, *Zwischen Ritual und Alltag: Der Traum von einer sozialistischen Persönlichkeit* (Frankfurt: Campus Verlag, 1997).

56. Udo Baron, *Die Wehrideologie der Nationalen Volksarmee der DDR* (Bochum: Universitätsverlag Dr. N. Brockmeyer, 1993); p. 51.

57. Baron 1993.

58. I. U. Korablev, *Lenin, the Founder of the Soviet Armed Forces* (Moscow: Progress Publishers, 1977), pp. 15–19.

59. SAPMO DY 30 1161:60.

60. SAPMO DY 30 1161:61.

61. Detlef Bald, ed., *Die Nationale Volksarmee: Beiträge zur Selbstverstandnis und Geschichte des deutschen Militärs von 1945–1990* (Baden-Baden: Nomos Verlag, 1992); P. Jüngermann, *Die Wehrideologie der SED und das Leitbild der Nationalen Volksarmee vom sozialistischen deutschen Soldaten* (Stuttgart: Degerloch, 1973); Gerhard Merkl and Wolfgang Wünsche, *Die Nationale Volksarmee der DDR-Legitimation und Auftrag: Alte und Neue Legenden kritisch hinterfragt* (Berlin: Forschungs und Diskussionskreis DDR Geschichte, 1996).

62. Beck 1983.

63. Vereinbarung der Ministerium für Volksbildung, Gesellschaft für Sport und Technik, Freie Deutsche Jugend, und Deutsches Rotes Kreuz, May 30, 1969; Diedrich, Ehlert, and Wenzke 1998, p. 651.

64. Diedrich, Ehlert, and Wenzke 1998, p. 651.

65. Only in the mid- and late 1980s did the NVA consider conscripting women; this was a result of demographic studies which showed that the military would not be able to meet its "manpower" requirements. Elaborate steps were taken to entice women to join the military, including promises of prized educational opportunities after military service. Honecker decided to slash the overall size of the NVA in 1988–89; consequently, a large number of women who had been promised military training and educational opportunities were told that they were not needed, and that they were no longer eligible for certain university slots.

66. Wehrdienstgesetz der Deutschen Demokratischen Republik, 1982.

67. SAPMO DY 30/IV/2/2039/201; Stefan Wolle, *Die heile Welt der Diktatur* (Munich: Econ, 1999), p. 259.

68. Boyer 2005, p. 102.

69. Karl-Heinz Freitag, personal communication, 1999.

70. See Fulbrook 2005, for her discussion of gender, women, and the family in the GDR.

71. Jack Zipes, *Fairy Tales and the Art of Subversion: The Classic Genre for Children and the Process of Civilization* (New York: Routledge, 2006), p. 35. The degree to which print media in the GDR was saturated with military themes is shown by a secret report

from a Meeting of the Secretariat of the Political Control Committee of the NVA (Sitzung des Sekretariats der PHV) from January 1988. "Anlage 17" (Attachment 17) of the report concerns the "activities of the Press Department of the Ministry of National Defense in the training year 1986–87."

From Attachment 1 of Attachment 17 of the report:

Quantitative Overview of Published Military-Political Articles

Military-Political Articles in toto	1,986	1,987
National press	2,301	2,345
District [Bezirk] press	4,651	3,783
Photographs		
National press	1,041	659
District press	4,651	1,344

The report then breaks down the newspapers, magazines, journals, and so on, in which these articles and photographs appeared:

Neues Deutschland	424	398
Junge Welt	349	368
Berliner Zeitung	326	344
National Zeitung	294	305
Tribuene	202	213
Der Morgen	211	208
Bauern-Echo	322	325
Neue Zeit	173	184
District Organs of the SED		
Ostsee Zeitung	349	317
Schweriner Volkszeitung	306	249
Freie Erde	270	227
Volksstimme	459	350
Neuer Tag	366	271
Märkische Volksstimme	352	308
Freiheit	307	240
Military-Political Articles on Specific Themes		
Every-day military life-recruitment	1,612	1,304
"Comrades-in-arms" [Waffenbruderschaft]	1,125	1,253
Military technology	133	179
Traditions	339	259
Culture	461	415
Sports	403	273

72. See SAPMO DY 30 901; BA-MA AZN P2 980; BA-MA DVW1/55631 for detailed discussions of how the NVA viewed the necessity of women for militarization programs.

73. Despite efforts to convince men of the need to defend socialism, the overwhelming majority of men remained skeptical of military service, and families were not interested in sending their sons to the army. Women, despite the best efforts of the SED and the NVA, were often particularly suspicious of the military, and openly rejected the NVA. Over 90 percent of the women at a factory in Wusterwitz openly rejected the NVA and

its recruitment efforts: "Most of us don't have husbands anymore, and we are not going to send our children into a new war" (Ross 1999: 118).

74. SAPMO DY 30 899:15.

75. SAPMO DY 30 901.

76. Enloe 1993; Cynthia Enloe, *Does Khaki Become You? The Militarization of Women's Lives* (Boston: South End Press, 1983).

77. Bernd Pröll, "Sozialistische Wehrerziehung in der DDR im Zeichen der Entspannung: Anachronismus oder unabdingbare Reaktion?" *IFSH-Diskussionsbeiträge* 40 (September 1985); See also Barbara Einhorn, *Cinderella Goes to Market: Citizenship, Gender, and Women's Movements in East Central Europe* (London: Verso, 1993), for a general discussion of families under socialism.

78. Christine Eifler, "Zur Weiblichkeitsklischees in der NVA-Propaganda," *Offiziersbrief* 28 (1996): 19–21.

79. Eifler 1996, p. 20.

80. *Armee Rundschau*, March 3, 1987, p. 12.

81. *Armee Rundschau* was also very concerned with portraying the "new socialist man." *Armee Rundschau* strove to regulate the male body, but in a manner that was not to be perceived as coercive, but rather as "helpful." Men were shown as dutiful soldiers and partners, politically interested and engaged, literate, athletic and in shape, and good domestic partners. *Armee Rundschau* consistently addressed questions of propriety, and even devoted question-and-answer sections to proper haircut styles for soldiers.

82. Thomas Spanier, "In Erinnerung an meine Dienstzeit: 18 Monate als Wehrpflichtiger in der NVA," in *NVA: Ein Rückblick für die Zukunft- Zeitzeugen berichten über ein Stuck deutscher Militärgeschichte*, ed. Manfred Backerra (Köln: Markus Verlag, 1992), pp. 27–42.

83. *Für Dich*, September 1975, as cited in Pröll 1985.

84. Marks 1970, p. 8.

85. *Manöver Schneeflocke Brigadetagebücher, 1960–90* (Berlin: n.p., 1994).

86. Elaine Scarry, *The Body in Pain: The Making and Unmaking of the World* (Oxford: Oxford University Press, 1985).

87. Cynthia Enloe, *Globalization and Militarism: Feminists Make the Link* (New York: Rowman and Littlefield, 2007).

88. Louis Althusser, *Ideology and Ideological State Apparatuses: Notes Towards an Investigation in Lenin and Philosophy and Other Essays* (New York: Monthly Review Press, 1971).

89. Anne Allison, "Japanese Mothers and Obentos: The Lunch Box as Ideological State Apparatus," *Anthropological Quarterly* 64, no. 4, *Gender and the State in Japan* (October 1991): 195–208.

90. Böhme and Spitzner 1977.

91. SAPMO DY 30 901:178.

92. Pröll 1985; Wolle 1999.

93. Wolle 1998, p. 258.

94. SAPMO DY 30/IV/2/2039/201.

95. SAPMO DY 30/IV/2/2039/201.

96. SAPMO DY 30 901:27.

97. SAPMO DY 30 901:35–36.

98. Ministerium für nationale Verteidigung, *Vom Sinn des Soldatenseins: Ein Ratgeber für den Soldaten* (Berlin: Militärverlag der DDR, 1983).

99. Dietrich, Ehlert, and Wenzke 1998.

100. Backerra 1992; Rüdiger Wenzke, "Die Nationale Volksarmee," in Dietrich, Ehlert, and Wenzke 1998.

101. SAPMO DY 30/IV/2/2039/182:108–10.

102. Susan Buck-Morss, *The Dialectics of Seeing: Walther Benjamin and the Arcades Project* (Cambridge, MA: MIT Press, 1992), p. 18.

103. Terry Eagleton, *The Ideology of the Aesthetic* (Hoboken, NJ: Wiley-Blackwell, 1988), p. 5.

104. SAPMO DY 30 902:48.

105. See Benno Hafeneger and Michael Fritz, *Sie starben für Führer, Volk, und Vaterland: Die Hitlerjugend* (Frankfurt am Main: Brandes und Apsel, 1993); and Benno Hafeneger and Michael Buddrus, *Militärische Erziehung in Ost und West: Ein Lesebuch zur Kriegsbegeisterung jünger Männer Band 4: Nachkriegszeit und fünfziger Jahre* (Frankfuft am Main: Brandes und Apsel, 1994).

106. SAPMO DY 30 864:51.

107. Ministerium für nationale Verteidigung 1983 (Walter Stranka).

108. Baron 1993, p. 53.

109. SAPMO DY 30 901:111–13. Werner Weihold was an East German Border Guard soldier who murdered two other Border Guards—Klaus Peter Seidel and Jürgen Lange—during his escape into West Germany. He was tried in West Germany on two counts of murder, but found innocent, as he had acted in "self-defense" during his escape.

110. SAPMO DY 30 901:119.

111. Linda Green, *Fear as a Way of Life* (New York: Columbia University Press, 1999), p. 6.

112. Lutz 2007.

113. T. J. Jackson Lears, "The Concept of Cultural Hegemony: Problems and Possibilities," *American Historical Review* 90, no. 3 (June 1985): 567–93.

114. Lears 1985, p. 572.

115. Gerald Sider, *Between History and Tomorrow: Making and Breaking Everyday Life in Rural Newfoundland* (Peterborough, Ont.: Broadview Press, 2003), p. 209.

116. SAPMO DY 30 899:113.

CHAPTER 3: COMING OF AGE IN THE NVA

1. There is a small but growing collection of memoirs about life in the NVA, written by both officers and conscripts. See, for example, Bernd Biedermann, *Offizier, Diplomat, und Aufklärer der NVA: Streiflichter aus dem Kalten Krieg* (Berlin: Verlag Dr. Köster, 2008); Harri Englemann, *Japanischer Garten: Reminiszenen an meine Verteidigungsbereitschaft* (Rostock: WeymannBauer Verlag, 2000); Hans Fricke, *Davor, Dabei, Danach: Ein ehemaliger Kommandeur der Grenztruppuen der DDR berichtet* (Köln: Verlag GNN, 1993); Joerg Waehner, *Einstrich—Keinstrich: NVA Tagebuch* (Köln: Kiepenhauer und Witsch, 2006). See also R. Gehler, "EK, EK, EK- bald bist du nicht mehr da!" in *Soldatenkultur in der Nationalen Volksarmee*, Schriftenreihe des Museums der Stadt Hagenow (Hagenow: Museum der Stadt Hagenow, 1998). Life in the NVA has also been turned into a film: in 2005, the German director Leander Hausmann released the comedy *NVA* (Berlin: Boje Buck Produktion GmbH).

2. Jay Lockenour, *Soldiers as Citizens: Former Wehrmacht Officers in the Federal Republic of Germany, 1945–1955* (Lincoln: University of Nebraska Press, 2001), p. 4; Emilio

Willems, *A Way of Life and Death: Three Centuries of Prussian-German Militarism; An Anthropological Approach* (Nashville, TN: Vanderbilt University Press, 1986).

3. Lockenour 2001, p. 4. See also Stephan Fingerle, *Waffen in Arbeiterhand? Die Rekrutierung des Offizierkorps der Nationalen Volksarmee und ihrer Vorläufer* (Berlin: Christoph Links Verlag, 2001).

4. Susan Jeffords, "The Remasculinization of Germany in the 1950s: Discussion," *Signs: The Journal of Women in Culture and Society* 24, no. 1 (Autumn 1998): 163–70; Roy Jerome, ed., *Conceptions of Postwar German Masculinity* (Albany: State University of New York Press, 2001).

5. Herspring 1998, pp. 159–60.

6. Fulbrook 2005, p. 188.

7. Eric Weitz, *Creating German Communism: From Popular Protests to Socialist State* (Princeton, NJ: Princeton University Press, 1997).

8. Fulbrook 2005, p. 30.

9. See Jeffords 1998.

10. Diedrich, Ehlert, and Wenzke 1998.

11. See Fulbrook 2005, p. 126, for a list of fears about military service and the decreasing appeal of a career in the NVA.

12. Allison 1991, p. 196; emphasis added.

13. Borneman 1992.

14. Borneman 1992, p. 46.

15. Sidney Mintz, *Sweetness and Power: The Place of Sugar in Modern History* (New York: Penguin Books, 1985).

16. Joan Scott, as quoted in Elaine Abelson, David Abraham, and Marjorie Murphy, "An Interview with Joan Scott," *Radical History Review* 45 (1989): 41–59.

CHAPTER 5: A WAR OF SIGNS, IMAGES, AND MEMORIES

1. See Andrew Bickford, "Soldiers, Citizens, and the State: East German Army Officers in Post-Unification Germany," *Comparative Studies in Society and History* 51, no. 2 (2009): 260–87.

2. Stuart Hall, "Cultural Identity and Diaspora," in *Colonial Discourse and Post-Colonial Theory: A Reader*, ed. Patrick Williams and Laura Christman (New York: Columbia University Press, 1994), pp. 392–403. See also Green 1999.

3. Paul Cooke, *From Colonization to Nostalgia: Representing East Germany Since Unification* (Oxford: Berg, 2005); Maier 1999; Roger Woods, "The East German Contribution to German Identity," in *Studies in GDR Culture and Society 13: Understanding the Past-Managing the Future: Integration of the Five New Lander into the Federal Republic of Germany*, ed. Margy Gerber and Roger Woods, selected papers from the Eighteenth New Hampshire Symposium (Lanham, MD: University Press of America, 1994), pp. 25–26.

4. Glaeser 2000, p. 99; see also Chris Flockton, Eva Kolinsky, and Rosalind Pritchard, *The New Germany in the East: Policy Agendas and Social Developments Since Unification* (London: Frank Cass, 2000), p. 1; Fulbrook 1995, 2005.

5. Flockton, Kolinsky, and Pritchard 2000, p. 2; Fulbrook 1995.

6. Boyer 2005, p. 7.

7. Glaeser 2000; Michael Brie, "The Difficulty of Discussing the GDR," in *Studies in GDR Culture and Society 13: Understanding the Past- Managing the Future: Integration of the Five New Lander into the Federal Republic of Germany*, ed. Margy Gerber and Roger

Woods, selected papers from the Eighteenth New Hampshire Symposium (Lanham, MD: University Press of America, 1994), pp. 1–23; Johannes L. Kuppe, "West German Policy Toward East Germany: A Motor of Unification?" in *German Unification: Process and Outcomes*, ed. M. Donald Hancock and Helga A. Walsh (Boulder, CO: Westview Press, 1994), pp. 35–51.

8. Andrew Beattie, *Playing Politics with History: The Bundestag Inquiries into East Germany* (New York: Berghahn Books, 2008).

9. Rede des Bundesministers der Verteidigung, Dr. Franz Josef Jung, anlässlich des XXXII, Internationalen Militärhistorikerkongresses am 21. August 2006 in Potsdam.

10. Woods 1994, p. 33.

11. Maier 1999; Stefan Berger, "Historians and Nation-Building in Germany After Unification," *Past and Present: A Journal of Historical Studies*, no. 148 (August 1995): 187–222.

12. Jarausch and Geyer 2003, p. 63.

13. Berger 1995; Bill Niven, *Facing the Nazi Past: United Germany and the Legacy of the Third Reich* (London: Routledge, 2002), p. 2.

14. Hans-Ulrich Wehler, *Deutsche Gesellschaftsgeschichte*, vol. 5, *Bundesrepublik und DDR, 1949–1990* (Munich: C. H. Beck, 2008); see also Donna Harsch, "Footnote or Footprint? The German Democratic Republic in History," Twenty-third Annual Lecture of the German Historical Institute, Washington, DC, November 12, 2009, *Bulletin of the German Historical Institute* (Spring 2010): 9–25.

15. Rogers Brubaker, *Citizenship and Nationhood in France and Germany* (Cambridge, MA: Harvard University Press, 1992), p. 169; see also Uli Linke, *German Bodies: Race and Representation After Hitler* (New York: Routledge, 1999); Stefan Senders, "Laws of Belonging: Legal Dimensions of National Inclusion in Germany," *New German Critique* 67 (Winter 1996):147–76.

16. Glaeser 2000; Kuppe 1994, pp. 41–42.

17. Deutscher Bundestag, Drucksache 14/8920, April 25, 2002, PDS Antrag: Deutsche Einheit in der Bundeswehr herstellen.

18. Jeffrey Peck, "Turks and Jews: Comparing Minorities in Germany after the Holocaust," in *German Cultures, Foreign Cultures: The Politics of Belonging*, AICGS research report no. 8, Humanities Program, Johns Hopkins University (Baltimore: American Institute for Contemporary German Studies, 1997), p. 12.

19. Dirk Philipsen, *We Were the People: Voices from East Germany's Revolutionary Autumn of 1989* (Durham, NC: Duke University Press, 1993), p. 5.

20. Walter Schmidt, as quoted in Berger 1995, p. 148.

21. Manfred Kossock, as quoted in Berger 1995, pp. 206–7.

22. K. Anthony Appiah, "Identity, Authenticity, Survival: Multicultural Societies and Social Reproduction," in *Multiculturalism*, ed. Amy Gutman (Princeton, NJ: Princeton University Press, 1994), p. 149.

23. Philipsen 1993, p. 3.

24. Brubaker 1992, p. 83.

25. Glaeser 2000, p. 181.

26. Niven 2002, p. 2.

27. Jarausch 2006, p. 40.

28. Maier 1999; Charles Maier, *The Unmasterable Past: History, Holocaust, and German National Identity* (Cambridge, MA: Harvard University Press, 1997); Jeffrey Herf, *Divided Memory: The Nazi Past in the Two Germanys* (Cambridge, MA: Harvard University Press, 1997); Weitz 1997.

29. Herspring 1998; Frederick Zilian, Jr., *From Confrontation to Cooperation: The Takeover of the National People's Army (East Germany) by the Bundeswehr* (London: Praeger, 1999).

30. See Herf 1997, pp. 23–25, for background on the founding of the NKFD.

31. Bald 1994; Daniel Giese, *Die SED und ihre Armee: Die NVA zwischen Politisierung und Professionalismus, 1956–1965*, Schriftenreihe der Vierteljahrshefte für Zeitgeschichte (Munich: R. Oldenbourg Verlag, 2002).

32. Giese 2002, p. 47.

33. Bald 1994, pp. 147–48.

34. Bald 1994, p. 148.

35. As of late 2010, Germany is considering abolishing conscription and moving toward an all-volunteer force.

36. Christoph Klessmann, *Zwei Staaten, Eine Nation: Deutsche Geschichte, 1955–1970* (Bonn: Bundeszentrale für politische Bildung, 1997), p. 146; Elmar Schmähling, *Ohne Glanz und Gloria: Die Bundewehr- Bilanz einer neurotischen Armee* (Düsseldorf: ECON Verlag, 1991).

37. Bald 2005.

38. In 1994, the German Constitutional Court ruled that the Bundeswehr could be deployed outside of the territorial boundaries of the Federal Republic. This ruling helped lead to an eventual change in the constitution of the Federal Republic, and allowed for the deployment of a German military outside of Germany for the first time since World War II. See Sameera Dalvi, "The Post–Cold War Role of the Bundeswehr: A Product of Normative Influences," *European Security* 7, no. 1 (Spring 1998): 97–116.

39. Meyer and Collmer 1993.

40. Egbert Fischer, *Ehemalige Berufssoldaten der NVA in der Bundesrepublik Deutschland, Report 1995: Ergebnisse einer Meinungsumfrage in Kamaradschaften "Ehemalige" des Landesverbandes Ost des Deutschen Bundeswehr—Verbandes e.V.* (Bonn:Karl-Theodor-Molinari Stiftung, 1995), pp. 153–54; Otto Wenzel, *Kriegsbereit: Der Nationale Verteidigungsrat der DDR, 1960–1989* (Köln: Verlag Wissenschaft und Politik, 1995), p. 77.

41. Wenzel 1995; Jörg Schönbohm, *Two Armies and One Fatherland* (Providence, RI: Berghahn Books, 1996).

42. Fischer 1995; Meyer and Collmer 1993; Baron 1993.

43. Generalmajor a.D. Peter Herrich, as quoted in Fischer 1995, p. 155.

44. Glaeser 2000, Pierre Bourdieu, as quoted in Michael Watts, "Living Under Contract: Work, Production Politics, and the Manufacture of Discontent in a Peasant Society," in *Reworking Modernity: Capitalism and Symbolic Discontent*, ed. Allen Pred and Michael Watts (New Brunswick, NJ: Rutgers University Press, 1992), p. 99.

45. Watts 1992, p. 99.

46. Niven 2002, p. 146; Berghahn 1987, p. 210.

47. Donald Abenheim, *Reforging the Iron Cross: The Search for Tradition in the West German Armed Forces* (Princeton, NJ: Princeton University Press, 1988), p. 53.

48. Abenheim 1988, p. 54.

49. Abenheim 1988, p. 55; Niven 2002, p. 146.

50. Abenheim 1988; Niven 2002, p. 146.

51. Abenheim 1988, p. 70.

52. Abenheim 1988; Large 1996.

53. Niven 2002, p. 146.

54. Abenheim 1988; Large 1996.

55. Niven 2002, p. 146; see also Omer Bartov, *Murder in Our Midst: The Holocaust, Industrial Killing, and Representation* (New York: Oxford University Press, 1996).

56. Edgar Doehler and Rudolf Falkenberg, *Militärische Traditionen der DDR und der NVA*, Serie Politik und Landesverteidigung (Berlin: Militärverlag der Deutschen Demokratischen Republik, 1979), p. 24.

57. Bundeswehr Web site, www.bundeswehr.de, Richtlinien zum Traditionsverständnis und zur Traditionspflege in der Bundeswehr, Grundsätze (accessed May 20, 2010).

58. Bundeswehr Web site, www.bundeswehr.de, Tradition der Bundeswehr, Eigene Geschichte (accessed May 20, 2010).

59. Eric Hobsbawm and Terence Ranger, eds., *The Invention of Tradition* (Cambridge: Cambridge University Press, 1988).

60. Holger Reimer, Deutscher Bundeswehrverband Landesverband Ost, personal communication 1998; Deutscher Bundestag Drucksache 14/8920, April 25, PDS Antrag: Deutsche Einheit in der Bundeswehr herstellen, press release.

61. Prof. Dr. Egbert Fischer, personal communication, 2006.

62. Meyer and Collmer 1993; Ralph Giordano, *Die Traditionslüge: Vom Kriegerkult in der Bundeswehr* (Köln: Kiepenheuer und Witsch, 2000), Volker Koop, *Abgewickelt? Auf den Spuren der Nationalen Volksarmee* (Bonn: Bouvier Verlag, 1995).

63. Niven 2002, p. 60.

64. See Niven 2002.

65. Volker Rühe, "'Aufstand des Gewissens': Gedenken an den militärischen Widerstand," *Presse- und Informationsamt der Bundesregierung*, bulletin, no. 68 (July 22, 1994), p. 648, as cited in Prof. Dr. Holger H. Herwig, *Aggression Contained? The Federal Republic of Germany and International Security*, final report, NATO research fellowship, n.d.

66. Wolfram Wette, *The Wehrmacht: History, Myth, Reality* (Cambridge, MA: Harvard University Press, 2006), p. 276.

67. Bald 1994; Niven 2002; Johannes Klotz, ed., *Vorbild Wehrmacht? Wehrmachtsverbrechen, Rechtsextrimismus und Bundeswehr* (Köln: PapyRossa Verlag, 1998); Wolfram Wette, "Wehrmachtstraditionen und Bundeswehr, Deutsche Machtphantasien im Zeichen der neuen Militärpolitik und des Rechstradikalismus," in Klotz 1998, pp. 126–54.

68. Niven 2002, p. 147.

69. Reinhard Günzel, Ulrich Wegener, and Wilhelm Walther, *Geheime Krieger—Drei Deutsche Kommandoverbände im Bild* (Selent: Pour le Mérite Verlag, 2005).

70. "Wehrmachtsemblem auf Jeep war nicht genehmigt," *Der Spiegel*, November 2, 2006.

71. "Hitler Apologist Wins Honor, and a Storm Breaks Out," *New York Times*, June 21, 2000.

72. Barthes 1972.

73. Reimer 1998; Deutscher Bundestag 2002.

74. Berger 1995.

75. Schönbohm 1996.

76. Rainer Wulf, personal communication, 1999.

77. Karin Hausen, "Histories of Mourning: Flowers and Stones for the War Dead, Confusion for the Living; Vignettes from East and West Germany," in *Between History and Histories: The Making of Silences and Commemorations*, ed. Gerald Sider and Gavin Smith (Toronto: University of Toronto Press, 1997), pp. 127–48.

78. Dr. Gerhard Kümmel, Universität der Bundeswehr, personal communication, 2003.

79. During the ceremony, Reagan stated: "I think there's nothing wrong with visiting that cemetery where those young men are victims of Nazism also, even though they were fighting in the German uniform, drafted into service to carry out the hateful wishes of the Nazis." Ronald Reagan, as quoted in Bartov 1996, p. 226, n. 8.

80. See Herf 1997, 351–54, for his discussion of Reagan's visit to Bitburg.

81. See Borneman 1992.

82. Glaeser 2000, p. 181

83. Glaeser 2000.

84. Johannes Fabian, *Time and the Other: How Anthropology Makes Its Object* (New York: Columbia University Press, 1983).

85. Linke 1999.

86. After unification, the release of declassified NVA documents and plans showed that the NVA did not cross into Czechoslovakia in 1968. NVA units were placed on alert and moved to the border as a reserve force, but the Soviet high command held them in reserve, and did not allow them to cross over as part of the invasion force. See Herspring 1998, p. 23.

87. Bald 2005.

88. See Bald 2005; Biess 2006; and Frank Biess, "Between Amnesty and Anti-Communism: The West German Kameradenschinder Trials, 1948–1960," in *Crimes of War: Guilt and Denial in the Twentieth Century*, ed. Omer Bartov, Atina Grossmann, and Mary Nolan (New York: New Press, 2002), pp. 138–60, for a discussion of the heated and bitter politics of "comradeship" in Germany between former Wehrmacht-SS soldiers and those who joined antifascist organizations founded in the Soviet Union (such as the NKFD).

89. Herbert Becker, Deutscher Bundeswehrverband, Landesverband Ost (informational memos-briefings written by Herbert Becker, and sent out to members of the veterans groups), "Sachstandsbericht Statusfragen," 1999.

90. See Omer Bartov's discussion and analysis of the Wehrmachtausstellung, "The Wehrmacht Exhibition Controversy: The Politics of Evidence," in Bartov, Grossmann, and Nolan 2002, pp. 41–60.

91. See Bartov 1996; Niven 2002.

CHAPTER 6: "UNIFICATION HAS RUINED MY LIFE"

1. Berdahl 1999; Flockton, Kolinsky, and Pritchard 2000.

2. Borneman 1992, 1993.

3. Deutscher Bundestag 1990, 224 Sitzung 1990/17744, September 13: Übernahme von Teilen der NVA durch die Bundeswehr.

4. Lapp 1992, p. 25. See also Bald 2005; Koop 1995.

5. Fischer 1995, pp. 153–54; Wenzel 1995, p. 18.

6. Fischer 1995, p. 18.

7. Maier 1999, p. 301; Einhorn 1993; Karen Remmler, "Deciphering the Body of Memory: Writing by Former East German Women Writers," in *Post-Communism and the Body Politic*, ed. Ellen E. Berry (New York: New York University Press, 1995), p. 138.

8. Berdahl 1999.

9. Berdahl 1999, p. 115.

10. Berdahl 1999, p. 115; see also Verdery 1996, p. 22.

11. Birgit Müller, *Disenchantment with Market Economics: East Germans and Western Capitalism* (New York: Berghahn Books, 2007), p. 29.

12. See Berdahl 1999; Müller 2007.

13. Derek Lewis and John R. P. McKenzie, eds., *The New Germany: Social, Political, and Cultural Challenges of Unification* (Exeter: University of Exeter Press, 1995), p. 147.

14. Holger Reimer, Deutscher Bundeswehr Landesverband Ost, personal communication, 1999.

15. For a discussion of the uses and politics of "culture" in the GDR, see David Bathrick, *The Powers of Speech: The Politics of Culture in the GDR* (Lincoln: University of Nebraska Press, 1995).

16. See Berdahl 1999; Einhorn 1993; Hermine DeSoto, "In the Name of the Folk: Women and the Nation in the New Germany," *UCLA Women's Law Journal* 5, no. 1 (1994): 83–101; Irene Dölling, "Gespaltenes Bewusstsein: Frauen und Männerbilder in der DDR," in *Frauen in Deutschland, 1945–1992*, ed. Gisela Helwig and Hildegard Maria Nickel, pp. 23–52 (Bonn: Bundeszentrale für politische Bildung); Susan Gal and Gail Kligman, *The Politics of Gender After Socialism: A Comparative Historical Essay* (Princeton, NJ: Princeton University Press, 2000); Eva Kolinsky, ed., *Between Hope and Fear: Everyday Life in Post-Unification Germany* (Keel: Keel University Press, 1995); Eva Kolinsky, ed., *Women in Contemporary Germany: Life, Work, and Politics* (Providence, RI: Berg, 1993); Hildegard Maria Nickel, "Women in the German Democratic Republic and in the New Federal States: Looking Backward and Forward (Five Theses)," in *Gender Politics and Post-Communism: Reflections from Eastern Europe and the Former Soviet Union*, ed. Nanette Funk and Magda Müller (New York: Routledge, 1993), pp. 138–50; Ilona Ostner, "Slow Motion: Women, Work, and the Family in Germany," in *Women and Social Policies in Europe*, ed. Jane Lewis (Hants: Edward Elgar, 1993), pp. 92–115; Dorothy Rosenberg, "Shock Therapy: GDR Women in Transition from a Socialist Welfare State to a Social Market Economy," *Signs: The Journal of Women in Culture and Society* 17, no. 1 (Autumn 1991): 129–51; Katherine Verdery, "From Parent-State to Family Patriarchs: Gender and Nation in Contemporary Eastern Europe," *East European Politics and Societies* 8, no. 2 (Spring 1994): 225–55.

17. BA-MA DVW1 55631:271.

18. Cynthia Enloe, *Bananas, Beaches, and Bases: Making Feminist Sense of International Politics* (Berkeley: University of California Press, 1990), p. 10.

19. See Linke 2002, pp. 165–66.

20. For discussions on the interplay between race, politics, and identity after unification, see Hermine DeSoto and Konstanze Plett, "Citizenship and Minorities in the Process of Nation Rebuilding in Germany," *PoLAR: Political and Legal Anthropology Review* 18, no. 1 (May 1995): 107–22; Mark Howard, "An East German Ethnicity? Understanding the New Division of Unified Germany," *German Politics and Society* 13, no. 4 (1995): 49–70; Uli Linke, "Murderous Fantasies: Violence, Memory, and Selfhood in Germany," *New German Critique* 64 (Winter 1995):37–59; Peter H. Merkl, "Reinventing German National Identity," introduction to *The Federal Republic of Germany at Forty Five: Union Without Unity*, ed. Peter H. Merkl (New York: New York University Press, 1995), pp. 1–30; Senders, 1996; Andreas Staab, *National Identity in Eastern Germany: Inner Unification or Continued Separation?* (London: Praeger, 1998); Woods 1994.

CHAPTER 7: AS GERMANS AMONG GERMANS

1. Herspring 1998, p. 145.

2. Jay Winter and Emmanuel Sivan, "Setting the Framework," in *War and Remembrance in the Twentieth Century*, ed. Jay Winter and Emmanuel Sivan (Cambridge: Cambridge University Press, 2000), p. 32.

3. Fischer 1995, pp. 153–54; Wenzel 1995, p. 5.

4. Herbert Becker, personal communication, 1999; see also the official Web site of the Initiativgemeinschaft zum Schutz der sozialen Rechte ehemaliger Angehöriger bewaffneter Organe und der Zöllverwaltung der DDR (ISOR), www.isor—sozialverein.de (accessed May 21, 2010).

5. I attempted to contact ISOR twice, but was unsuccessful.

6. Fischer 1995, p. 5.

7. The Mildtätige Stiftung (Charity Foundation), was established to help soldiers and their families in financial difficulties.

8. Herbert Becker, "Sachstandsbericht Statusfragen," press release of the Landesverband Ost der Deutschen Bundeswehrverband, December 1999.

9. *Unser Fallschirm*, September 1999.

10. *Unser Fallschirm*, September 1999.

11. Becker 1999.

12. Deutschen Bundeswehrverband 1999.

13. Becker 1999.

14. See Berdahl 1999; Shapiro 1997.

15. "Ehemaliger U.S. Sergeant untersucht Gefühle der NVA Soldaten: Ungleichbehandlung sorgt immer noch für Ärger," *Ostsee Zeitung*, March 23, 2000.

16. Gerd Richter, public address to the meeting of the Kameradschaft Ehemalige Rostock, March 23, 2000, transcript in author's possession.

17. The militarization of the United States–Mexico border was a constant topic of discussion with former officers. Many drew connections between the Berlin Wall and the construction of a border fence by the United States, and many wondered why they were punished or held accountable for the Wall while the United States was building what they saw as the equivalent.

18. Questions of "will" were very important in the NVA, as the NVA as a coherent, effective fighting force was only expected to last three to five days before it was completely destroyed. The Border Guards referred to themselves as the "suicide soldiers of the first hour," and expected to take 90 percent casualties within the first twenty-four hours of combat.

19. See Bald 2005; Herf 1997; Weitz 1997.

20. See Michel Foucault, *History of Sexuality, Volume 1* (New York, Vintage Books, 1980).

CHAPTER 8: "WE'RE THE JEWS OF THE NEW GERMANY"

1. Paul Connerton, *How Societies Remember* (New York: Cambridge University Press, 1989); Hobsbawm and Ranger 1988.

2. See Andrew Bickford, "'The Red General': German Unification, Fallen Elites, and the Time-Shift of Heroic Victimhood," *Anthropology Now* 2, no. 2 (September 2010): 42–51.

3. Baumgarten and other high-ranking East German officials vehemently denied—and continue to deny—that there was ever a "shoot-to-kill order" issued in the GDR. However, in 2007, a document dated 1 October 1973 was found in Magdeburg, authorizing the use of deadly force by the Border Guards, including the use of deadly force to stop women and children attempting to escape to the West. See "E. German License to Kill Found," BBC report, 12 August 2007.

4. See Paige West, "Holding the Story Forever: The Aesthetics of Ethnographic Labour," *Anthropological Forum* 15, no. 3 (November 2005): 267–75.

5. Fabian 1983; Glaeser 2000.

6. See Bartov 1992; Herf 1997; Wette 2006.

7. Aleida Assmann and Ute Frevert, *Geschichtsvergessenheit/Geschichtsverssenheit: Vom Umgang mit deutschen Vergangenheiten nach 1945* (Stuttgart: Deutsche Verlags-Anstalt, 1999), pp. 42–44.

8. Alison Landsberg, *Prosthetic Memory: The Transformation of American Remembrance in the Age of Mass Media* (New York: Columbia University Press, 2004), p. 25.

9. Bartov, Grossmann, and Nolan 2002, p. xxiii.

10. Dominic Boyer, "Conspiracy, History, and Therapy at a Berlin Stammtisch." *American Ethnologist* 33, no. 3 (2006): 327–39.

11. Tzvetan Todorov, as quoted in Bartov, Grossmann, and Nolan 2002, p. xxiii.

12. Giorgio Agamben, *Homo Sacer: Sovereign Power and Bare Life* (Stanford, CA: Stanford University Press, 1998).

13. Agamben 1998.

14. Giorgio Agamben, *State of Exception* (Chicago: University of Chicago Press, 2005).

15. John Borneman, "State Formation," in *International Encyclopedia of the Social and Behavioral Sciences*, ed. Neil J. Smelser and Paul B. Baltes (Amsterdam: Elsevier Sciences).

16. Brubaker 1992; Linke 1999; Senders 1996.

CHAPTER 9: DEATH AND ALLEGIANCE

1. Catherine Lutz, "Making War at Home in the United States: Militarization and the Current Crisis," *American Anthropologist* 104, no. 3 (2002): 723–35.

2. Enloe 2007.

3. Sheehan 2008, p. 17.

4. Kertzer 1989, p. 8.

5. See Michael Taussig, *The Magic of the State* (New York: Routledge, 1997).

Works Cited

ARCHIVAL SOURCES

BA-MA AZN P2 98079. PHV Soziologische Untersuchungen 1976–79, GVS, PHV Abt. Soz. Analyse, VVS, Ergebnisse von Untersuchungen über die Bewahrung der OS während der Berufs- und Hochschulreifeausbildung.

BA-MA DVW1 55631:271. Protokoll der Sitzung des Kollegiums des MfnV vom 30.09.1983, Geheime Verschlusssache, MfnV Chef Kader, Information an des Kollegium des Ministeriums für Nationale Verteidigung, Über die Entwicklung der Entlassungen aus disziplinarischen Grunden der Berufsoffiziere Am 23.09.1983.

BA-MA DVW 1/55636:000019. Geheime Verschlusssache, Sitzung des Kollegiums des MfNV vom 11.12.1985, Information über die Ergebnisse der Sicherung des militärischen Berufsnachwuchses im Ausbildungsjahr 1984–85.

BA-MA DVW 1/55638:000050. Geheime Verschlusssache, Sitzung des Kollegiums des MfNV vom 11.12.1985, Information über die Ergebnisse der Sicherung des militärischen Berufsnachwuchses im Ausbildungsjahr 1984–85, Entwicklung der Nachwuchsgewinnung.

SAPMO DY 30 1161:60–61. SED Abteilungs Sicherheitsfragen, Sozialistische Wehrerziehung in Weissenfels.

SAPMO DY 30/IV/2/2039/201. Gewinnung des militärischen Berufsnachwuches, Ministerium für Volksbildung/Hauptabteilung Oberschulen.

SAPMO DY 30/IV/2/2039/182:97. Ministerrat der DDR/Der Vorsitzender, Geheime Verschlusssache,GVS-NR: ZV 003 294 Verfügung Nr. S 5/84 Über Massnahmen zur Gestaltung der Zivilverteidigung vom 27. Marz 1984.

SAPMO DY 30/IV/2/2039/182:108–110. Ministerrat der DDR/Der Vorsitzender, Geheime Verschlusssache,GVS-NR: ZV 003 294, Verfügung Nr. S 5/84 Über Massnahmen zur Gestaltung der Zivilverteidigung vom 27. Marz 1984.

SAPMO DY 30 899:15. SED Abteilung Sicherheitsfragen, Konzeption für die Beratung mit staatlichen Leitern in der KEL-Sitzung am 29.05.1981.

SAPMO DY 30 899:113. SED Abteilung Sicherheitsfragen, Sektor Wehrpolitische Massenarbeit,Berlin, den 21.Oktober 1983, Vom operativen Einsatz zum Studium der Erfahrungen bei der wehrpolitischen Massenarbeit der Kreisleitung Schwedt und der Betriebsparteiorganisation PCK Schwedt (5 Sept. u. 17—19 Okt. 1983).

SAPMO DY 30 901:111–13. Rat des Bezirkes Suhl Stellvertreter des Vorsitzenden für Inneres 19.09.85, Ministerrat der DDR, Ministerium des Inneren, Leiter der Hauptabteilung Innere Angelegenheiten, Erfahrungen und Ergebnisse in der Arbeit der Kommission sozialistische Wehrerziehung.

SAPMO DY 30 901:119. Rat des Bezirkes Suhl Stellvertreter des Vorsitzenden für Inneres 19.09.85, Ministerrat der DDR,Ministerium des Inneren, Leiter der Hauptabteilung,Innere

Angelegenheiten, Erfahrungen und Ergebnisse in der Arbeit der Kommission sozialistische Wehrerziehung.

SAPMO DY 30 901:27. Rat der Stadt Plauen, Stellvertreter des Oberburgermeisters für Inneres 2.9.1985, Vortrag: Erfahrungen und Ergebnisse in der Arbeit der Kommission sozialistische Wehrerziehung.

SAPMO DY 30 901:35–36. Rat der Stadt Plauen, Stellvertreter des Oberburgermeisters für Inneres 2.9.1985, Vortrag: Erfahrungen und Ergebnisse in der Arbeit der Kommission sozialistische Wehrerziehung.

SAPMO DY 30 901:178. SED Abteilung Sicherheitsfragen, 6 Okt 1986, Information zum Erfahrungsaustausch der Bezirkskommission für sozialistische Wehrerziehung and Nachwuchsgewinning am 1.10.86 in Halle.

SAPMO DY 30 902:48. SED Abteilung Sicherheitsfragen, Sektor Wehrpolitische Massnahmen,Berlin 1 Okt 1981 Aktennotiz, Zur Situation an der Fammschirmsprungschule Halle/Oppin.

SAPMO DY 30/IV/2/2039/201. SED, Buro Krenz,2, 29.9.1982, An: ZK der SED Horst Dohlus von Margot Honecker, Information über die formalistischen Methoden bei der Gewinnung des militärischen Berufnachwuchses.

SAPMO DY 30864:43. SED Abteilung Sicherheitsfragen, Meldung über die Ergebnisse des 13ten Politlehrgangs (1981–83), 13 Polit. Lehrgang Jahresarbeit.

SAPMO DY 30864:51. SED Abteilung Sicherheitsfragen, Meldung über die Ergebnisse des 13ten Politlehrgangs (1981–83), Die kulturpolitische Arbeit im Politlehrgang.

PERSONAL COMMUNICATIONS

Albers, Lt. Col. Bernd. 2002. Assistant Military Attaché, German Embassy, Washington DC, July 2.

Becker, Herbert. 1999.

Fischer, Prof. Dr. Egbert. 2006.

Freitag, Karl-Heinz. 1999.

Kümmel, Dr. Gerhard. 2003. Universität der Bundeswehr.

Müller, Oberst a.D. Dieter. 2006. Deutscher Bundeswehrverband Landesverband Ost.

Reimer, Holger. 1998. Deutscher Bundeswehrverband Landesverband Ost.

———. 1999. Deutscher Bundeswehr Landesverband Ost.

Wulf, Rainer. 1999.

OTHER SOURCES

Abelson, Elaine, David Abraham, and Marjorie Murphy. 1989. "An Interview with Joan Scott." *Radical History Review* 45: 41–59.

Abenheim, Donald. 1988. *Reforging the Iron Cross: The Search for Tradition in the West German Armed Forces.* Princeton, NJ: Princeton University Press.

Abrams, Philip. 1988 (1977). "Notes on the Difficulty of Studying the State." *Journal of Historical Sociology* 1, no. 1 (March): 58–89.

Agamben, Giorgio. 1998. *Homo Sacer: Sovereign Power and Bare Life.* Stanford, CA: Stanford University Press.

———. 2005. *State of Exception.* Chicago: University of Chicago Press.

Allison, Anne. 1997. "Japanese Mothers and Obentos: The Lunch Box as Ideological State

Apparatus." *Anthropological Quarterly* 64, no. 4, *Gender and the State in Japan* (October 1991): 195–208.

Althusser, Louis. 1971. *Ideology and Ideological State Apparatuses: Notes Towards an Investigation in Lenin and Philosophy and Other Essays.* New York: Monthly Review Press.

Anderson, Benedict. 1991. *Imagined Communities.* London: Verso.

Appiah, K. Anthony. 1994. "Identity, Authenticity, Survival: Multicultural Societies and Social Reproduction." In *Multiculturalism,* ed. Amy Gutman, pp. 149–63. Princeton, NJ: Princeton University Press.

Arkin, William, and Lynne R. Dobrovsky. 1978. "Military Socialization and Masculinity." *Journal of Social Issues* 34, no. 1 (Winter): 151–68.

Armee Rundschau. 1980–90. East German military magazine for civilians.

Assmann, Aleida, and Ute Frevert. 1999. *Geschichtsvergessenheit/Geschichtsvesessenheit: Vom Umgang mit deutschen Vergangenheiten nach 1945.* Stuttgart: Deutsche Verlags-Anstalt.

Backerra, Manfred. 1992. *NVA: Ein Ruckblick für die Zukunft- Zeitzeugen berichten über ein Stuck deutscher Militärgeschichte.* Köln: Markus Verlag.

Bald, Detlef, ed. 1992. *Die Nationale Volksarmee: Beiträge zur Selbstverstandnis und Geschichte des deutschen Militärs von 1945–1990.* Baden-Baden: Nomos Verlag.

———. 1994. *Militär und Gesellschaft, 1945–1990: Die Bundeswehr in Bonner Republik.* Baden-Baden: Nomos Verlag.

———. 2005. *Die Bundeswehr: Eine kritische Geschichte, 1955–2005.* Munich: C. H. Beck.

Baron, Udo. 1993. *Die Wehrideologie der Nationalen Volksarmee der DDR.* Bochum: Universitätsverlag Dr. N. Brockmeyer.

Barthes, Roland. 1972. *Mythologies.* New York: Hill and Wang.

Bartov, Omer. 1992. *Hitler's Army: Soldiers, Nazis, and War in the Third Reich.* Oxford: Oxford University Press.

———. 1996. *Murder in Our Midst: The Holocaust, Industrial Killing, and Representation.* New York: Oxford University Press.

———. 2002. "The Wehrmacht Exhibition Controversy: The Politics of Evidence." In *Crimes of War: Guilt and Denial in the Twentieth Century,* ed. Omer Bartov, Atina Grossmann, and Mary Nolan, pp. 41–60. New York: New Press.

Bartov, Omer, Atina Grossmann, and Mary Nolan, eds. 2002. *Crimes of War: Guilt and Denial in the Twentieth Century.* New York: New Press.

Bathrick, David. *The Powers of Speech: The Politics of Culture in the GDR.* Lincoln: University of Nebraska Press, 1995.

Beattie, Andrew. 2008. *Playing Politics with History: The Bundestag Inquiries into East Germany.* New York: Berghahn Books.

Beck, T. 1983. *Liebe zum Sozialismus-Hass auf dem Klassenfeind: Sozialistisches Wehrmotiv und Wehrerziehung in der DDR.* Luneburg: n.p.

Becker, Herbert. 1999. "Sachstandsbericht Statusfragen" (Progress Report on the Status Question). Press release of the Deutscher Bundeswehrverband Landesverband Ost, December.

———. 2000. "Gedanken zur Traditionspflege" (Thoughts on Maintaining Tradition). Press Release of the Deutscher Bundeswehrverband Landesverband Ost, February 2000.

Berdahl, Daphne. 1999. *Where the World Ended: Re-Unification and Identity in the German Borderland.* Berkeley: University of California Press.

Berger, Stefan. 1995. "Historians and Nation-Building in Germany After Unification." *Past and Present: A Journal of Historical Studies*, no. 148 (August): 187–222.

Berghahn, Volker. 1987. *Modern Germany: Society, Economy, and Politics in the Twentieth Century*. Cambridge: Cambridge University Press.

Berry, Ellen E., ed. 1995. *Post-Communism and the Body Politic*. New York: New York University Press.

Bickford, Andrew. 2001. "Male Identity, the Military, and the Family in the former German Democratic Republic." *Anthropology of East Europe Review* 19, no. 1 (Spring): 1–11.

———. 2009. "Soldiers, Citizens, and the State: East German Army Officers in Post-Unification Germany." *Comparative Studies in Society and History* 51, no. 2: 260–87.

———. 2010. "'The Red General': German Unification, Fallen Elites, and the Time-Shift of Heroic Victimhood." *Anthropology Now* 2, no. 2 (September): 42–51.

Biedermann, Bernd. 2008. *Offizier, Diplomat, und Aufklärer der NVA: Streiflichter aus dem Kalten Krieg*. Berlin: Verlag Dr. Köster.

Biess, Frank. 2002. "Between Amnesty and Anti-Communism: The West German Kameradenschinder Trials, 1948–1960." In *Crimes of War: Guilt and Denial in the Twentieth Century*, ed. Omer Bartov, Atina Grossmann, and Mary Nolan, pp. 138–60. New York: New Press.

———. 2006. *Homecomings: Returning POWs and the Legacies of Defeat in Postwar Germany*. Princeton, NJ: Princeton University Press.

Böhme, Gunther, and Wolfgang Spitzner. 1977. "Schutz des Sozialismus- Recht und Ehrenpflicht." *Einheit* (May). Ministerium für nationale Verteidigung der DDR, Berlin.

Borneman, John. 1992. *Belonging in the Two Berlins: Kin, State, Nation*. New York: Cambridge University Press.

———. 1993. "Uniting the German Nation: Law, Narrative, and Historicity." *American Ethnologist* 20, no. 2: 288–311.

———. 2001. "State Formation." In *International Encyclopedia of the Social and Behavioral Sciences*, ed. Neil J. Smelser and Paul B. Baltes. Amsterdam: Elsevier Sciences.

Boyer, Dominic. 2005. *Spirit and System: Media, Intellectuals, and the Dialectic in Modern German Culture*. Chicago: University of Chicago Press.

———. 2006. "Conspiracy, History, and Therapy at a Berlin Stammtisch." *American Ethnologist* 33, no. 3: 327–39.

Braudy, Leo. 2005. *From Chivalry to Terrorism: War and the Changing Nature of Masculinity*. New York: Vintage Books.

Brie, Michael. 1994. "The Difficulty of Discussing the GDR." In *Studies in GDR Culture and Society 13: Understanding the Past- Managing the Future: Integration of the Five New Länder into the Federal Republic of Germany*, ed. Margy Gerber and Roger Woods, pp. 1–23. Selected papers from the Eighteenth New Hampshire Symposium. Lanham, MD: University Press of America.

Brigadebefehl 01/99 der Logistikbrigade 4 (Bridade Order Number 01/99 of the Fourth Logistics Brigade of the Bundeswehr). As cited in Herbert Becker, Deutscher Bundeswehrverband Landesverband Ost (informational memo-briefings written by Herbert Becker, and sent out to members of the veterans groups), "Gedanken zur Traditionspflege." 2000.

Brubaker, Rogers. 1992. *Citizenship and Nationhood in France and Germany*. Cambridge, MA: Harvard University Press.

Buck-Morss, Susan. 1992. *The Dialectics of Seeing: Walther Benjamin and the Arcades Project*. Cambridge, MA: MIT Press.

Bundesverfassungsgericht, Beschl. v. 10.10.1995-1 BvR 1476191, 1 BvR 1980191, 1 BvR 102192, 1 BvR 221192. German Supreme Court decision on the "Soldiers are Murderers" debate.

Bundeswehr Web site, www.bundeswehr.de. Richtlinien zum Traditionsverständnis und zur Traditionspflege in der Bundeswehr, Grundsätze (accessed May 20, 2010).

———. Tradition der Bundeswehr, Eigene Geschichte (accessed May 20, 2010).

Carrigan, Tim, et al. 1985. "Towards a New Sociology of Masculinity." *Theory and Society* 14, no. 5: 551–603.

Carrier, Peter. 2005. *Holocaust Monuments and National Memory: France and Germany Since 1989*. New York: Berghahn Books.

Cohn, Carol. 1987 (2004). "Sex and Death in the Rational World of Defense Intellectuals." In *Violence in War and Peace*, ed. Nancy Scheper-Hughes and Philippe Bourgois, pp. 354–61. Malden, MA: Blackwell Publishing.

Collier, Jane, and Sylvia Yanagisako, eds. 1987. *Gender and Kinship: Essays Toward a Unified Analysis*. Stanford, CA: Stanford University Press.

Connell, R. W. 1995. *Masculinities*. Berkeley: University of California Press.

Connerton, Paul. 1989. *How Societies Remember*. New York: Cambridge University Press.

Cooke, Paul. 2005. *From Colonization to Nostalgia: Representing East Germany Since Unification*. Oxford: Berg.

Cornwall, Andrea, and Nancy Lindisfarne. 1994. *Dislocating Masculinity: Comparative Ethnographies*. New York: Routledge.

Corrigan, Phillip, and Derek Sayer. 1985. *The Great Arch: English State Formation as Cultural Revolution*. Oxford: Basil Blackwell.

Dalvi, Sameera. 1998. "The Post–Cold War Role of the Bundeswehr: A Product of Normative Influences." *European Security* 7, no. 1 (Spring): 97–116.

Dengel, Sabine. 2005. *Untertan, Volksgenosse, Sozialistische Persönlichkeit: Politische Erziehung im Deutschen Kaiserreich, dem NS-Staat, und der DDR*. Frankfurt am Main: Campus Forschung.

Deutscher Bundestag. 1990. 224 Sitzung 1990/17744, 13 September: Übernahme von Teilen der NVA durch die Bundeswehr. Press release.

———. 2002. Drucksache 14/8920, April 25, PDS Antrag: Deutsche Einheit in der Bundeswehr herstellen (PDS motion: Create German unity in the Bundeswehr). Press release.

DeSoto, Hermine. 1994. "In the Name of the Folk: Women and the Nation in the New Germany." *UCLA Women's Law Journal* 5, no. 1: 83–101.

DeSoto, Hermine, and Konstanze Plett. 1995. "Citizenship and Minorities in the Process of Nation Rebuilding in Germany." *PoLAR: Political and Legal Anthropology Review* 18, no. 1 (May): 107–22.

Diedrich, Torsten, Hans Ehlert, and Rüdiger Wenzke, eds. 1998. *Im Dienste der Partei: Handbuch der bewaffneten Organe der DDR*. Berlin: Christoph Links Verlag.

Doehler, Edgar, and Rudolf Falkenberg. 1979. *Militärische Traditionen der DDR und der NVA*. Serie Politik und Landesverteidigung. Berlin: Militärverlag der Deutschen Demokratischen Republik.

Dölling, Irene. 1993. "Gespaltenes Bewusstsein: Frauen und Männerbilder in der DDR." In *Frauen in Deutschland, 1945–1992*, ed. Gisela Helwig and Hildegard Maria Nickel, pp. 23–52. Bonn: Bundeszentrale für politische Bildung.

Eagleton, Terry. 1988. *The Ideology of the Aesthetic.* Hoboken, NJ: Wiley-Blackwell.
———. 1991. *Ideology: An Introduction.* London: Verso.
"E. German License to Kill Found." 2007. BBC Report, August 12.
"Ehemaliger U.S. Sergeant untersucht Gefühle der NVA Soldaten: Ungleichbehandlung sorgt immer noch für Ärger" (Former U.S. Sergeant Examines the Feelings of NVA Soldiers: Unequal Treatment Still Causes Bitterness). Newspaper article. 2000. *Ostsee Zeitung,* March 23.
Ehlert, Hans, and Matthias Rogg, eds. 2004. *Militär, Staat, und Gesellschaft in der DDR: Forschungsfelder, Ergebnisse, Perspektiven.* Berlin: Christoph Links Verlag.
Eifler, Christine. 1996. "Zur Weiblichkeitsklischees in der NVA-Propaganda." *Offiziersbrief* 28: 19–21.
Einhorn, Barbara. 1993. *Cinderella Goes To Market: Citizenship, Gender, and Women's Movements in East Central Europe.* London: Verso.
Englemann, Harri. 2000. *Japanischer Garten: Reminiszenen an meine Verteidigungsbereitschaft.* Rostock: WeymannBauer Verlag.
Enloe, Cynthia. 1983. *Does Khaki Become You? The Militarization of Women's Lives.* Boston: South End Press.
———. 1990. *Bananas, Beaches, and Bases: Making Feminist Sense of International Politics.* Berkeley: University of California Press.
———. 1993. *The Morning After: Sexual Politics and the End of the Cold War.* Berkeley: University of California Press.
———. 2007. *Globalization and Militarism: Feminists Make the Link.* New York: Rowman and Littlefield.
Evans, Peter B., Dietrich Rueschemeyer, and Theda Skocpol, eds. 1999. *Bringing the State Back In.* Cambridge: Cambridge University Press.
Fabian, Johannes. 1983. *Time and the Other: How Anthropology Makes Its Object.* New York: Columbia University Press.
Fehrenbach, Heide. 1998. "Rehabilitating Fatherland: Race and German Remasculinization." *Signs: The Journal of Women in Culture and Society* 24, no. 1 (Autumn): 107–28.
Fenemore, Mark. 2009. *Sex, Thugs, and Rock 'n Roll: Teenage Rebels in Cold War East Germany.* New York: Berghahn Books.
Fingerle, Stephan. 2001. *Waffen in Arbeiterhand? Die Rekrutierung des Offizierkorps der Nationalen Volksarmee und ihrer Vorläufer.* Berlin: Christoph Links Verlag.
Fischer, Egbert. 1995. *Ehemalige Berufssoldaten der NVA in der Bundesrepublik Deutschland, Report 1995: Ergebnisse einer Meinungsumfrage in Kamaradschaften "Ehemalige" des Landesverbandes Ost des Deutschen Bundeswehr—Verbandes e.V.* Bonn: Karl-Theodor-Molinari Stiftung.
Flockton, Chris, Eva Kolinsky, and Rosalind Pritchard. 2000. *The New Germany in the East: Policy Agendas and Social Developments Since Unification.* London: Frank Cass.
Foster, T. M. 1980. *The East German Army.* London: George Allen and Unwin.
Foucault, Michel. 1980. *History of Sexuality, Volume 1.* New York: Vintage Books.
Fricke, Hans. 1993. *Davor, Dabei, Danach: Ein ehemaliger Kommandeur der Grenztruppen der DDR berichtet.* Köln: Verlag GNN.
Frühstuck, Sabine. 2007. *Uneasy Warriors: Gender, Memory, and Popular Culture in the Japanese Army.* Berkeley: University of California Press.
Frykman, Jonas, and Orvar Lofgren. 1987. *The Culture Builders: A Historical Anthropology of Middle Class Life.* New Brunswick, NJ: Rutgers University Press.

Fulbrook, Mary. 1995. *Anatomy of a Dictatorship: Inside the GDR, 1949–1989*. Oxford: Oxford University Press.

———. 2005. *The People's State: East German Society from Hitler to Honecker*. New Haven, CT: Yale University Press.

Funk, Nanette and Magda Müller, eds. 1993. *Gender Politics and Post-Communism: Reflections from Eastern Europe and the Former Soviet Union*. New York: Routledge.

Gal, Susan, and Gail Kligman. 2000. *The Politics of Gender After Socialism: A Comparative Historical Essay*. Princeton, NJ: Princeton University Press.

Gehler, R. 1998. "EK, EK, EK- bald bist du nicht mehr da!" In *Soldatenkultur in der Nationalen Volksarmee*, Schriftenreihe des Museums der Stadt Hagenow. Hagenow: Museum der Stadt Hagenow.

Gerber, Margy, and Roger Woods, eds. 1994. *Studies in GDR Culture and Society 13: Understanding the Past- Managing the Future; Integration of the Five New Länder into the Federal Republic of Germany*. Selected papers from the Eighteenth New Hampshire Symposium. Lanham MD: University Press of America.

Giese, Daniel. 2002. *Die SED und ihre Armee: Die NVA zwischen Politisierung und Professionalismus, 1956–1965*. Schriftenreihe der Vierteljahrshefte für Zeitgeschichte. Munich: R. Oldenbourg Verlag.

Gill, Lesley. 1997. "Creating Citizens, Making Men: The Military and Masculinity in Bolivia." *Cultural Anthropology* 12, no. 4: 527–50.

———. 2004. *The School of the Americas: Military Training and Political Violence in the Americas*. Durham, NC: Duke University Press.

Gillis, John R., ed. 1989. *The Militarization of the Western World*. New Brunswick, NJ: Rutgers University Press.

Giordano, Ralph. 2000. *Die Traditionslüge: Vom Kriegerkult in der Bundeswehr*. Köln: Kiepenheuer und Witsch.

Glaeser, Andreas. 2000. *Divided in Unity: Identity, Germany, and the Berlin Police*. Chicago: University of Chicago Press.

Green, Linda. 1999. *Fear as a Way of Life*. New York: Columbia University Press.

Günzel, Reinhard, Ulrich Wegener, and Wilhelm Walther. 2005. *Geheime Krieger: Drei Deutsche Kommandoverbände im Bild*. Selent: Pour le Mérite Verlag.

Gusterson, Hugh. 2007. "Anthropology and Militarism." *Annual Review of Anthropology* 36: 155–75.

Gutman, Amy, ed. 1994. *Multiculturalism*. Princeton, NJ: Princeton University Press.

Gutmann, Matthew. 1997. "Trafficking in Men: The Anthropology of Masculinity." *Annual Review of Anthropology* 26: 385–409.

———. 2006. *The Meaning of Macho: Being a Man in Mexico City*. Berkeley: University of California Press.

Hafeneger, Benno, and Michael Buddrus. 1994. *Militärische Erziehung in Ost und West: Ein Lesebuch zur Kriegsbegeisterung jünger Männer Band 4: Nachkriegszeit und fünfziger Jahre*. Frankfurt am Main: Brandes und Apsel.

Hafeneger, Benno, and Michael Fritz. 1993. *Sie starben für Führer, Volk, und Vaterland: Die Hitlerjugend*. Frankfurt am Main: Brandes und Apsel.

Hagemann, Karen. 2002. *Home/Front: The Military, War, and Gender in Twentieth Century Germany*. Oxford: Berg.

Hall, Stuart. 1994. "Cultural Identity and Diaspora." In *Colonial Discourse and Post-*

Colonial Theory: A Reader, ed. Patrick Williams and Laura Christman, pp. 392–403. New York: Columbia University Press.

Harrison, Hope. 2003. *Driving the Soviets Up the Wall: Soviet-East German Relations, 1953–1961*. Princeton, NJ: Princeton University Press.

Harsch, Donna. 2010. "Footnote or Footprint? The German Democratic Republic in History." Twenty-third Annual Lecture of the German Historical Institute, Washington, DC, November 12, 2009. *Bulletin of the German Historical Institute* (Spring): 9–25.

Hausen, Karin. 1997. "Histories of Mourning: Flowers and Stones for the War Dead, Confusion for the Living; Vignettes from East and West Germany." In *Between History and Histories: The Making of Silences and Commemorations*, ed. Gerald Sider and Gavin Smith, pp. 127–48. Toronto: University of Toronto Press.

Hausmann, Leander. 2005. *NVA*. Berlin: Boje Buck Produktion GmbH.

Heider, Paul. 2004. "Ideologische Indoktrination und Traditionspflege in der Nationalen Volksarmee." In *Militär, Staat, und Gesellschaft in der DDR: Forschungsfelder, Ergebnisse, Perspektiven*, ed. Hans Ehlert and Matthias Rogg, pp. 303–21. Berlin: Christoph Links Verlag.

Herf, Jeffrey. 1997. *Divided Memory: The Nazi Past in the Two Germanys*. Cambridge, MA: Harvard University Press.

Herspring, Dale. 1998. *Requiem for an Army: The Demise of the East German Military*. Lanham, MD: Rowman and Littlefield.

Herzfeld, Michael. 2001. *Anthropology: Theoretical Practice in Culture and Society*. Malden, MA: Blackwell Publishing.

Higate, Paul, et al. 2003. *Military Masculinities: Identity and the State*. Santa Barbara, CA: Praeger Press.

"Hitler Apologist Wins Honor, and a Storm Breaks Out." 2000. *New York Times*, June 21.

Hobsbawm, Eric, and Terence Ranger, eds. 1988. *The Invention of Tradition*. Cambridge: Cambridge University Press.

Hodgson, Dorothy. 2004. *Once Intrepid Warriors: Gender, Ethnicity, and the Cultural Politics of Maasai Development*. Bloomington: Indiana University Press.

Howard, Mark. 1995. "An East German Ethnicity? Understanding the New Division of Unified Germany." *German Politics and Society* 13, no. 4: 49–70.

Hübner, Werner. 1998. "Zur Rolle der Partei in der Nationalen Volksarmee." In *Rührt Euch! Zur Geschichte der NVA*, ed. Wolfgang Wünsche, pp. 412–31. Berlin: Edition Ost.

Huizinga, Johan. 1954. *The Waning of the Middle Ages*. New York: Doubleday Anchor.

Initiativgemeinschaft zum Schutz der sozialen Rechte ehemaliger Angehöriger bewaffneter Organe und der Zöllverwaltung der DDR (ISOR) Web site, www.isor-sozialverein. de (accessed May 21, 2010).

Janowitz, Morris. 1960. *The Professional Soldier: A Social and Political Portrait*. New York: Free Press.

Jarausch, Konrad. 2006. *After Hitler: Recivilizing Germans, 1945–1995*. Oxford: Oxford University Press.

Jarausch, Konrad, and Michael Geyer. 2003. *Shattered Past: Reconstructing German Histories*. Princeton, NJ: Princeton University Press.

Jeffords, Susan. 1998. "The Remasculinization of Germany in the 1950s: Discussion." *Signs: The Journal of Women in Culture and Society* 24, no. 1 (Autumn): 163–70.

Jerome, Roy, ed., 2001. *Conceptions of Postwar German Masculinity*. Albany: State University of New York Press.

Judt, Tony. 2005. *Postwar: A History of Europe Since 1945*. New York: Penguin Books.

Jüngermann, P. 1973. *Die Wehrideologie der SED und das Leitbild der Nationalen Volksarmee vom sozialistischen deutschen Soldaten*. Stuttgart: Degerloch.

Kanaaneh, Rhoda. 2005. "Boys or Men? Duped or 'Made'? Palestinian Soldiers in the Israeli Military." *American Ethnologist* 32, no. 2: 260–75.

Karlson, Holger Jens, and Jörg Juderslehen. 1994. "Die Soldatensprache der NVA: Eine Wortschatzbetrachtung." *Muttersprache* 104: 143–65.

Keen, Sam. 1991. *Faces of the Enemy: Reflections of the Hostile Imagination*. San Francisco: Harper and Row.

Kertzer, David I. 1989. *Ritual, Power, and Politics*. New Haven, CT: Yale University Press.

Klessmann, Christoph. 1997. *Zwei Staaten, Eine Nation: Deutsche Geschichte, 1955–1970*. Bonn: Bundeszentrale für politische Bildung.

Klotz, Johannes, ed. 1998. *Vorbild Wehrmacht? Wehrmachtsverbrechen, Rechtsextremismus und Bundeswehr*. Köln: PapyRossa Verlag.

Kolinsky, Eva, ed. 1993. *Women in Contemporary Germany: Life, Work, and Politics*. Providence, RI: Berg.

———, ed. 1995. *Between Hope and Fear: Everyday Life in Post-Unification Germany*. Edinburgh: Keele University Press.

Koop, Volker. 1995. *Abgewickelt? Auf den Spuren der Nationalen Volksarmee*. Bonn: Bouvier Verlag.

Korablev, I. U. 1977. *Lenin, the Founder of the Soviet Armed Forces*. Moscow: Progress Publishers.

Künhe, Thomas, ed. 1996a. *Männergeschichte-Geschlechtergeschichte: Männlichkeit im Wandel der Moderne*. Frankfurt am Main: Campus Verlag.

———. 1996b. "'. . . Aus diesem Krieg werden nicht nur harte Männer heimkehren': Kriegskameradschaft und Männlichkeit im 20. Jahrhundert." In *Männergeschichte-Geschlechtergeschichte: Männlichkeit im Wandel der Moderne*, ed. Thomas Künhe, pp. 174–92. Frankfurt am Main: Campus Verlag.

Kuppe, Johannes L. 1994. "West German Policy Toward East Germany: A Motor of Unification?" In *German Unification: Process and Outcomes*, ed. M. Donald Hancock and Helga A. Walsh, pp. 35–51. Boulder, CO: Westview Press.

Ladd, Brian. 1997. *The Ghosts of Berlin: Confronting German History in the Urban Landscape*. Chicago: University of Chicago Press.

Lancaster, Roger. 1994. *Life Is Hard: Machismo, Danger, and the Intimacy of Power in Nicaragua*. Berkeley: University of California Press.

———. 2003. *The Trouble with Nature: Sex in Science and Popular Culture*. Berkeley: University of California Press.

Landsberg, Alison. 2004. *Prosthetic Memory: The Transformation of American Remembrance in the Age of Mass Media*. New York: Columbia University Press.

Lapp, Peter Joachim. 1992. *Ein Staat—eine Armee: Von der NVA zur Bundeswehr*. Bonn-Bad Godesberg: Friedrich-Ebert Stiftung.

Large, David Clay. 1996. *Germans to the Front: West German Rearmament in the Adenauer Era*. Chapel Hill: University of North Carolina Press.

Lears, T. J. Jackson. 1985. "The Concept of Cultural Hegemony: Problems and Possibilities." *American Historical Review* 90, no. 3 (June): 567–93.

Lee, Martyn J. 1993. *Consumer Culture Reborn: The Cultural Politics of Consumption*. New York: Routledge.

Leonhard, Nina. 2004. "Biographische Lebenskonstruktionen ehemaliger NVA-Soldaten." In *Militär, Staat, und Gesellschaft in der DDR: Forschungsfelder, Ergebnisse, Perspektiven,* ed. Hans Ehlert and Matthias Rogg, pp. 717–33. Berlin: Christoph Links Verlag.

Lerner, Max. 1941. *Ideas for the Ice Age.* New York: Viking Press.

Lewis, Derek, and John R. P. McKenzie, eds. 1995. *The New Germany: Social, Political, and Cultural Challenges of Unification.* Exeter: University of Exeter Press.

Lewis, Jane. 1993. ed., *Women and Social Policies in Europe.* Hants: Edward Elgar.

Linke, Uli. 1995. "Murderous Fantasies: Violence, Memory, and Selfhood in Germany." *New German Critique* 64 (Winter): 37–59.

———. 1999. *German Bodies: Race and Representation After Hitler.* New York: Routledge.

Lockenour, Jay. 2001. *Soldiers as Citizens: Former Wehrmacht Officers in the Federal Republic of Germany, 1945–1955.* Lincoln: University of Nebraska Press.

Lutz, Catherine. 2001. *Homefront: A Military City and the American 20th Century.* Boston: Beacon Press.

———. 2002. "Making War at Home and in the United States: Militarization and the Current Crisis." *American Anthropologist* 104, no. 3: 723–35.

———. 2007. "Militarization." In *A Companion to the Anthropology of Politics,* ed. David Nugent and Joan Vincent, pp. 318–31. Malden, MA: Blackwell Publishing.

Mählert, Ulrich, and Gerd-Rüdiger Stephan. 1996. *Blaue Hemden, Rote Fahnen: Die Geschichte der Freien Deutschen Jugend.* Opladen: Leske und Budrich.

Maier, Charles. 1997. *The Unmasterable Past: History, Holocaust, and German National Identity.* Cambridge, MA: Harvard University Press.

———. 1999. *Dissolution: The Crisis of Communism and the End of East Germany.* Princeton, NJ: Princeton University Press.

Manöver Schneeflocke Brigadetagebücher, 1960–90. Berlin: n.p., 1994.

Marcus, George E., and Michael M. J. Fisher. 1986. *Anthropology as Cultural Critique: An Experimental Moment in the Human Sciences.* Chicago: University of Chicago Press.

Marks, Heinz. 1970. *Gesellschaft für Sport und Technik: Vormilitärische Ausbildung in der DDR.* Köln: Markus Verlag.

McAdams, A. James. 2001. *Judging the Past in Unified Germany.* Cambridge: Cambridge University Press.

Merkl, Gerhard, and Wolfgang Wünsche. 1996. *Die Nationale Volksarmee der DDR-Legitimation und Auftrag: Alte und Neue Legenden kritisch hinterfragt.* Berlin: Forschungs und Diskussionskreis DDR Geschichte.

Merkl, Peter H. 1995a. "Reinventing German National Identity." Introduction to *The Federal Republic of Germany at Forty Five: Union Without Unity,* ed. Peter H. Merkl, pp. 1–30. New York: New York University Press.

———, ed. 1995b. *The Federal Republic of Germany at Forty Five: Union Without Unity.* New York: New York University Press.

Meyer, Georg-Maria, and Sabine Collmer. 1993. *Kolonisierung oder Integration: Bundeswehr und Deutsche Einheit: Eine Bestandaufnahme.* Opladen: Westdeutscher Verlag.

Ministerium für nationale Verteidigung. 1983. *Vom Sinn des Soldatenseins: Ein Ratgeber für den Soldaten.* Berlin: Militärverlag der DDR.

Mintz, Sidney. 1985. *Sweetness and Power: The Place of Sugar in Modern History.* New York: Penguin Books.

Moeller, Robert. 1998. "The Remasculinization of Germany in the 1950s: An Introduction." *Signs: The Journal of Women in Culture and Society* 24, no. 1 (Autumn): 101–6.

———. 2003. *War Stories: The Search for a Usable Past in the Federal Republic of Germany*. Berkeley: University of California Press.

Moon, Seungsook. 2005. *Militarized Modernity and Gendered Citizenship in South Korea*. Durham, NC: Duke University Press.

Mosse, George. 1975. *The Nationalization of the Masses: Political Symbolism and Mass Movements In Germany from the Napoleonic Wars Through the Third Reich*. Ithaca, NY: Cornell University Press.

———. 1985. *Nationalism and Sexuality: Middle-Class Morality and Sexual Norms in Modern Europe*. Madison: University of Wisconsin Press.

———. 1990. *Fallen Soldiers: Reshaping the Memory of the World Wars*. New York: Oxford University Press.

———. 1996. *The Image of Man: The Creation of Modern Masculinity*. New York: Oxford University Press.

Müller, Birgit. 2007. *Disenchantment with Market Economics: East Germans and Western Capitalism*. New York: Berghahn Books.

Müller, Maria Elisabeth. 1997. *Zwischen Ritual und Alltag: Der Traum von einer sozialistischen Persönlichkeit*. Frankfurt: Campus Verlag.

Nader, Laura. 1974. "Up the Anthropologist: Perspectives Gained from Studying Up." In *Reinventing Anthropology*, ed. Dell Hymes, pp. 284–311. New York: Vintage Books.

Nickel, Hildegard Maria. 1993. "Women in the German Democratic Republic and in in the New Federal States: Looking Backward and Forward (Five Theses)." In *Gender Politics and Post-Communism: Reflections from Eastern Europe and the Former Soviet Union*, ed. Nanette Funk and Magda Müller, pp. 138–50. New York: Routledge.

Niven, Bill. 2002. *Facing the Nazi Past: United Germany and the Legacy of the Third Reich*. London: Routledge.

Nordstrom, Carolyn, and Antonius Robben, eds. 1995. *Fieldwork Under Fire: Contemporary Studies of Violence and Survival*. Berkeley: University of California Press.

Nugent, David, and Joan Vincent, eds. 2007. *A Companion to the Anthropology of Politics*. Malden, MA: Blackwell Publishing.

Ostner, Ilona. 1993. "Slow Motion: Women, Work, and the Family in Germany." In *Women and Social Policies in Europe*, ed. Jane Lewis, pp. 92–115. Hants: Edward Elgar.

Peck, Jeffrey. 1997. "Turks and Jews: Comparing Minorities in Germany After the Holocaust." In *German Cultures, Foreign Cultures: The Politics of Belonging*, ed. Jeffrey Peck, pp. 1–16. AICGS research report no. 8, Humanities Program, Johns Hopkins University. Baltimore: American Institute for Contemporary German Studies.

Philipsen, Dirk. 1993. *We Were the People: Voices from East Germany's Revolutionary Autumn of 1989*. Durham, NC: Duke University Press.

Poiger, Ute. 1998. "A New, 'Western' Hero? Reconstructing German Masculinity in the 1950s." *Signs: The Journal of Women in Culture and Society* 24, no. 1 (Autumn): 147–62.

Pred, Allen, and Michael Watts, eds. 1992. *Reworking Modernity: Capitalism and Symbolic Discontent*. New Brunswick, NJ: Rutgers University Press.

Pröll, Bernd. 1985. "Sozialistische Wehrerziehung in der DDR im Zeichen der Entspannung: Anachronismus oder unabdingbare Reaktion?" *IFSH-Diskussionsbeiträge* 40 (September).

Rede des Bundesministers der Verteidigung, Dr. Franz Josef Jung, anlässlich des XXXII. Internationalen Militärhistorikerkongresses am 21. August 2006 in Potsdam. Address of the Federal Minister of Defense, Dr. Franz Josef Jung, at the Thirty-second International Congress of Military Historians, August 21, in Potsdam, Germany.

Remmler, Karen. 1995. "Deciphering the Body of Memory: Writing by Former East German Women Writers." In *Post-Communism and the Body Politic*, ed. Ellen E. Berry, pp. 134–63. New York: New York University Press.

Richter, Gerd. 2000. Public address to the meeting of the Kameradschaft Ehemalige Rostock, March 23. Transcript in author's possession.

Robben, Antonius. 1995. "The Politics of Truth and Emotion Among Victims and Perpetrators of Violence." In *Fieldwork Under Fire: Contemporary Studies of Violence and Survival*, ed. Carolyn Nordstrom and Antonius Robben, pp. 81–104. Berkeley: University of California Press.

Rosenberg, Dorothy. 1991. "Shock Therapy: GDR Women in Transition from a Socialist Welfare State to a Social Market Economy." *Signs: The Journal of Women in Culture and Society* 17, no. 1 (Autumn): 129–51.

Ross, Corey. 1999. "What About Peace and Bread? East Germans and the Remilitarization of the GDR, 1952–1962." *Militärgeschichtliche Zeitschrift* 58, no. 1: 111–35. Munich: Oldenburg.

Rueschemeyer Dietrich, and Peter B. Evans. 1999. "The State and Economic Transformation: Toward an Analysis of the Conditions Underlying Effective Intervention." In *Bringing the State Back In*, ed. Peter B. Evans, Dietrich Rueschemeyer, and Theda Skocpol, pp. 44–77. Cambridge: Cambridge University Press.

Rühe, Volker. 1994. "'Aufstand des Gewissens': Gedenken an den militärischen Widerstand." *Presse- und Informationsamt der Bundesregierung*, bulletin, no. 68, July 22, 1994, p. 648, as cited in Prof. Dr. Holger H. Herwig, *Aggression Contained? The Federal Republic of Germany and International Security*. Final report, NATO research fellowship, n.d.

Scarry, Elaine. 1985. *The Body in Pain: The Making and Unmaking of the World*. Oxford: Oxford University Press.

Scheper-Hughes, Nancy, and Philippe Bourgois, eds. 2004. *Violence in War and Peace*. Malden, MA: Blackwell Publishing.

Schmähling, Elmar. 1991. *Ohne Glanz und Gloria: Die Bundewehr- Bilanz einer neurotischen Armee*. Düsseldorf: ECON Verlag.

Schönbohm, Jörg. 1996. *Two Armies and One Fatherland*. Providence, RI: Berghahn Books.

Scott, James. 1987. *Weapons of the Weak: Everyday Forms of Peasant Resistance*. New Haven, CT: Yale University Press.

Seifert, Ruth. 1996. *Militär—Kultur—Identität: Individualisierung, Geschlechtsverhältnisse und die soziale Konstruktion des Soldaten*. Bremen: Edition Themen.

Senders, Stefan. 1996. "Laws of Belonging: Legal Dimensions of National Inclusion in Germany." *New German Critique* 67 (Winter): 147–76.

Shapiro, Michael J. 1997. *Violent Cartographies: Mapping Cultures of War*. Anne Arbor: University of Michigan Press.

Sharma, Aradhana, and Akhil Gupta, eds. 2006a. "Rethinking Theories of the State in an Age of Globalization." Introduction to *The Anthropology of the State: A Reader*, ed. Aradhana Sharma and Akhil Gupta, pp. 1–41. Malden, MA: Blackwell Publishing.

———, eds. 2006b. *The Anthropology of the State: A Reader*. Malden, MA: Blackwell Publishing.

Sheehan, James J. 2008. *Where Have All the Soldiers Gone? The Transformation of Modern Europe.* Boston: Houghton Mifflin.

Sider, Gerald. 2003. *Between History and Tomorrow: Making and Breaking Everyday Life in Rural Newfoundland.* Peterborough, Ont.: Broadview Press.

Sitzung des Sekretariats der PHV (Meeting of the Secretariat of the Political Control Committee of the NVA), January 1988. *Anlage* 17 (Attachment 17) of the report concerns the "activities of the Press Department of the Ministry of National Defense in the training year 1986–87." Formerly classified NVA report.

Spanier, Thomas. 1992. "In Erinnerung an meine Dienstzeit: 18 Monate als Wehrpflichtiger in der NVA." In *NVA: Ein Rückblick für die Zukunft- Zeitzeugen berichten über ein Stück deutscher Militärgeschichte,* ed. Manfred Backerra, pp. 27–42. Köln: Markus Verlag.

Staab, Andreas. 1998. *National Identity in Eastern Germany: Inner Unification or Continued Separation?* London: Praeger.

Taussig, Michael. 1997. *The Magic of the State.* New York: Routledge.

Taylor, Charles. 2004. *Modern Social Imaginaries.* Durham, NC: Duke University Press.

Theweleit, Klaus. 1987–89. *Male Fantasies.* 2 vols. Minneapolis: University of Minnesota Press.

Tilly, Charles. 1999. "War Making and State Making as Organized Crime." In *Bringing the State Back In,* ed. Peter B. Evans, Dietrich Rueschemeyer, and Theda Skocpol, pp. 169–91. Cambridge: Cambridge University Press.

Unser Fallschirm. 1999. Newsletter of former NVA paratrooper veterans group. September.

Verdery, Katherine. 1994. "From Parent-State to Family Patriarchs: Gender and Nation in Contemporary Eastern Europe." *East European Politics and Societies* 8, no. 2 (Spring): 225–55.

———. 1996. *What Was Socialism, and What Comes Next?* Princeton, NJ: Princeton University Press.

Vereinbarung der Ministerium für Volksbildung. 1969. Gesellschaft für Sport und Technik, Freie Deutsche Jugend, und Deutsches Rotes Kreuz, May 30.

Voloshinov, V. I. 1973 (1929). *Marxism and the Philosophy of Language.* Cambridge, MA: Harvard University Press.

Waehner, Joerg. 2006. *Einstrich—Keinstrich: NVA Tagebuch.* Köln: Kiepenhauer und Witsch.

Walzer, Michael. 1967. "On the Role of Symbolism in Political Thought." *Political Science Quarterly* 82: 191–205.

Watts, Michael. 1992. "Living Under Contract: Work, Production Politics, and the Manufacture of Discontent in a Peasant Soceity." In *Reworking Modernity: Capitalism and Symbolic Discontent,* ed. Allen Pred and Michael Watts, pp. 65–105. New Brunswick, NJ: Rutgers University Press.

Weber, Eugen. 1976. *Peasants into Frenchmen: The Modernization of Rural France, 1870–1914.* Stanford, CA: Stanford University Press.

Wehler, Hans-Ulrich. 2008. *Deutsche Gesellschaftsgeschichte.* Vol. 5, *Bundesrepublik und DDR, 1949–1990.* Munich: C. H. Beck.

Wehrdienstgesetz der Deutschen Demokratischen Republik. 1982. March 25.

"Wehrmachtsemblem auf Jeep war nicht genehmigt" (Wehrmacht Emblem on Jeep Was Not Authorized). 2006. *Der Spiegel,* November 2.

Wenzel, Otto. 1995. *Kriegsbereit: Der Nationale Verteidigungsrat der DDR, 1960–1989.* Köln: Verlag Wissenschaft und Politik.

Wenzke, Rüdiger. 1998. "Die Nationale Volksarmee." In *Im Dienste der Partei: Handbuch der bewaffneten Organe der DDR,* ed. Torsten Diedrich, Hans Ehlert, and Rüdiger Wenzke, pp. 423–535. Berlin: Christoph Links Verlag.

West, Paige. 2005. "Holding the Story Forever: The Aesthetics of Ethnographic Labour." *Anthropological Forum* 15, no. 3 (November): 267–75.

Wette, Wolfram. 1998. "Wehrmachtstraditionen und Bundeswehr. Deutsche Machtphantasien im Zeichen der neuen Militärpolitik und des Rechstradikalismus." In *Vorbild Wehrmacht? Wehrmachtsverbrechen, Rechtsextremismus und Bundeswehr,* ed. Johannes Klotz, pp. 126–54. Köln: PapyRossa Verlag.

———. 2006. *The Wehrmacht: History, Myth, Reality.* Cambridge, MA: Harvard University Press.

Weitz, Eric. 1997. *Creating German Communism: From Popular Protests to Socialist State.* Princeton, NJ: Princeton University Press.

Willems, Emilio. 1986. *A Way of Life and Death: Three Centuries of Prussian-German Militarism; An Anthropological Approach.* Nashville, TN: Vanderbilt University Press.

Williams, Patrick, and Laura Christman, eds. 1994. *Colonial Discourse and Post-Colonial Theory: A Reader.* New York: Columbia University Press.

Winter, Jay, and Emmanuel Sivan. 2000. "Setting the Framework." In *War and Remembrance in the Twentieth Century,* ed. Jay Winter and Emmanuel Sivan, pp. 6–39. Cambridge: Cambridge University Press.

Wolf, Eric. 1982. *Europe and the People Without History.* Berkeley: University of California Press.

———. 1999. *Envisioning Power: Ideologies of Dominance and Resistance.* Berkeley: University of California Press.

———. 2001. *Pathways of Power: Building an Anthropology of the Modern World.* Berkeley: University of California Press.

Wolle, Stefan. 1999. *Die heile Welt der Diktatur.* Munich: Econ.

Woods, Roger. 1994. "The East German Contribution to German Identity." In *Studies in GDR Culture and Society 13: Understanding the Past- Managing the Future: Integration of the Five New Länder into the Federal Republic of Germany,* ed. Margy Gerber and Roger Woods, pp. 53–70. Selected papers from the Eighteenth New Hampshire Symposium. Lanham MD: University Press of America.

Zilian, Frederick, Jr. 1999. *From Confrontation to Cooperation: The Takeover of the National People's Army (East Germany) by the Bundeswehr.* London: Praeger.

Zipes, Jack. 2006. *Fairy Tales and the Art of Subversion: The Classic Genre for Children and the Process of Civilization.* New York: Routledge.

Index